Citizen Participation
in Science Policy

Citizen Participation in Science Policy

edited by
James C. Petersen

The University of Massachusetts
Press Amherst, 1984

128716

Earlier versions of the chapters by Sheldon
Krimsky, Frederick A. Rossini and Alan L. Porter,
Rachelle Hollander, Jane C. Kronick, and Barry
Checkoway appeared in the *Journal of Voluntary
Action Research* (Jan.–March 1982), and are re-
printed here by permission. An earlier version of
the chapter by Dorothy Nelkin was printed in
Five-Year Outlook, vol. 2, published 1980 by the
National Science Foundation.

To
Linda, Eric,
and Kurt

Acknowledgments

The idea for this book was born while I was editing a special issue of the *Journal of Voluntary Action Research* (JVAR). Earlier versions of five of the chapters in the book appeared in the special issue (Vol. 11, no. 1, 1982). Jon Van Til, editor of JVAR, was an important source of advice and encouragement during that project. The Association of Voluntary Action Scholars, sponsor of JVAR, has for many years provided me with an important network of scholarly colleagues and friends.

Much of the initial work on the book was done while I was a Visiting Fellow at the Lincoln Filene Center for Citizenship and Public Affairs at Tufts University. Stuart Langton, the center's director, and his outstanding staff have created a very productive and congenial environment. My year at the Filene Center provided me with that most perfect of academic settings—great resources and few obligations.

My colleagues at Western Michigan University have also contributed to the completion of this work. David Chaplin and Stanley Robin were generous in providing administrative and clerical support, and Gerald Markle supplied helpful comments on parts of the manuscript.

Contents

I

An Overview

1

Citizen Participation
in Science Policy

James C. Petersen

One of the ironies of the 1970s was
that while social commentators
were decrying the rise of self-ab-
sorption and the abandonment of
social responsibility, the citizen
participation movement in the
United States was flourishing as
never before (Langton, 1978). An
emphasis on self-gratification was
certainly prominent in the past decade. Pop psychologists played on
the themes of self-awareness and
self-fulfillment to their great financial gain. A mass-circulation magazine emerged with the improbable
title of *Self*. Social critics warned of
the development of a "me generation" and the creation of a "culture
of narcissism" (Lasch, 1979). And,
indeed, there was at least some empirical evidence of the abandonment of collective responsibilities.
Sociologists and political scientists
documented the "white flight"
from American cities that occurred

during the seventies, and the decline in voter turnout that has been continuing for the past two decades.

At the same time, however, the seventies was a period of rapid growth for neighborhood associations, special-interest or single-issue politics, citizen participation in many federal and state programs, and public involvement in a number of large-scale social movements. No account of the past decade would be complete without mention of the pro- and antiabortion forces, the organizations favoring and opposing the Equal Rights Amendment, the antinuclear power groups, and the environmental movement. Indeed, by 1978, one-eighth of all Americans regarded themselves as active participants in the environmental movement (Public Opinion on Environmental Issues, 1980). This decade saw citizen participation written into law, conferences held on the topic, and the establishment of a publication devoted to the subject—*Citizen Participation* newsmagazine.

Many of the citizen participation efforts of the past decade involved issues of science or technology policy. During the late 1970s Americans watching network news slowly grew accustomed to the sight of farmers being arrested as they tried to block the construction of a high-energy powerline across western Minnesota. While these Minnesota farmers were engaging in a kind of guerrilla warfare against the survey and construction crews, other energy-related protests were taking place in New England. In June 1978 thousands of demonstrators and spectators descended upon Seabrook, New Hampshire, to oppose the Seabrook Nuclear Power Plant and to advocate alternative energy sources. During this same summer, Love Canal and the hazards of toxic wastes became part of the national consciousness, largely through the protest efforts of Lois Gibbs and the Love Canal Homeowners' Association. Dramatic though these stories were, they represented but a tiny part of the vast amount of citizen participation.

Some public involvement efforts were government mandated, as in the network of Health Systems Agencies established in 1974. The legislation creating these health planning agencies required that health-care consumers make up a majority of the board of directors of each HSA. In other cases, the government facilitated citizen participation efforts. For example, the National Science Foundation's Science for Citizens Program established a series of pilot Science for Citizens Centers to provide technical assistance to citizens who wanted significant input in the policy-making process. In many instances, public participation was more emergent. Citizens became concerned about airport siting, landfill locations, toxic waste disposal, and a host of other issues, and attempted to influence policy both through traditional means such as public hearings and petitions or through varied forms of protest. Most of these events never attracted network news coverage and yet were in the best tradition of American democracy.

This book is a collection of essays and case studies on these citizen participation efforts. Together, the chapters place citizen involvement in science policy in the context of larger participatory movements, explore the variety of forms which citizen participation may take, consider new alternatives for public involvement, and provide case studies detailing the promise and problems of citizen participation in issues with a heavily technical content. Few areas have been less receptive to public participation than the formulation of technical policy. The public has been frequently excluded from such decision making by leaders who generally define decisions as technical questions. The issues at stake are too critical to permit any but the most thorough of debates. It is my hope that the analyses collected here will not only increase our understanding of citizen participation in science policy, but will also increase the effectiveness of citizens who wish to help shape the outcome of questions of science and technology policy.

The Rise of Citizen Participation

Citizen participation is nearly synonymous with American democracy. Its roots run deep in American culture. Whereas traditional forms of political participation have received extensive attention from scholars (Milbrath and Goel, 1977), other forms of public involvement have not been subject to comparable scrutiny. Much basic information about the extent and form of participation in neighborhood groups, voluntary associations, and social movements remains to be collected. Still, we know that from our earliest days as a nation, voluntary citizen action has been important to our way of life. Travel accounts by such nineteenth-century visitors as French aristocrat Alexis de Tocqueville and Britain's Lord Bryce contain observations on the extensive associational activity in the United States.

In more recent years survey researchers have conducted studies of the public's involvement in formal voluntary associations. The results of these surveys vary widely, partly because of the different ways they pose questions on involvement and partly because some researchers exclude union or church participation while others include these activities. In summarizing the research on extent of participation, David Sills (1968) suggests that probably more than three-quarters of American adults are at least inactive members of associations, but perhaps fewer than one-quarter are really active members. Data from national surveys conducted during the 1950s and 1960s indicate that the percentage of adult Americans who were members of voluntary associations increased somewhat during this period (Hyman and Wright, 1971).

In the 1970s there seems to have been a virtual explosion of citizen activity. Block clubs and neighborhood associations gained great prominence along with citizen organizations, public interest groups, and other forms of grassroots activity. By 1975, the Alliance for Voluntarism estimated that there were 6 million voluntary associations in the United States. There was also a great deal of informal activity which is more difficult to accurately quantify.

One of the unique features of the seventies was that the impetus for greater citizen participation and involvement came from both grassroots citizen action and governmental initiatives. In this decade government at all levels increasingly encouraged and sometimes mandated citizen participation in the decision-making process. Thus the 1970s witnessed the growth of two citizen participation movements: a government-initiated movement and a citizen-initiated movement.

Government-mandated participation   Until the early 1960s the guidelines for citizen involvement in federal agencies were set by the Administrative Procedures Act. Agencies were generally required to provide for public notice, to allow groups the opportunity to make presentations during hearings, and, when appropriate, to hold public hearings. Under this act, the responsibility for initiating participation rested with the public, and involvement was generally confined to a late stage of policy development (Rosenbaum, 1978).

The Economic Opportunity Act of 1964 was to change all this with its famous and controversial requirement that the Office of Economic Opportunity achieve "maximum feasible participation" among the poor in its programs. Here a federal agency was required to encourage participation among the people it served. When OEO officials attempted to aggressively mobilize the poor in community development activities, the programs came under a great deal of criticism. Still, an important principle was established: "Participation was now a right rather than a privilege" (Rosenbaum, 1978:83).

Federal legislation in the seventies retained the principle that agencies are responsible for encouraging public participation. Much of the legislation affected groups ranging from the poor to the wealthy. Most aspects of agency planning were opened to citizen involvement. "Sunshine" legislation may also have had the effect of increasing the importance of citizen participation. The extensive array of government-mandated citizen participation was largely a creation of the 1970s. Of the more than 200 public participation programs in place in federal agencies at the end of the seventies, 61 percent had been created during that decade. Furthermore, 80 percent of the federal grant-in-aid programs that required public participation were established in the 1970s (Rich and Rosenbaum, 1981).

It is clear that federally mandated citizen participation will not be as prominent in the 1980s as it was in the previous decade. The Reagan administration has systematically been dismantling the federal citizen participation programs. At the Environmental Protection Agency, for example, public participation requirements were rolled back to speed up the approval process for construction projects. Where the Community Development Block Grant Program had previously required written citizen participation plans, now only a single public hearing is required for a CDBG proposal. Under the guise of deregulation and budget trimming, the Reagan administration has been gutting the citizen participation programs established in the 1970s (Berry, 1981).

It is difficult to assess the impact of government-initiated citizen participation for several reasons: many of the programs have been in place for relatively short periods of time; others are currently being sharply curtailed or eliminated and will thus never develop much of a record to assess; some agencies have notoriously poor participation programs and yet these programs have not been altered. Government may properly have a responsibility to facilitate participation by citizens, especially those who are disadvantaged socially or economically. Yet, at the same time, there is a risk that government sponsorship could restrict the freedom of citizens to openly criticize their sponsors.

Grassroots participation　As is perhaps appropriate for our technological era, many citizen-initiated movements of the 1970s and 1980s have grown up around disputes involving science or technology. Thus individuals have organized citizen organizations to protest and oppose the siting of new airports, the development of nuclear power plants, the mandatory use of automobile airbags, and the installation of high-energy powerlines. Among the core concerns in these disputes are questions of equity, fears of risk, and infringements on personal freedoms and traditional values (Nelkin, 1979).

In *The Dynamics of Technical Controversy*, Allan Mazur (1981) identifies three major steps in the growth of such protests. Initially a warning is brought to the attention of the public. Such warnings may be issued by individual critics, watchdog groups, agencies involved in risk assessment, whistleblowers, or as a result of tragic events. The second step is reached if a small number of protesters emerge in response to the public warning. These individuals or groups serve as adversaries to the promoters of the technology in question. In many cases, however, public warnings attract little attention and no opponents emerge. Finally, some protests grow up to become mass movements. Typical features of successful national movements include a coalition of local protest groups and an active presence in Washington.

Of course not all citizen efforts are in opposition to new products or technologies. In recent years groups of citizens have opposed the threatened ban of saccharin by the Food and Drug Administration (Petersen and Markle, 1981), and the creationist forces have demanded equal time in textbooks for the biblical story of creation (Nelkin, 1981). Occasionally citizens have organized to champion new techniques, as with Laetrile. Although claims about Laetrile were labelled a hoax by the U.S. Food and Drug Administration, the American Medical Association, and most of the American medical community, a large social movement developed in the mid-seventies around this purported cancer treatment. A number of voluntary associations including the International Association of Cancer Victims and Friends, the Cancer Control Society, and the Committee for Freedom of Choice in Cancer Therapy were formed to promote Laetrile and other "underground" cancer therapies. Tens of thousands of Americans became supporters of Laetrile and opposed the federal government's ban on the substance. Since 1976, as a result of lobbying by pro-Laetrile organizations, about half of the states have legalized Laetrile despite opposition from the federal government. Supporters of Laetrile also won several battles in the courts, although they lost a case argued before the U.S. Supreme Court (Petersen and Markle, 1979; Markle and Petersen, 1980).

Clearly the involvement of large numbers of citizens and citizen groups in technical controversies is no guarantee that wise policy will always result. Citizens have advocated questionable techniques, like Laetrile, and have, on occasion, unduly delayed legitimate projects. Still, substantial public input ensures a more thorough and open debate on questions of science and technology policy. This is especially important in that the public has so frequently been excluded from decisions on technical questions. In this context, extraordinary measures may be required to facilitate effective citizen participation to counterbalance the current elite domination of technical policy making.

Forms of Citizen Input

Few values in American society are held more deeply than the right of citizens to participate in decisions on matters that directly affect them. Yet effective public participation on toxic waste disposal, nuclear plant siting, energy conservation, drug regulation, and a host of contemporary concerns is difficult due to the scientific and technical content of such issues. Specialized scientific knowledge and impenetrable technical jargon are barriers to meaningful participation by a public that is frequently placed at risk by the decisions of technical experts or governmental officials. If the public is to have significant input into the environmental, medical, and science-related problems confronting society, mechanisms must be developed to facilitate meaningful participation by citizens and citizen groups.

Many traditional forms of citizen participation—public hearings, advisory boards, and study groups—often give the appearance of citizen input but actually lack much substance. Barry Checkoway (1980) has noted that hearings are often the only participation method used in many decisions. Despite this fact, they are frequently held at times and locations that severely limit access. Furthermore, the formal language and procedural rules make communication difficult, especially for some low-income and minority citizens. Even when special care is taken to make meetings accessible to the public, hearings are often held at such a late stage in the decision-making process that possibilities for change are sharply circumscribed.

Barry Casper and David Wellstone's (1981) powerful account of the Minnesota powerline protests illustrates many of the shortcomings of the public hearing. Well before Minnesota farmers turned to mass protest and sabotage in their attempt to stop the construction of high-energy powerlines across western Minnesota, they participated in a series of public hearings. The Minnesota Environmental Quality Control Council held numerous hearings in order to involve the public in the routing of the powerline. Farmers were unimpressed with the results. As one protest leader put it, "They say they're giving the people input or whatever; they'd be a lot better off just to decide to put it over here, because we had no say-so anyway."

As is often the case, the range of options had been severely limited by the time the hearings occurred. The end points of the powerline were taken as fixed, and key concerns of the farmers—environmental effects and safety issues—were defined as irrelevant by those in charge. At the hearings, the farmers lacked the resources to challenge the technical experts brought in by the power cooperatives planning to construct the line. Once again, technical expertise proved to be a potent political resource. The power co-ops were granted a certificate of need and a route was designated for the powerline.

By 1976 Minnesota farmers were using force to drive survey crews from their land. When attempts to stop construction crews failed, direct action increased: many powerline towers toppled after being unbolted from their bases by "bolt weevils"; the insulators that supported the line proved susceptible to "insulator disease" and thousands were shattered; and the line itself became a target for local marksmen.

At several points in the dispute, Governor Rudy Perpich advocated the use of a science court to try to resolve the conflict. The idea of a science court had been developed in 1976 by a White House task force. The science court process would first identify significant scientific and technical questions associated with a policy dispute. Then an adversary proceeding would take place before a panel of scientist-judges. Finally, the judges would issue a report as to the scientific facts related to the controversy. In Minnesota, however, Perpich was unable to convince the farmers and power co-ops to agree on arrangements for a science court. The science court concept assumes that fact and value can be separated in disputes. Often this proves difficult, if not impossible. Ronnie Brooks, a special assistant to the governor, recognized this when she observed, "Perhaps part of our failure was due to the attempt to impose a rational decision-making process on an already value-laden issue. If, in fact, the issue all along was one of intrusion on the land, then our attempts to address technological questions were at best irrelevant" (Casper and Wellstone, 1981:246).

As the Minnesota experience indicates, when traditional forms of citizen input such as hearings are perceived as biased, and innovations such as the science court are seen as irrelevant, the demand for input will still find expression. Public protest, nonviolent direct action, and even the use of violence have at times in our history served to convey the sentiments of those who felt they lacked other effective ways of communicating their needs. No nation born of revolution can totally deny the legitimacy of such forms of political expression. At the same time, I do not think many Americans would welcome the use of violence as a normal way to provide input into the decision-making process.

Clearly, we need to develop mechanisms that provide citizens with real opportunities to shape policies before the basic parameters become fixed. Public hearings can be improved through such devices as advance publicity in nontechnical language, interactive procedures, technical assistance to participants, and posthearing follow-ups (Checkoway, 1980). Less familiar forms of citizen input—such as citizen courts, citizen review boards, referenda, and other participatory experiments—should also be considered. The discussions of these devices in the following chapters are a starting point. A decade ago Carroll (1971) analyzed the "incipient emergence of participatory technology"—the mechanisms for including the public in the development, implementation, and regulation of technology. Our problem is that technology continues to develop far more rapidly than "participatory technology."

Issues for Citizen Involvement

Issues of power and control permeate most conflicts related to science and technology. In some instances, such as the Minnesota powerline controversy, the political nature of the conflict is quite open. In the Minnesota case, major state politicians became deeply involved in the dispute, and a protest leader sought the Democratic-Farmer-Labor nomination for governor in the 1978 primary. In other science-related controversies, however, the political nature of the decision-making process may be more hidden, often concealed behind claims of technical complexity and scientific objectivity. Such claims warrant a skeptical view, for as Dorothy Nelkin (1975) has detailed, technical expertise is itself politicized. In the cases Nelkin examined—the expansion of an airport and the siting of a power plant—the developers sought expertise to legitimize their plans, and then attempted to use their control of technical knowledge to exclude the public from the decision-making process.

Citizens who wish to influence decisions involving science and technology must confront the political aspects of the process. What resources are available and how can they be mobilized? The range of resources that can be used in political confrontations is broad. Among those commonly used are money, prestige, political access, control of the media, legality, knowledge and expertise, and numbers of people. Until mobilized, however, resources remain but a potential. Those who want more effective citizen participation in technical matters must find better ways to locate and mobilize political resources.

Such resources need not be material. The role of values in science-related controversies is poorly understood, but values seem to play a part in the expansion of disputes among experts into public controversies. When value claims are consistent with prominent social values, they may serve as potent political resources. In the case of both public opposition to a threatened ban of saccharin and interest group advocacy of Laetrile, appeals were made to "freedom of choice." This ideal, consistent with the dominant American value of individualism, was an effective tool in confronting claims of special expertise by scientists and government officials (Petersen and Markle, 1981).

Expertise, however, is a potent resource, and the public can ill afford to let utilities, developers, and corporations purchase a virtual monopoly of technical expertise. A key issue for citizen activists must be how to develop mechanisms to redistribute expertise more equitably. The notion that the public—like government and industry—should have scientific advisers was a central theme in the public interest science movement of the 1970s (von Hippel and Primack, 1972; Primack and von Hippel, 1974). Since the early 1970s, some professional societies—most notably the American Association for the Advancement of Science—have become more concerned with the issue of the social responsibilities of scientists. Public interest scientists have founded a few organizational bases, as in the Union of Concerned Scientists, the Center for Science in the Public Interest, and the various Public Interest Research Groups. Still, most citizens have no idea where to turn for assistance in disputes involving scientific or technical issues.

An experiment in providing technical assistance to local citizens was launched by the federal government in 1977. As a result of a congressional mandate growing out of the public interest science movement, the National Science Foundation established the Science for Citizens Program. Rachelle Hollander's account of the program (see chapter 5) details the shaping of its policies and programs. In 1980 the Science for Citizens Program awarded six operational grants for the establishment of public service science centers whose purpose was to (1) provide scientific and technical assistance to citizens and (2) increase the level and quality of citizen and scientist involvement in the resolution of science-related policy issues. When the 1982 NSF budget eliminated funding for the Science for Citizens

Program, it cut short this experiment in the redistribution of expertise. Inadequate funding has been a chronic problem for public interest science efforts, and greater attention will have to be paid to finding stable sources of funds to support technical assistance programs.

Although it will never eliminate the need for technical assistance on specific policy issues, increasing the public's level of awareness and understanding of science could substantially increase the effectiveness of citizen participation in science policy matters. Certainly improvements in the extent and quality of science teaching in the schools could eventually produce a public better prepared to grapple with issues that have a strong technical component. In the short run, however, improving the quality of science reporting in the mass media may be one of the most effective ways of capacity building in the public.

Opportunities for learning about science and technology through the media have increased dramatically in recent years. Such publications as *Science 84, Discover, Science Digest, Technology Illustrated,* and *High Technology* are glossy publications filled with dramatic graphics. They are aimed at the public, not at professional scientists. Television has also increased coverage of science with such shows as "Nova," "Omni," "Universe," and "Cosmos," as well as special series like "The Body in Question" and "Connections." Although these media efforts at popularizing science have many supporters, they have not met with universal praise. Some critics charge that science is being transformed into entertainment in order to make it sell (Bernstein, 1981). In fact, there has long been a strong "gee whiz" tradition in science reporting that resulted in uncritical coverage of the highly dramatic.

Science journalists are aware of the need for improving media coverage of science. The National Association of Science Writers and the Science Writing Educators Group are working in a variety of ways to upgrade the quality of science reporting. Several scientific societies have also provided guidance for their members on how to more effectively communicate with the media. Recently the Scientists' Institute for Public Information published a handbook on dealing with the media titled "The Scientist's Responsibility for Public Information." One of the real difficulties for both scientists and the public, however, is that only perhaps fifty newspapers in the United States have a full-time science reporter on their staffs. If citizens were to demand more extensive and higher quality science coverage from their local newspapers, this situation could be improved dramatically.

Even if higher levels of public understanding result from improvements in science education and media coverage, citizens should expect continued opposition to public involvement in questions of science and technology policy. Opponents of public participation will continue to attempt to restrict decision making to a scientific elite. Citizens who wish to open up this decision-making process will have to make the case for citizen participation. As the chapters in this book detail, such a case can be made on the basis of democratic values, tax support of research, increasing public understanding, and shared risk. Furthermore, public participation may have important benefits for science itself. Halsted Holman and Diana Dutton (1978) describe a number of contributions citizens could make to scientific investigation, from the actual selection of the problem to the application of results. Finding ways to make an effective case for citizen participation in technical issues is likely to remain a central problem for citizen activists until mechanisms which build in citizen input become institutionalized.

The Organization of the Book

This book is divided into three sections. The first is an overview of the central issues involved in citizen participation in science policy; it also serves as an introduction to the other chapters. The second section examines the different forms of citizen input into science policy, and explores options for the future. The final section is composed of three case studies of citizen participation in the development of health policy and three papers on public involvement in nuclear policy.

Dorothy Nelkin's essay on technical policy and the democratic process completes the overview section. Nelkin, one of the keenest observers of the science policy scene, considers the factors behind the increased demand for public involvement in the making of science and technology policy. Chief among these were changes in the public's perception of science, technology, and expertise. Nelkin also describes channels of influence open to citizens, including models drawn from Europe. Her essay concludes with an exploration of the implications of participatory politics for the conduct of science.

The second section of the book opens with Sheldon Krimsky's exploration of the role of citizen participation in social risk assessment. Conventional approaches of public access are compared with some recent experiments that have included lay members on technical advisory boards. Krimsky urges the improvement of access to decision making for those who face special risks, but who are unorganized, powerless, and lacking in technical expertise. He also examines how to increase the effectiveness of citizen involvement in science and technology policy.

As a result of federal and state legislation, environmental impact statements must be prepared before major actions that affect the environment can be taken. Impact assessment began in the United States in the early 1970s as an activity conducted by professionals with limited public input. Frederick Rossini and Alan Porter consider the increasing role of public involvement in impact assessment and technology assessment. They identify three broad approaches: professional-dominant assessments, participant-dominant assessments, and a partnership mode. Rossini and Porter view both professionalism and participation as essential in assessment, and consider the implications of different mixes. Their essay concludes with a discussion of the factors that may shape the selection of an assessment approach.

The Science for Citizens program at the National Science Foundation was a major experiment in providing technical assistance to citizens and citizen groups. The program, initiated in 1977, was eliminated from the 1982 NSF budget. Rachelle Hollander recounts the history of Science for Citizens, describes its program elements, and provides views of six NSF-funded public service science centers. She also discusses the future of these centers in light of the termination of NSF funding.

The second section of the book concludes with a view of the role of science policy in third-world countries. Jayanta Bandyopadhyay and Vandana Shiva examine the legitimacy of public participation in the formulation of science and technology policy, with special attention to the ecological movement in India. The roots of this movement are considered in a discussion of problems produced by planned forest management. The growth of the "Chipko" movement—a grassroots protest against forest destruction—is explored, and justifications for public participation in technological decisions are provided.

The case studies in the third section of the book provide opportunities to view the successes and failures of citizen participation efforts in two major areas: health policy and nuclear policy. The six papers provide fascinating insights into how public involvement efforts have actually worked. The apparent impact of citizen participation varies widely from case to case. In several instances, formidable barriers to significant citizen input limited public access. As the authors point out, however, substantial social costs result from the exclusion of the public.

Daryl Chubin's case study of the Virus Cancer Program at the National Cancer Institute explores one pattern of the relationship of scientists and the public in the establishment of research priorities. Because no disease is more feared than cancer, the public is more susceptible to manipulation. Research missions emerge from the relations between science and politics. This country's war on cancer has been propelled by an alliance of politicians and technical experts articulating a rhetoric of need. Chubin charges that research progress on cancer was "overpromised" to the public in order to ensure generous funding of cancer research.

The National Health Planning and Resources Development Act of 1974 created a national network of Health Systems Agencies which emphasized consumer participation in health planning, a field long dominated by medical providers and hospitals. Thus far, the record of consumer participation in the Health Systems Agencies has been uneven. On the one hand, considerable dissatisfaction with the agencies has been expressed from various quarters. On the other hand, health consumer groups have been able to organize independently of, but with reference to, health planning. Barry Checkoway examines the increased number and capacity of these groups, the major issues with which they have been concerned, and the opportunities and resources that have helped make group formation possible. In Checkoway's view, federal legislation has provided an avenue by which citizens can move beyond their traditional subservience to health professionals.

The final essay on health policy provides a view of public involvement in four cases of biomedical policy making. Diana Dutton examines different forms of direct intervention by citizens in the decision making on DES—a synthetic hormone used to prevent miscarriages and as a "morning-after pill" contraceptive—recombinant DNA research, the nationwide swine flu immunization program of 1976, and the government-funded artificial heart research program. Among the prominent barriers to public involvement in these cases were apathy, incomplete data, diffuse issues, backlash from established interests, and the secrecy of developments in the private sector. Dutton's chapter closes with a thoughtful analysis of the reasons for and against public participation in the development of biomedical policy.

Though nuclear policy was once determined in secrecy by the Great Powers, the rules of the international nuclear market are becoming targets of an ever-growing number of actors ranging from governments of developing nations, to corporations, legislative committees, and public interest groups. Randy Rydell explores the expansion of participants in the debate over tomorrow's nuclear world order, and provides a framework of analysis to understand this expansion. He includes brief accounts of the role of public participation in three nuclear power controversies: the Three Mile Island accident, the Clinch River Breeder Reactor project, and the control of nuclear proliferation.

In the second essay on nuclear policy, Jane Kronick contrasts the nature of interest group participation in legislative hearings on nuclear power with that occurring in hearings on toxic substances. In the latter case, both public interest groups and labor unions have made a strong case for collective welfare and responsibility of government. As a result of substantive and procedural constraints, neither public interest groups nor unions have participated to the same extent in legislative hearings on nuclear power development. In the absence of effective public input, a narrow government-industry dialogue has been able to ignore key issues and values.

The final entry on nuclear policy considers the ways in which a nonviolent protest influenced public opinion on the construction of a nuclear power plant. In June 1978 a large antinuclear rally in Seabrook, New Hampshire, attracted national attention. John Hunt and Neil Katz conducted telephone interviews of a sample of Seabrook-area residents during the month following the protest. Their study examines the views of local residents toward the protesters, the appeal of the protest actions, and opinions of the power plant construction. They suggest that perceived legitimacy of the protest was related to predisposing ideologies and prior contact with the protest group. Young people were the social category most likely to respond to the protest's appeal.

Given the current prominence of social controversies over nuclear power development, energy policy, toxic waste disposal, and new medical technologies like in vitro fertilization, the essays comprising this book could hardly have been written at a more appropriate time. Each illuminates an aspect of citizen participation in science policy. Taken together, they provide significant insight into the strengths and limitations of different mechanisms for citizen input. A brief afterword sets out a few of the major commonalities of the papers. There are lessons here for both scholarship and social action.

References

Bernstein, Jeremy. 1981. "Can TV Really Teach Science?" *Dial* (June):46–49.

Berry, Jeffrey M. 1981. "Maximum Feasible Dismantlement." *Citizen Participation* 3:3–5.

Carroll, James D. 1971. "Participatory Technology." *Science* 171:647–53.

Casper, Barry M., and Wellstone, Paul David. 1981. *Powerline: The First Battle of America's Energy War.* Amherst: University of Massachusetts Press.

Checkoway, Barry. 1980. "Public Hearings Are Not Enough." *Citizen Participation* 1:6–7, 20.

Holman, Halsted R., and Dutton, Diana B. 1978. "A Case for Public Participation in Science Policy Formation and Practice." *Southern California Law Review* 51:1505–34.

Hyman, Herbert, and Wright, Charles. 1971. "Trends in Voluntary Association Memberships of American Adults." *American Sociological Review* 36:191–206.

Langton, Stuart, ed. 1978. *Citizen Participation in America.* Lexington, Massachusetts: Lexington Books.

Lasch, Christopher. 1979. *The Culture of Narcissism.* New York: Warner Books.

Markle, Gerald E., and Petersen, James C., eds. 1980. *Politics, Science, and Cancer: The Laetrile Phenomenon.* Boulder, Colorado: Westview.

Mazur, Allan. 1981. *The Dynamics of Technical Controversy.* Washington, D.C.: Communications Press.

Milbrath, Lester, and Goel, M. L. 1977. *Political Participation*, 2d ed. Chicago: Rand McNally.

Nelkin, Dorothy. 1975. "The Political Impact of Technical Expertise." *Social Studies of Science* 5:35–54.

———. 1977. *Science Textbook Controversies and the Politics of Equal Time.* Cambridge, Massachusetts: MIT Press.

———, ed. 1979. *Controversy: Politics of Technical Decisions.* Beverly Hills: Sage Publications.

Petersen, James C., and Markle, Gerald E. 1979. "Politics and Science in the Laetrile Controversy." *Social Studies of Science* 9:139–66.

———. 1981. "Expansion of Conflict in Cancer Controversies." In *Research in Social Movements, Conflicts and Change*, ed. Louis Kriesberg. Greenwich, Connecticut: JAI Press.

Primack, Joel, and von Hippel, Frank. 1974. *Advice and Dissent: Scientists in the Political Arena.* New York: New American Library.

Public Opinion on Environmental Issues. 1980. Washington, D.C.: Government Printing Office.

Rich, Richard C., and Rosenbaum, Walter A. 1981. "Introduction." *Journal of Applied Behavioral Science* 17:439–45.

Rosenbaum, Walter A. 1978. "Public Involvement as Reform and Ritual: The Development of Federal Participation Programs." In *Citizen Participation in America*, ed. Stuart Langton. Lexington, Massachusetts: Lexington Books.

Sills, David L. 1968. "Voluntary Associations: Sociological Aspects." In *International Encyclopedia of the Social Sciences*. New York: Macmillan and Free Press.

von Hippel, Frank, and Primack, Joel. 1972. "Public Interest Science." *Science* 177:1166–71.

2

Science and Technology Policy and the Democratic Process

Dorothy Nelkin

Summary

This paper reviews the issues involved in the demands for greater public participation in science and technology policy. Numerous controversies suggest that the sources of "participatory politics" lie in the changing public image of science and technology and especially in the changing attitudes toward expertise as a source of political legitimacy. The paper analyzes these sources of conflict and the various "publics" involved, describing diverse fears about science and technology that lead to participatory demands. While surveys indicate that most people perceive science and technology as instrumental in achieving important social goals, specific concerns persist. The central and pervasive issue—the source of many conflicts—is the question of who controls crucial policy decisions.

As various groups seek greater participation in science and technology policy, governments have expanded participatory channels both within the representative system and through administrative reforms. In addition, participatory experiments outside of official administrative channels have proliferated. Describing experiments in the United States and Western Europe, this essay suggests the range of options available to accommodate participatory demands. It also analyzes some of their difficulties, as the complexity of science and technology and the expectations of efficiency associated with technical planning obstruct efforts to develop participatory procedures.

The demands for participation can affect the application of resources to research, the strength of research institutions, and the way scientists choose their topics and conduct their work. And participation can influence the general climate—political, social, and intellectual—in which research takes place. Thus its implications warrant special attention in the coming years.

Introduction

Everywhere symbols of progress are under public scrutiny. Technologies of speed and power—airports, highways, nuclear plants—provoke antagonism as local communities protest against noise and disruption. Science-based programs such as genetic screening are a source of public debate. And important areas of research face persistent opposition: note, for example, disputes over fetal research, recombinant DNA, and studies of the genetic origins of human behavior. Technical problems that were once considered the preserve of experts are increasingly forced into the political arena as many interests seek greater control over the direction of science and technology (Nelkin, 1979).

Until recently, most questions of public control focused on technological applications, but public scrutiny has come to rest on science as well. Given the policy importance of many areas of scientific research and the growing concern in the biological sciences with basic life processes, such scrutiny is inevitable. Indeed the relationship between science and the public appears to be in the process of significant renegotiation.

Despite the intensity of some disputes, few people seek to impose major restrictions on science and its applications; most areas of science and technology are valued as instrumental in achieving important social goals. Rather, the negotiation is over *who* should participate in establishing policies and controls, how these controls will be organized, and how much they should influence decisions concerning the direction and conduct of research. Reflected in these questions is a troublesome feature of contemporary society—the impact of increased complexity and specialization on the decision-making process. The power afforded to those who control technical information reduces public control over many public policy choices, and technical complexity appears to limit effective political choice. This concern is ubiquitous in the controversies over science and technology. The key slogans in these disputes are "public accountability of scientists," "demystification of expertise," and "lay participation." Local groups demand a voice in the location and design of nuclear power plants. Patients seek greater control over their medication. Parents insist on influencing the science textbooks used in schools. Consumers raise questions about the validity of the data that back government regulation of drugs such as cyclamates, saccharin, and Laetrile. Citizens seek to participate in shaping the rules and standards that control science and technology or the conditions of work in the laboratory.

Participatory demands have focused both on the conduct of research (the recombinant DNA and fetal research disputes) and on its public consequences (research on genetic manipulation or on the sources of criminal violence). Indeed, a new field, "the social assessment of science," is emerging to examine "the involvement of non-scientists in the assessment, judgment and criticism of science" (Mendelsohn and Weingart, 1978).

While the concern in this review is more with policies that affect the conduct of research than with the management of technology, it includes examples of the latter. It is often hard to distinguish science from its applications, and public concern about technology extends to science, especially in those areas perceived to have eventual application. People are clearly more concerned about technology than about science, but when asked in a public opinion survey whether it is more important for society to control science or technology, 59 percent responded that both must be controlled equally (20 percent that neither should be controlled at all) (Opinion Research Corp., 1976).

This essay, then, analyzes the politics of participation in both science and technology policy. It describes the sources of participatory demands, the existing procedures and some recent experiments in accommodating those who wish to participate, some of the obstacles to greater participation, and, finally, some of the potential implications of greater public involvement.

Sources of Participatory Politics

Demands for greater public involvement in science and technology reflect the convergence of a heightened sensitivity to the environmental and social implications of science and technology with a changing view of expertise. These are the preconditions for participatory politics as people seek greater control over decisions that affect their lives.

Changing images of science and technology   Attitudes toward science and technology are ambivalent: optimistic expectations about potential social good are mixed with concern about undesirable consequences. Surveys indicate that most people view science as instrumental in achieving important social goals, yet only a small majority (52 percent) of respondents in a 1976 survey said they believed that science and technology have produced more good than harm. By far the greatest perceived benefits were in the field of medicine (81 percent); in other areas—improved living conditions, environmental conservation, energy programs, and improved communication—science and technology were reported as beneficial only 10–14 percent of the time. A review of longitudinal data on the public's confidence in people who run institutions found that the proportion of respondents expressing "a great deal of confidence" in the scientific community declined from 56 percent to 43 percent between 1966 and 1976 (National Science Board, 1977).[1] However, in gauging the public's esteem for science relative to other occupations in 1976, science ranked second (behind medicine) and engineering third. Public regard for scientists has declined in absolute terms, but this reflects the declining trust in most major institutions. Between 1966 and 1976 those expressing a great deal of confidence in Congress declined from 42 percent to 14 percent, the heads of major corporations from 55 percent to 22 percent, the U.S. Supreme Court from 51 percent to 35 percent, and educators from 61 percent to 37 percent. In this context scientists have fared rather well.

But opposition to specific projects persists. Science and technology are often blamed for environmental pollution, loss of privacy and civil liberties, the impersonal character of medical care, the routine character of work, and the threat of greater social control.

Concerns about science and technology extend beyond the fear of risk.

Some critics (e.g., those opposing fetal research or the teaching of evolution) feel that science has ethical implications that threaten deeply held personal beliefs. Others worry about the potential misuse of scientific findings: for example, critics of research on recombinant DNA, on the XYY chromosome, and on the relationship between genetics and intelligence question the implications of relating genetically mediated characteristics to human behavior. Biology, they claim, is "a social weapon." "Can future generations cope with the possibilities science opens up today?" Still others are concerned about equity both in the allocation of resources to science and technology and in the distribution of social and environmental costs.

It is often argued that changing attitudes toward science reflect disappointed expectations. Atomic energy and the space program brought science from the obscurity of the university laboratory to the forefront of American consciousness, creating optimistic expectations—the so-called "Moon-Ghetto syndrome": given enough support, science and technology can solve all problems (Richard, 1977). Yet the 1960s also brought the realization that science and technology not only failed to solve social problems but often contributed to them.

The changing image of science and technology also reflects reaction to the increased role of the federal government in this sector. The rate of technological change, the scale of scientific and technical projects, the rapid diffusion of technology to new areas, and the high costs associated with R&D have necessitated increasing federal commitment to develop and regulate many technologies and some areas of scientific research as well. These have essentially moved from the private to the public sector.

This has happened at a time when public interest in playing a role in major policy decisions at all levels has reached a high point. Science and technology, of course, have not been immune. Demands for public accountability and questions about the appropriate focus of authority in science and technology policy reflect a more general loss of confidence in established institutions and a concomitant concern with public or consumer influence.

Changing images of expertise As technical knowledge assumes growing policy importance, scientists and engineers are increasingly active in public policy decisions through advisory boards, special commissions, staffs, and consultant groups (Gianos, 1974; Benveniste, 1972). Federal government expenditures for consultants have been estimated at over $1.8 billion a year. Moreover, there has been a general evolution from ad hoc advisory activity to the institutionalization of an "intellectual technocracy." Federal government employment of scientists grew by 49 percent from 1960 to 1970; for social scientists the increase was an even greater 52 percent. (Total federal government employment grew by only 30 percent during the same period.)

The implications of the growing policy role of expertise are not clear. Some perceive evidence of a growing technocratic elite—a new source of power with decisive influence over both politicians and the public (Meynaud, 1968; Ellul, 1970). Political power, it is argued, has shifted significantly from political and corporate decision makers to "knowledge elites" who derive their authority from the cultural emphasis on rationality, efficiency, and technological progress, and from the specialization inherent in bureaucratic organization.

An alternative view sees the technical elite essentially as a "mandarin" class, beholden to the existing establishment and commanding little or no independent power (Noble, 1977; Winner, 1977; McCrae, 1973). Experts, it is claimed, use their specialized knowledge to serve the established institutions in industrial society. They are said to be effective only insofar as politicians and entrepreneurs allow them to be, and they pose no real threat to entrenched forms of power. It is further argued that existing institutions legitimize themselves by enlisting technical expertise and using it selectively to give the appearance of objectivity, to support predetermined decisions, to maintain secrecy, or to "buy time" when opposition is anticipated (Primack and von Hippel, 1974; Benveniste, 1972; Lakoff, 1977).

Both views of the experts' role have increased apprehension about an erosion of democratic values. Metaphors of "the priesthood" or "the new Brahmans" are used to describe the function of the "knowledge elite" in a social system where authority is based on information, and many policy choices are reduced to technical decisions (Klaw, 1969; Lapp, 1965). The power afforded to those who control technical information reduces public influence. Thus, just as people are more aware of the potential harm associated with science and technology, they also feel they have fewer ways to directly influence them. This structural dilemma creates demands for greater public involvement.

The "Public" and the Participatory Impulse

Controversies over science and technology involve a variety of groups concerned with greater influence over the direction and control of science and its applications. As they organize, their concerns are translated into participatory demands.

Who is involved? The most obvious "public" concerned about science and technology are those persons who are directly affected by land expropriation, immediate risk, or rapid local economic, environmental, or social change. Residents of urban neighborhoods often claim that technological developments neglect their needs. They question the justice of the anticipated distribution of costs and benefits from a technology: Can any reduction in some citizens' welfare be justified by greater advantage to others? Can the magnitude or intensity of harm borne by neighbors of a noxious facility be reasonably incorporated into cost-benefit calculations? These questions are expressed in organized opposition to the expansion of airports and the siting of highways or power plants. Recently, similar arguments have confronted plans for siting biology laboratories to host recombinant DNA research. Indeed, most participatory demands come from the "neighbors" of science and technology, those directly affected by a planned project and unable to avoid its present impact or potential risks (Nelkin, 1971 and 1975; Hirshman, 1970).

In addition, a well-defined "concerned public" includes direct recipients of such professional services as health care. Mental or medical patients are directly affected by the availability of new drugs, new biomedical technologies, and trends in the use of health care techniques (Alford, 1975). They may also be subjects of clinical research. Here the demands for participation, based on the rights of individuals to have some voice in their own treatment, are often expressed in proposals for changes in professional-client relationships.

A far more vaguely defined public is made up of the consumers of the products of science and technology. Here the participatory impulse is often reflected in protest against government regulation of technology. The Laetrile dispute and the debates over regulation of saccharin and cyclamates raise questions about government intrusion and the limits of individual choice. In such cases, the opportunities opened up by science and technology and the potential risks involved in innovation exacerbate this classic political dilemma.

Other groups critical of science and technology share rather global concerns based on ideological or moral principles. These include members of major environmental and public interest associations who seek to influence national policy.

Finally, an important source of criticism has come from the scientific community itself. Many scientists became politicized during the 1960s. At that time, they focused on antiwar activities and the issue of military research in universities. More recently, their attention has turned to the environment, nuclear power, or biomedical research. These scientists question the potential risks in areas often obscured from public knowledge (Mazur, 1973).

As differences between experts rise to public visibility, science no longer appears as an objective and compelling basis for policy. Disputes among experts, encouraged by the intrinsic uncertainty concerning the impact of science and technology, call attention to this limited ability to predict potential risks. Controversy thus demystifies expertise, exposing the nontechnical and political assumptions that influence technical advice and encouraging the transfer of problems from the technical to the political arena.

From public concern to participatory demands   Technological controversies are marked by the proliferation of citizen groups. Most are temporary coalitions formed to challenge specific decisions, often disbanding once the issue is resolved. But some groups maintain themselves with a core of activists who remain interested in other projects affecting the community and who can mobilize a larger constituency when specific issues arise.

Sustaining these local groups are the large national associations such as the Sierra Club and Friends of the Earth, whose membership has more than tripled since the 1960s. Their relatively stable constituency can be mobilized to intervene in diverse technical areas, and they seek to increase public participation in areas of science and technology that present potential risk. They were, for example, among the active participants in the recombinant DNA dispute.

Consumer protection and public interest science groups have also proliferated. Such organizations as the Center for Science and the Public Interest, the Center for Concerned Engineers, the Coalition for Responsible Genetic Research, the Clearinghouse for Professional Responsibility, and Science for the People call attention to the social impacts and political dimensions of science and technology, and they try to provide citizen groups with the technical expertise necessary to challenge policy decisions (Ann Arbor Science for the People Editorial Collective, 1977).

The interest of these various groups extends beyond specific policies to the broader issue of decision-making power. Controversies are pervaded by questions of responsibility and control; "expert accountability" is a central theme. The demands of local community groups often resemble a kind of "mininationalism," as they seek to protect themselves by greater local control against the intrusions of technology. Expertise, they claim, should rest with those affected: "We need no experts"; it is an "arrogant assumption" to leave decisions to scientists. Thus citizen groups call for better information, provisions for "counterexpertise" and greater opportunities for participation.

Participatory Mechanisms and Administrative Reforms in Science and Technology Policy

Demands for greater participation have coincided with congressional qualms about the increasing power of administrative agencies. To sustain the authority of the representative system over decisions in technical areas, the Congress has built up its own technical competence, and it has also imposed legislative requirements on agencies to involve citizens more directly in the formulation and implementation of science and technology policies.

Participation and the representative system   Increasingly involved in decisions concerning science and technology, Congress has greatly expanded its technical staff: between 1947 and 1976 the combined staffs of the Senate and House increased from 2,513 to 13,272. Staff appointments have included specialized science-trained consultants who gather technical information and select technical witnesses for public hearings. The many hearings on recombinant DNA, for example, were largely structured by professional staff through the selection of key witnesses. A number of these hearings were specifically organized as a means to brief special congressional committees on various technical and political aspects of this controversial issue.

To improve its technical competence, Congress has also established several research services (Carpenter, 1970; Casper, 1977; Fox and Hammond, 1977). The Congressional Research Service was created in 1970 to provide information on special issues. The Office of Technology Assessment (OTA) was established in 1972 to assist Congress in evaluating and planning specific technologies. These technical services allow Congress to reassert legislative control and oversight over issues that have previously been delegated to administrative agencies.

The primary congressional response to anxiety about democratic representation has been through legislation. The Airport and Airways Development Act, the Federal Water Pollution Control Act, the Coastal Zone Management Act, the Highway Safety Act, the National Environmental Policy Act, and the Energy Reorganization Act all contain requirements for greater direct participation in administrative agency decisions.

Administrative channels of participation Administrative agencies are a major arena for political action, often replacing legislative bodies in defining policy problems and devising their solutions (Lowi, 1972; La Porte, 1971). Yet agency commitment to rational, efficient decision making usually precludes significant public involvement, except in a few highly politicized proceedings such as the power plant siting hearings of the Nuclear Regulatory Commission (Scott, 1969; Cramton, 1972; Gelhorn, 1972). Participatory reforms are mostly intended to expand the information available to the public and to channel information about public preferences to decision-making agencies. However, some procedural reforms seek to open the administrative process to negotiation and compromise, allowing public representatives to take part in the development of policies. I will briefly review some of these procedures, suggesting why critics often dismiss them as inadequate and seek participation through other means.

Participatory reforms have provided greater public access to data and reports that underlie the decision-making process. The Administrative Procedures Act requires administrative agencies to publish proposed rulemaking in the *Federal Register* and invite public comment. These comments are then taken into account when final regulations are developed. The *Register* contains drafts of controversial proposals; for example, HEW published early drafts of proposed regulatory guidelines for the use of human subjects in research in order to solicit public comments and to test public acceptability of HEW procedures. The National Research Act of 1974 extended this use of the *Federal Register*, as a forum as well as a bulletin board, by creating the National Commission for the Protection of Human Subjects of Biomedical and Behavioral Research to advise HEW. It required the Secretary of HEW to publish the commission's reports and recommendations prior to announcing his proposed rules and to respond if he failed to follow them.

The Freedom of Information Act further extended public access to government reports, as did the requirements for Environmental Impact Statements (EIS). Under the EIS requirements, agencies must publicize the existence of documents and actively disseminate them. This model has generated proposals for "Scientific Impact Statements" that would similarly evaluate the potential effects of research and solicit public review.

These participatory channels can provide useful information and also inform decision makers of citizen concerns, but critics contend that considerable initiative, money, and access to expertise are necessary to seek out and utilize useful material. The *Federal Register* is available in libraries and is indexed, but with 60,000 three-column pages per year it is a cumbersome document. Agencies must disclose information on request, but sometimes charge search and copy fees. Citizens unfamiliar with what is available or lacking access to expertise are often unable to request material with sufficient specificity, and crucial material on controversial topics is often withheld as proprietary information (Wade, 1972; Kolata, 1975). Thus, it is argued, although legislative reforms provide greater legal access to information, they are intended more to reduce conflict than to devolve power. More collaborative modes of participation include having citizen representatives, not simply as informants, but as partners with some power to exercise direct influence.

Advisory boards are a frequent channel for such collaborative participation. In 1975, forty-five agencies employed 1,267 advisory committees with 22,246 members. However, a 1976 survey of sixteen federal energy agency advisory boards reported that nearly 50 percent of the board members were industry representatives, while consumer and environmental representation comprised 4 percent and 3 percent respectively (Sullivan, 1977). Agencies justified this balance by arguing that citizens' groups were not interested, lacked technical qualifications, or were simply inappropriate; citizens' groups, however, charged agencies with trying to close their deliberations to "outsiders." Their arguments have had increasing effect on increasing citizen representation on advisory boards.

For example, the Federal Energy Administration advisory committees doubled their consumer and environmental representation to 10.8 percent and 7 percent respectively. The FDA has paid consumer representatives elected by consumer groups on its advisory panels. Of the eighteen members of the National Council on Health Care Technology appointed to assess the safety, the effectiveness, and the social impacts of health technologies, two must be from law, one from the field of ethics, and three from "members of the general public who represent the interests of consumers of health care." The National Institutes of Health (NIH) has experimented with consumer representation on advisory panels that are responsible for reviewing research proposals. NIH uses two stages of review: the first by study sections composed of scientists who judge the technical competence of proposals, the second by advisory councils composed of scientists and informed laymen who decide the allocation of funds on the basis of NIH priorities and social considerations.

Disputes over controversial areas of biomedical research have brought expanded public participation in the NIH advisory groups. The twenty-five people composing NIH's Recombinant DNA Advisory Committee, for example, include several lawyers and ethicists, a scientist from a public interest organization, and several nonscientists who have been actively critical of existing controls over this research. Similarly, the National Commission for the Protection of Human Subjects of Biomedical and Behavioral Research includes five scientists, three lawyers, two ethicists, and one public representative. It has sought to enhance public involvement through open meetings where public comment was encouraged, through surveys of national opinion to evaluate its own effectiveness as perceived by the public, and through the creation of five independent public information centers. In addition, NIH and NSF require that institutions seeking federal funds form Institutional Review Boards (IRBs) to monitor all research proposals involving human experimentation. These IRBs include lay participants: a recent study found that most members (50 percent) were biomedical scientists, 21 percent were social scientists, and the rest included administrators, lawyers, clergymen, and other nonscientists (Gray et al., 1978). New policy proposals call for including more lay members on the IRBs and opening IRB meetings to the public.

Some see this form of participation as a desirable way to forestall potentially harmful consequences of research and to ensure scientific work of greater social utility. But others fear that participation will lead to administrative delays, excessive constraint based on short-sighted goals, and, ultimately, to dangerous social control over scientific inquiry. Thus, the response to legislative mandates for greater participation proceeds with caution.

Other Channels of Public Influence over Science
and Technology Policy

The structure and responsibilities of government institutions place important constraints on meaningful public participation through administrative procedures. Thus critics of science and technology have developed their own channels of participation through the courts and special referenda, and this in turn has inspired a number of participatory experiments, outside the usual government channels but intended to increase public influence over government policy.

Litigation and referenda   Litigation has been a major means for citizens to restrict and direct technological change.[2] The courts may define responsibilities for damages caused by technology; they can improve injunctions against proposed technologies that may be harmful; and they can galvanize administrative agencies and regulatory commissions into more effective action by reaffirming standards.

The ability of citizens to use the courts has expanded with the extension of the legal doctrine of standing which determines who has a right to be heard. "Standing" to sue varies from state to state, but the rules of standing have generally been liberalized to allow a private citizen without an alleged personal economic injury to present a grievance as an advocate of the public interest. Moreover, in environmental litigation, the courts have accepted as cause for standing not only damage to property rights but some of the more subtle health and aesthetic impacts of technology.

Citizen litigation as a means of policy influence has focused mostly on technological applications, but occasional cases—e.g., the Boston "grave-robbing" trial of medical researchers studying aborted fetuses—focus on science as well. Medical malpractice suits may be extended to clinical research or genetic experimentation. And the growing concern over the adequacy of safety precautions in the laboratory opens possibilities for legal action.

The role of the courts in cases associated with science and technology poses considerable problems. Despite a well-developed system of using expert witnesses, the courts cannot easily deal with esoteric scientific information that involves uncertainty. Many of the problems of science and technology require evaluation of potential risk at some future date. Weighing cancer risks, for example, requires judgments based on statistical evidence. Yet judges are accustomed to ruling on the basis of precedent.

Moreover, developments in science and technology raise problems that require reanalysis of legal principles. What, for example, is the appropriate role of law in controlling genetic experimentation? How can the courts deal with new questions that arise in the wake of expanded clinical research without stifling scientific progress? These are some of the issues confronting the courts as they are increasingly used to influence decisions about science and technology.

The referendum is a prominent and growing feature of the United States political landscape and, significantly, technological decisions such as airport expansion, nuclear plant siting, and nuclear waste disposal plans are appearing on ballots. The direct citizen vote is a form of participatory democracy within representative governments, and it is intended to preempt administrative authority. Although using referenda for technical issues poses problems of representation, adequate information, and co-optation, its growing popularity suggests an interest in shifting technical decisions to a more participatory framework.

Participatory experiments   The current surge of participatory demands reflects the decline in public confidence in decision-making authorities. Concern with this trend has shaped a number of experimental efforts to establish the procedural conditions that would encourage public acceptance of technology and restore trust. For example, agencies search for ways to gain information about actual public preferences. Opinion polls are the most common technique, but in 1970 the U.S. Forest Service employed an instrument called "code-involve" to uncover public attitudes about its proposed use of DDT to protect Douglas Firs (Clark and Stankey, 1976). Code-involve is an applied content analysis system designed to transfer large quantities of information from written statements in diverse sources (e.g., editorials, petitions, letters) into a condensed form for policy review. Condensing scattered statements into clusters of opinions, the system offers a wider spectrum of attitudes than may emerge from other procedures such as public hearings, and the frequency of a given view as it appears in written statements provides a measure of its prevalence.

Some "quasi-experiments" attempt to use systematic observations of the actual behavior of individuals as evidence of policy choices. For example, to assess the social impact of power plants, investigators measure actual reactions to siting policies as an indicator of public preferences (Murray et al., 1976). Participation in such experiments is random and mediated by the procedure: the only questions answered are those that are raised by the researchers and their sponsors. Nevertheless, social research techniques are increasingly exploited as a surrogate for direct involvement —as a way to increase public influence while avoiding the problems of representation inherent in many participatory procedures.

A number of experiments employ mediation procedures. Modeled after industrial-labor negotiations, they are intended to promote constructive dialogue among contesting parties to a controversy. The process is based on the voluntary participation of groups concerned about a project; they meet to debate the issues with a third party who facilitates arbitration of the dispute. Mediation procedures have helped to reach settlement in several environmental cases.[3]

Another participatory procedure emerged from the recombinant DNA dispute when citizen review boards formed to advise the city councils in several communities on policies for allowing the research to go on. The first of these, in Cambridge, Massachusetts, was organized on the principle that decisions about risks and benefits are questions not for scientists but for laymen, and that laymen are able to face technical matters, educate themselves, and reach just decisions (Cambridge Experimentation Review Board, 1976). This review board, composed entirely of nonscientists, discussed complex questions about the risks of DNA research for four months and, with a modification requiring local monitoring, approved the research under the federal guidelines set down by the National Institutes of Health. A similar citizen review structure has been proposed by a study group at the Oak Ridge National Laboratory to resolve nuclear siting disputes.

Some European models   Several European experiments are worth noting (Nelkin, 1978). In the Netherlands, an elaborate public inquiry system was developed on the principle that the public must be consulted on all decisions affecting the environment. Government plans are preceded by the publication of "policy intentions" dealing with political and philosophical questions: the objectives of growth, the goals of particular technological projects, and their likely impacts. These are widely distributed for public comment. Local governments organize discussion groups, information evenings, and photo and sound shows on the plan. Television programs present alternatives and encourage people to send in their written comments. Reactions are analyzed by a representative advisory group, and the appropriate minister must answer criticism and either reformulate or justify his policy. The entire dossier developed through this process serves as a basis for parliamentary decision making.

The Austrian government set up a series of structured public debates between scientists with opposing views on nuclear policy. The purpose was to highlight controversial dimensions of the nuclear program and to clarify the areas of persistent disagreement. This was mainly intended to inform parliament but also to engage public reaction.

In 1974, disturbed by the growing antinuclear movement, the Swedish government initiated an experiment in public education. Using an existing system of study groups managed by the principal popular organizations and political parties, the government financed a program to inform broad segments of the public about energy and nuclear power. The program involved some 8,000 study circles, each with about ten members who met together to discuss those energy-related questions they felt to be most important.

The Burgerdialog in Germany, first organized in 1974, represents a similar effort to involve broad sectors of the public in an information program. Organizations such as churches, unions, and adult education groups have been funded to organize discussion groups and meetings which include speakers both for and against nuclear power. The goal is to strengthen confidence in the democratic process and to restore public confidence in the administrative authorities.

These information efforts are for the most part intended less to ascertain public opinion than to inform citizens about the value of specific technology policies and to convince them that risk is minimal. Informing the public is equated with participation, even though its aim is to create more favorable attitudes. Although in most cases opposition persists, such experiments are important to observe for the insights they provide into diverse ways of accommodating greater public involvement.

Special Problems of Participation in Science and Technology Policy

Democratic ideology requires participation in decision making by affected interests. But in the arena of science and technology there are special problems in expanding political choice—for citizens seeking to influence policies involving complex technical material, for bureaucracies responsible for efficient technological development, and for scientists concerned about the progress of research.

Problems of citizen influence   Citizen involvement in science and technology policy depends on many of the same factors that affect political participation: leadership, community organization, access to the media, and the visibility and urgency of the immediate issue. However, other factors, such as the availability of information and the distribution of expertise, assume special importance in this policy area. In order to have any real influence in the process, citizen groups must cope with complex and often uncertain technical material. And they must have access to experts who can help to analyze the material and maintain control of the information and grasp of the policy choices. Thus access to technical resources is a key problem for citizen groups.

A related problem lies in the complex network of decisions that contribute to technical policies. Citizens seeking to influence nuclear energy policy, for example, must focus their resources on very diverse areas: federal research policy, licensing procedures, fuel supply, and waste management decisions. But also they must try to influence state regulations on utility rates, permit procedures, federal and state environmental legislation, and local government land use regulations. Participation on all these fronts is costly, especially in that those who intervene must be able to present an informed and technically valid case.

The fuzzy boundaries between the technical and political dimensions of science policy compound the difficulties of expanding public choice. Too often political issues, such as the tradeoffs betwen risks and benefits, are defined as technical, and technical questions of feasibility become confused with political acceptability.

Finally, administrative ambivalence may limit public choice. Agencies control the agenda of hearings and select the members of committees. The timing of public involvement—often late in the decision process—puts citizens at a disadvantage where they can only react to proposals already accepted and even already underway.

Administrative concerns   Participation presents administrative authorities with a dilemma. They have likely judged the propriety of their policies according to their contribution to general economic growth, only to discover that their activities are perceived as allied to special interests. They have likely assumed that legitimacy would flow from their technical competence, only to find critics insisting that legitimacy must rest on public consent. Expertise remains central to insuring the efficiency of administrative and legislative procedures, yet deeply rooted democratic values hold that public consent is a "right," and that procedures including more direct citizen involvement are intrinsically "better."

Administrative agencies try to avoid political conflict by following procedures that are limited to those who share common assumptions. Demands for involvement by citizens' groups with different assumptions disrupt procedures, preclude accommodation, and raise political dilemmas. Participatory measures, it is feared, will encourage endless demands from private interests or from self-appointed public representatives who lack the technical knowledge necessary to assess decisions (U.S. Senate, 1976). This will lead, they fear, to impossible expectations for risk-free technologies and unresolvable polarization: "environment vs. jobs," "local costs vs. regional benefits," "individual choice vs. public interest." There is concern that such participants will seriously obstruct the decision-making process, causing costly delays and precluding the long-range perspectives necessary for effective technical planning. Indeed, those who manage the scientific and technological enterprise feel constant tension between the ideal of participation as a source of legitimacy and its practical consequences.

The Implications of Participatory Politics

Scientist, regulator, lawyer, and layman must work together to reconcile the sometimes conflicting values that underlie their respective interests, perspectives, and goals. [Brazelon, 1979]

As governments fumble to accommodate participatory demands in different political and administrative situations, difficult questions remain. What form can lay participation take in complex technical areas? Who should be involved? What are its implications for the representative process? And, of particular concern to this report, what are the implications of greater lay involvement for the application of resources to research, for the strength of the research institutions, for the way scientists choose their topics and conduct their work, and for the general climate—political, social, and intellectual—in which research takes place?

Perceptions of the consequences of greater participation reflect quite different political perspectives on the nature of the scientific enterprise and the appropriate relationship between science and the citizen. Some argue that the layman, unable to deal with the complex technical material necessary to evaluate science and technology, must leave responsibility to the scientists. Others claim that the political and moral implications of science and technology are matters of central public concern that require political, not technical, competence: hence the citizen must be involved.

Many scientists have interpreted demands for participation as an indication of antiscience attitudes. They fear that lay involvement would threaten their autonomy and bring external controls that would infringe on freedom of inquiry and virtually paralyze the research process (*Daedalus*, 1978; Nobel Symposium, 1979). However, experience suggests that even the critical public does not want to stop either science or technology, although particular projects may be under attack. Lay involvement in the NIH advisory review boards has not destroyed the grant review system; study sections continue to review the scientific merit of individual proposals and control the quality of research. Although the existence of institutional review boards to monitor human experimentation is still viewed by many scientists as an "unwarranted intrusion" that impedes research, lay participation in these boards has not significantly obstructed research. Indeed, nonscientists have been generally less active and less influential than scientists.[4] Even the Cambridge Review Board supported the continuation of recombinant DNA research under the NIH guidelines, clearly accepting the premises of the scientific community about the value of research. And, in the end, the intense public concern over this issue abated, while control remained with the NIH as before.

Attitudes toward participation also remain ambivalent among those with political concerns. Some criticize participatory procedures as simply another means to maintain the existing structure of influence. Participatory procedures are easily co-opted; token participation can simply reinforce the status quo, providing means for informed consent rather than expanding democratic choice. Others suggest that participation provides a means to protect minority interests and to include a wider range of issues in the policy agenda. These arguments develop in all policy areas—and as science and technology assume growing social and political importance, they are no exception. Democratic ideals imply that science policy be subject to greater public scrutiny and political control. Indeed, a fundamental source of public concern about science and technology is their implication for political choice. Accommodating these demands of democracy while maintaining the best of scientific learning is a key and growing challenge that will warrant careful attention over the coming years.

Notes

1 Similar ambivalence shows up in European surveys. See Commission of the European Communities (1977). A more recent survey focusing specifically on medical research shows greater confidence in this field than others. Most respondents felt medical research has changed life for the better (very much better—59 percent, somewhat for the better— 34 percent). But 49 percent agreed that in deciding what to do, scientists are more concerned with their own research interests than with public benefits (National Commission for the Protection of Human Subjects, 1978).

2 See Dimento (1977) for a review and bibliography on citizen litigation. See Carroll (1971), for the difficulty of finding conceptual correspondence between scientific developments and legal concepts.

3 For reviews of environmental mediation efforts, see the EIA Review published at MIT.

4 A study of IRBs found that, although accepting the legitimacy of the IRBs, 25 percent of the 940 biomedical scientists and 38 percent of the 395 behavioral and social scientists interviewed felt the review procedures are an unwarranted intrusion of the investigator's autonomy; 43 percent of the biomedical scientists and 54 percent of the behavioral scientists felt the procedure had impeded the progress of research (National Commission for the Protection of Human Subjects, 1978).

References

Alford, R. 1975. *Health Care Politics: Ideology and Interest Group Barriers to Reform.* Chicago: University of Chicago Press.

Ann Arbor Science for the People Editorial Collective. 1977. *Biology as a Social Weapon.* Minneapolis: Burgess.

Bazelon, David L. 1979. "Risk and Responsibility." *Science* 205:278.

Benveniste, G. 1972. *The Politics of Expertise.* Berkeley: Glendessary Press.

Cambridge Experimentation Review Board. 1976. "Guidelines for the Use of Recombinant DNA Molecule Technology in the City of Cambridge." December 21.

Carpenter, Richard. 1970. "Information for Decisions in Environmental Policy." *Science* 168:1316–22.

Carroll, James. 1971. "Participatory Technology." *Science* 171:647–53.

Casper, Barry M. 1977. "Scientists on the Hill." *Bulletin of the Atomic Scientists* 33:8–15.

Clark, Roger, and Stankey, George. 1976. "Analyzing Public Input to Resource Decisions: Criteria, Principles, and Case Examples of the Codeinvolve System." *Natural Resources Journal* 16:197–212.

Commission of the European Communities. 1977. *Science and European Public Opinion.* Brussels.

Cramton, Roger. 1972. "The Why, Where, and How of Broadening Public Participation in the Administrative Process." *Georgetown Law Journal* 60:3.

Daedalus. 1978. "Limits of Scientific Inquiry." March.

DiMento, J. 1977. "Citizen Environmental Litigation and Administrative Process." *Duke Law Journal* 22:409–52.

Ellul, Jacques. 1970. *The Technological Society.* New York: Alfred A. Knopf.

Fox, Harrison, Jr., and Hammond, Susan W. 1977. *The Invisible Force in American Lawmaking.* New York: The Free Press.

Gelhorn, Ernest. 1972. "Public Participation in Administrative Proceedings." *Yale Law Journal* 81:367.

Gianos, P. 1974. "Scientists as Policy Advisors: The Context of Influence." *Western Political Quarterly* (September):429–56.

Gray, Bradford; Cooke, Robert A.; and Tannenbaum, Arnold S. 1978. "Research Involving Human Subjects." *Science* 201:1094–1104.

Hirschman, Albert. 1970. *Exit, Voice and Loyalty.* Cambridge, Massachusetts: Harvard University Press.

Klaw, Spencer, 1969. *The New Brahmans: Scientific Life in America.* New York: Morrow.

Kolata, G. 1975. "Freedom of Information Act: Problems at the FDA." *Science* 189:32–33.

Lakoff, S. 1977. "Scientists, Technologists and Political Power." In *Science, Technology and Society*, ed. I. S. Rosing and D. Price. Beverly Hills: Sage Publications, pp. 355–92.

LaPorte, Todd. 1971. "The Study of Public Organizations." In *Towards a New Public Administration*, ed. Frank Marini. Scranton: Chandler, p. 20.

Lapp, R. 1965. *The New Priesthood.* New York: Harper and Row.

Lowi, Theodore. 1972. "Four Systems of Policy, Politics and Choice." *Public Administration Review* (July/August):298–309.

Mazur, A. 1973. "Disputes between Experts." *Minerva* 11:213–62.

McCrae, D. 1973. "Science and the Formation of Policy in a Democracy." *Minerva* 11:228–42.

Mendelsohn, Everett, and Weingart, Peter. 1978. "The Social Assessment of Science: Issues and Perspectives." In *The Social Assessment of Science*, ed. E. Mendelsohn, D. Nelkin, and P. Weingart. Conference Proceedings, University of Bielefeld.

Meynaud, Jacques. 1968. *Technocracy.* London: Faber and Faber.

Murray, B. et al. 1973. "Peaking Plant Environment Report" (September). Reported in Heberkin, Thomas. 1976. "Some Observations on Alternative Mechanisms for Public Involvement: The Hearing, Public Opinion Poll, the Workshop, and the Quasi-Experiment." *Natural Resources Journal* 16:197–212.

National Commission for the Protection of Human Subjects. 1978. *Special Study.* DHEW Publication No. (OS) 78–0015.

———. 1978. *Report and Recommendations on Institutional Review Boards.* DHEW (OS) 78–0008, p. 75.

National Science Board. 1977. *Science Indicators 1976.* USGPO, pp. 168–82.

Nelkin, Dorothy. 1971. *Nuclear Power and Its Critics*. Ithaca: Cornell University Press.

———. 1975. *Jetport*. New Brunswick: Transaction Books.

———. 1978. *Technological Decisions and Democracy*. Beverly Hills: Sage Publications.

———, ed. 1979. *Controversy: Politics of Technical Decisions*. Beverly Hills: Sage Publications.

Nelson, Richard. 1977. *The Moon and the Ghetto*. New York: W. W. Norton.

Nobel Symposium. 1979. Vol. 44. *Ethics for Science Policy*. New York: Pergamon Press.

Noble, D. 1977. *America by Design*. New York: Alfred A. Knopf, Inc.

Opinion Research Corporation. 1976. *Attitudes of the U.S. Public Towards Science and Technology*, Study 3, p. 51.

Primack, Joel, and von Hippel, Frank. 1974. *Advice and Dissent: Scientists in the Political Arena*. New York: Basic Books.

Scott, William. 1969. "Organizational Government: The Prospects for a Truly Participatory System." *Public Administration Review* (January/February):43–53.

Sullivan, J. 1977. In Boasbug, Tersch. "Implications of NSF Assistance to Non-Profit Organizations." *Report to NSF*. Washington, D.C., p. 64.

U.S. Senate. 1976. Committee on Government Operations. *Public Participation in Government Proceedings Act of 1976, Hearings*. Washington, D.C.: Government Printing Office.

Wade, Nicholas. 1972. "Freedom of Information." *Science* 175:493–502.

Winner, L. 1977. *Autonomous Technology*. Cambridge: MIT Press.

II

Varieties of Citizen Participation

3

Beyond Technocracy: New Routes for Citizen Involvement in Social Risk Assessment

Sheldon Krimsky

Introduction

Over the past decade and a half, several pieces of federal legislation established an initial framework for improving public access to information and public input into federal regulatory policy. Of special significance in this regard are the National Environmental Policy Act [NEPA] (1969), the Freedom of Information Act (1974), amendments to the Administrative Procedure Act (1966), and the Federal Advisory Committee Act (1972). NEPA requires that governmental agencies avail themselves of commentary from various sectors of society on their policies before final decisions are made. The Freedom of Information Act and the Executive Department's requirements for "government in the sunshine" have made further contributions to an open process of decision making, where the evidence, justification, and procedural issues are available for public review. The Administrative Procedure Act requires that the opinions, policy statements, rules, and procedures of federal agencies be a matter of public record. Under the Federal Advisory Committee Act, the deliberations and reports of federal advisory committees are open to public review.

Despite these reforms and others in the rule-making process, in the access to information, and in the format of open hearings, public skepticism over the soundness of governmental decisions has not waned; it may even be rising. The aforementioned reforms have themselves contributed to broadening the avenues for dissent. With greater accessibility to information, dissenting parties have the opportunity to present their cases more effectively.

Recent federal policies involving the site of the Seabrook nuclear power facility, off-shore oil drilling on Georges Bank, the Three Mile Island incident, the landing of the SST at New York's JFK Airport, and the NIH guidelines regulating the production of and work with recombinant DNA molecules have been met with widespread criticism—and in some cases, mass protest. These and related actions begin to place in doubt the degree to which governmental decisions that seek to balance the risks and benefits of a technology have been successful in gaining the public confidence when conventional access routes are available to the citizenry. Some may argue that expanding democratic rights results in less efficient and more costly decision making. Nevertheless, the primary good of democratic process is not the optimization of efficiency, but the promotion of fairness and objectivity. Furthermore, from a pragmatic standpoint, narrowly drawn decision processes which fail to take account of the full potential of citizen participation may, in the long run, be quite costly in the event of mounting opposition.

Attaining public confidence in federal regulatory decisions on the impacts of risk-bearing technologies is of paramount importance. When public confidence begins to erode, it is time to reexamine the conventional systems of decision making and to test appropriate modifications. One relevant consideration is the degree and form of citizen involvement. Can we improve public confidence by providing citizens better access to the decision process? At what point can we comfortably say that we have achieved optimum participation? If we liken the participation process to due process in our legal proceedings, then its justness must be judged independently of the outcome. However, the analogy falls short in places. Whereas the onus of proof is clear in our system of jurisprudence, in decisions where there are social risks, the burden of proof may depend on where the balance of political power lies.

This essay examines some new developments in citizen participation in technological decisions involving highly specialized areas of knowledge. It analyzes the role of nonexperts on technical advisory committees or risk assessment panels. The form and legitimacy of citizen involvement is addressed through a set of general principles. The following pages emphasize the desirability of improving access to the decision-making process for those segments of society which endure special risks, but are unorganized, lack technical expertise, or are relatively powerless.

Forms of Participation

In considering meaningful and effective forms of public participation in technological decisions, it is useful to start by examining the determinants that distinguish alternative models. The type of public involvement should, in some sense, match the nature of the problem. Three factors are important in this regard: the entrance points into the decision process; the structural form of participation; and the types of citizens who participate. The following table illustrates some cardinal elements within these categories.

Active vs. reactive participation Most opportunities for public participation in social risk assessment restrict citizens to playing a reactive role in decisions. Accordingly, the public responds to a proposal or a set of guidelines or regulations after they have been drawn up by technical committees. The open hearing is the conventional vehicle for this mode of public input, as is the solicitation of responses to regulations published in the *Federal Register*. The passive mode of participation has drawn criticism because fundamental issues have already been factored into the decision by the time the public is asked to react. Thus, within this reactive mode, the permitted changes are usually marginal. To achieve the full benefits of participation by citizens, early access routes to the decision-making process should be developed, possibly even during the stage at which the problem is defined.

The Environmental Impact Statement (EIS) process is a case in point. By the time an EIS is introduced for public comment, the salient issues have already been developed. Active participation by the public would include its involvement in the scoping session for the EIS. It is in this early period that the impact parameters are established and the boundaries of discourse set.

Advisory panel This format for public involvement permits citizens to participate at the highest levels of policy making. Although it responds to the criticism that the narrow interests of technical experts dominate the decision-making process, it should not be seen as a substitute for the public hearing where a broader involvement from public constituencies is pos-

Table 1
Modalities of Citizen Participation

I. *Entrance Points for Citizen Involvement*
   a. Definition of the Problem
   b. Data Collection and Analysis
   c. Risk Assessment
   d. Technical Alternatives/Solutions
   e. Policy Implications
   f. Policy Alternatives
   g. Resolution: Choice of Policy

II. *Form of Citizen Involvement*
   a. Hearings
   b. Task Force
   c. Advisory Board
   d. Referendum
   e. Mediation/Arbitration
   f. Review Board
   g. Science Court
   h. Citizen Court
   i. Prehearings for Major Constituencies

III. *Types of Citizens Involved*
   a. Disinterested Laypersons
   b. Laypersons with a Vested Interest
   c. Technically Sophisticated but Disinterested Parties
   d. Technically Sophisticated and Interested Parties
   e. Representatives of Constituencies Most Impacted by the Decision
   f. Members of Public Interest Groups

---

sible. An example of such a panel is the Recombinant DNA Advisory Committee, chartered by the Secretary of HEW in 1974, to advise the director of the National Institutes of Health on the regulation of genetic research. Another model in the area of research involving human subjects is the National Commission for the Protection of Human Subjects of Biomedical and Behavioral Research (Yesley, 1978). The limitation of such bodies is that the lay members are at a disadvantage with respect to the scientific and technological issues. In such situations, technical language should be interpreted to intelligent lay representatives. Public members should be in a position to reach decisions based upon arguments they hear from different technical experts. In addition, the lay members may offer expertise in procedural areas or broaden the scope of social impacts addressed.

Science Court   Modeled on a legal adversary proceeding, the Science Court would establish a panel of distinguished scientists, presumably disinterested in the issue under consideration. This panel would listen to testimony orchestrated by two opposing teams of "scientific lawyers." The outcome of such a proceeding would be a ruling by the scientific judges on the factual situation with respect to the risks and benefits in question. Although the concept of the Science Court has been discussed in science policy circles for six years, it has not been put to a test. The assumptions underlying its successful operation are that factual claims and value judgments can be separated in a controversy involving the risks of a given technology. Moreover, the model assumes that the public policy makers need only possess the relevant factual information provided by the scientific experts to deliver a rational decision on the appropriate course of action (Kantrowitz, 1975; 1977).

The Science Court does address several important problems in decisions over risk assessment. It embodies the notion of the disinterested, astute technical generalist. It also incorporates the skills of scientists who specialize in an area of research or technology other than the one in question. It recognizes that an adversary proceeding (i.e., getting the best minds to address each side of the question) is the most promising means of flushing out all the hidden assumptions and speculative hypotheses passing for ineluctable truth. As a vehicle through which the public can obtain a better grasp of the nature of a controversy, it is much superior to a public hearing.

However, the Science Court concept is built upon some tenuous assumptions. It does not promote broad public participation, but draws heavily on the idea that "scientists know best" regarding issues related to the conceptualization of risk and the selection of relevant evidence (Nelkin, 1977). In cases where there is significant disagreement among the scientific experts, public confidence may not be secured by appealing to yet another subset of that community of elites.

Citizen panel   This form of participation has been used with some degree of success for setting policies or resolving disputes involving differential impacts on selected communities. Where complex scientific and technological questions are at issue and require in-depth study, local public officials may designate a citizen panel as an advisory body. As distinguished from a Science Court or technical advisory board, this group is selected to represent diverse sectors of the community—and therefore to promote public confidence, when a narrower selection of scientists might not be successful in achieving the same objectives (Krimsky, 1978a). Another asset of this model is that it brings opposing views into a negotiating framework.

There are some serious limitations in having a panel review a technical problem when the panel is composed exclusively of laypersons. The issues may be too complex for nontechnical persons to understand. The time it might take the lay citizenry to become well versed in the issues could be prohibitive, given their work schedules. Also, laypersons may be more vulnerable to persuasion by exaggerated claims, especially when they are made by scientists or technical persons, than individuals who are trained in a technical discipline.

Arbitration/mediation   The American Arbitration Association has supported the use of arbitration and mediation techniques to resolve intractable disputes of an environmental nature. The principal idea behind this strategy is to adapt a procedure that has been successful in labor negotiations and business conflicts. Inasmuch as environmental controversies involve many constituencies, the design of arbitration or mediation modes must incorporate multilateral negotiations (Suskind, 1978). The advantage of such negotiating mechanisms is that those constituencies that are recognized as important segments of the impacted population will be treated on par with other parties, including public agency heads. However, for the powerless and unrepresented, arbitration offers no entry points into the decision-making process. Thus, while it may not broaden participation of the citizenry, it may deepen the quality of participation for some well-established groups in the community. In addition, arbitration may help to remove the impasse between formidable opponents.

Informal hearings and gripe sessions   The public hearing has become a great American institution, but many people have been frustrated by its limitations. First, it is an imposing atmosphere—threatening to those who have not achieved a certain level of competence in public speaking. Second, the citizen is at considerable disadvantage with respect to the decision authority. It is the latter that controls the timing and can shape the nature of the questioning. Third, there is no opportunity for citizens to engage the decision makers in a dialogue where issues can be pursued in greater depth and with less formality. The prehearing (or posthearing) is designed to augment important agency proceedings where informal procedures can permit representatives of key constituencies to have special access to the decision authority.

A posthearing was used effectively by HEW Secretary Joseph A. Califano after a public hearing was held in September 1978 on revised guidelines for recombinant DNA research. Outspoken critics of the proposed guidelines were brought together with HEW and NIH agency personnel to express their concerns about procedural and safety issues. The setting was informal and conducive to in-depth discussion between citizen advocates and public agency officials. One of the results of that session was an increase in the number of public members on the HEW–NIH Recombinant DNA Advisory Committee.

Some Successes and Failures in Present Efforts at Public Participation

The grounds for broad public participation in policy decisions involving the risks and benefits of technology are similar to those that have been cited for urban revitalization programs, water quality planning, or transportation planning. They fall into three areas: justice, knowledge, and pragmatism.

It is a simple matter of justice that those who are the prime targets of technologies' adverse effects have some representation in the decision that weighs risks against benefits. Too often the most vulnerable groups in our society are burdened with additional risks they did not choose.

Richer resources of ideas and perspectives on troublesome problems are gained by soliciting help from diverse constituencies. Even in cases where the issues are highly technical and specialized, broadening the range of inputs into decision making invariably adds some special dimension to the process. The experience of laboratory technicians is quite different from that of scientists; consequently, they are likely to have unique insights into the actual safety operations of a laboratory. Policies that address the spraying of insecticides on crops can benefit from the views of migrant farm workers. They, after all, are among the ones at greatest risk and can offer valuable personal knowledge about exposure that could complement the knowledge of the toxicologist. The personal experiences of workers at risk can often provide the earliest advanced warning that something is amiss. The case histories of how asbestos, vinyl chloride, and the soil fumigant DBCP were discovered to cause occupational disease, show that workers were among the first to understand the relationships between chemical exposure and morbidity (Epstein, 1978).

The third justification for public participation is a pragmatic one. It is desirable if policy decisions on technological risk achieve public confidence. By broadening the opportunities for public participation, the likelihood for improving public confidence is surely higher than were such decisions the work of narrowly defined interests (Carroll, 1971).[1]

The areas which illustrate failures or limitations in present efforts at public participation in technology policy include (1) entrance points, (2) vehicles for participation, and (3) who participates. Several examples of the entrance points are listed in table 1.

Entrance points For meaningful participation, the public must have access to the decision-making process in the early stages, when it can make a difference. Once the problem is defined, and the questions set, a decision-making body may exhibit considerable inertia in returning to a more fundamental examination of the issue.

One rationale for scheduling public input late in the process is that the determination of policy is separate and independent of the scientific and technological analysis which precedes it. This rationale is severely limited in the following respect: it is very unusual for a clear demarcation to exist between technical issues and policy issues with regard to the assessment of risk. Consequently, restricting public input to the later stages of such a decision results in delegating policy-making authority to a group of technical experts, thereby limiting the alternatives of the final outcome.

In the early stages of the recombinant DNA debate, scientists acted as if they were providing only technical knowledge to the National Institutes of Health. A careful analysis of the role of scientific decision making during that period reveals that many policy decisions were being made, highlighted by the way the problem of risk was initially defined (Krimsky, 1978b). Had there been broader participation by diverse sectors of the scientific community, environmental groups, bioethicists, and ecologists, certain issues would not have been factored out of the DNA discussion at the outset—such issues as the relationship between recombinant DNA research and genetic engineering, the impact of the new technology on the physical environment, and the desirability of long-term epidemiological studies.

We also face the prospect that diversifying participation on technical advisory bodies can delay new advances in biomedical science. More interests and perspectives involved in the assessment of risks and benefits could slow down the process. Pluralism can translate into a go-slow attitude when it comes to introducing new technologies.

Vehicles for participation   Little attention has been given to creating effective modes for citizen involvement in public policy decisions involving science and technology. Our experience with the passive-reactive mode of participation reveals a high probability of public cynicism accompanied by a lack of public confidence. Without participatory vehicles for becoming educated about a technological innovation, the public is likely to oversimplify the issues and respond in a polarized manner. In the recombinant DNA episode, wherever citizens were engaged in what was primarily a reactive type of participation, and were basically uninformed about this highly specialized area of knowledge, the consequent polarized choices were to call for a ban on the research, or to act uncritically by placing public trust in the scientists.

As an overall objective, the vehicle for public participation should be chosen to optimize the attainment of public confidence. That is to be distinguished from a call for an efficient outcome. Four factors that can help insure public confidence are accountability, openness, objectivity, and awareness of the social good. Accountability means knowing who is responsible for the decision and understanding the avenues for review, modification, and reversal. Openness refers to the degree to which (1) the public, on its own initiative, can learn the reasons why certain decisions are made, (2) meetings are held in the open, and (3) all the factors which play a role in the decision are open to examination by the public.

Objectivity in the decision-making process implies that the decision-making body or individual does not enter the process with a bias that selects out information and resists rational argument. Where objectivity is difficult to achieve because any single individual has special interests, pluralistic bodies are clearly preferable to single-interest decision makers. Finally, the forms of decision analysis and policy determination should instill in the public the confidence that the social good is being sought. To this end, there must be an unambiguous statement about how the instruments of science and technology will be used, especially when public funds are the source of support.

Another factor to consider in the choice of a vehicle for participation is whether the impacts of a policy are differential (substantially affect some distinct population or community more than others) or uniform. Recent trends in decisions involving the siting of a facility suggest some type of partnership model between the federal government and the community in question. This could mean two types of participatory processes—one at the federal level and one at the local level. To insure an element of justice and secure public confidence in the decisions, safeguards must be built into the process to avoid a partnership of elites. Diverse groups in the community should be effectively represented, especially those who would bear disproportionately more risk.

Special difficulties arise when local communities wish to have veto power over federal siting decisions, or wish to impose more restrictive regulations for greater margins of safety than those issued by the federal government. A balance must be found between the rights of communities to decide the level of risk they are willing to tolerate and the interests and needs of the larger society. More than a dozen states and local communities held hearings on local proposals for regulating recombinant DNA research. These hearings are a concrete expression that reviewing federal regulations is an appropriate response to concerns of local constituencies. In these communities, federal preemption was viewed as a serious infringement on the authority of these states and local municipalities to promote public health and safety.

In the summer of 1976, the Cambridge (Massachusetts) City Council was faced with a controversy over the construction of a physical containment facility to be used for moderate risk recombinant DNA research. The council, recognizing the complexity of the issues, called for a study panel. The city manager avoided selecting a panel of distinguished scientists, because—in his view—these scientists already disagreed about the interpretation of the potential hazards of the research to the community. The manager chose a board of citizens to investigate the public health hazards of the new gene-splicing techniques developed by molecular biologists. The Cambridge Experimentation Review Board (CERB) functioned like a citizen court, and proved to be a reasonably sound representative of community interests. Its purpose was to hear the arguments first hand from the scientists and decide what recommendations to make to the city council. The soundness of this process became evident when the CERB issued its report, for the citizen review board inspired a high degree of confidence among elected officials and the general public. Although not everyone agreed with the outcome, even those most polarized on the issues believed that the members of the citizens' panel had no vested interests in the outcome of the decision, and that their overriding concern was the community's public safety. The process was interpreted as fair in the context of the issues and the circumstances of the debate.

Clearly, CERB members were limited in their ability to understand either the technical complexities or the subtle nuances in NIH regulations. But on broad policy questions—such as the need for risk assessment, public accountability of local institutions, enforcement, and the concerns over the unregulated sectors—such a citizen board can be effective.

Who participates? Next to the issue of how much participation, the question of who participates is the most perplexing. If we are considering a reactive mode of participation exclusively—e.g., a public hearing or solicited comments on a proposed regulation—then the response to the question of who participates is: anyone who wishes to. But when we enter into participatory modes that make citizen input a more integral part of the decision-making process, other determinations must be made. What factors should guide such selectivity?

The moving forces in society have always found means of getting their point across. There is a natural advantage to participation by individuals and organizations which possess economic resources. But it is society's powerless and unorganized who have difficulty gaining entry into the decision-making process, even at the reactive level. Consider, for example, chemical workers who do not have environmental health experts at their disposal; nonunionized migrant farmworkers who have no direct representation in pesticide hearings; nonorganized laboratory technicians working with biological agents. Present efforts do not ensure participation by those groups that will bear the greatest human risk. The open hearing by itself is insufficient because these power-poor sectors lack organization, resources for technical assistance, or political influence.

In decisions regarding who participates, special consideration should be given to the particular population groups most severely at risk. Risk is interpreted to mean adverse effects on health and well-being. The fact that a decision's positive benefits are likely to accrue to a larger population should not override the importance of the minority at risk. Representation in decision making should be skewed in favor of those who must bear the greatest risks.

Merely including laypersons with an alternative perspective or those who represent a particular population group does not insure that they will be effective. Public representatives are generally at a disadvantage with respect to the technical members of policy boards or advisory bodies. This is true whether it is the consumer representatives on Health Systems Agencies sitting with the providers, the public members on Institutional Review Boards, or the community advocates on Institutional Biosafety Committees. Because these individuals must interact with scientists or technically trained medical persons, their effectiveness depends on an ability to learn quickly, to break through the technical jargon, and to refuse to be intimidated by titles and letters. When filling such slots for public representation, it is incumbent on the agency head to select individuals who are credible, effective spokespersons with a definite potential for technical learning.

Some Caveats for Public Participation in Technological Decisions Involving Risks and Benefits

I have argued that serious attention given to citizen involvement in technology assessment is in the interest of both social equity and of achieving broad public confidence in public policy. Some sectors of government—especially agencies that deal with policy matters of broad application—have made an effort to incorporate diverse viewpoints in their rule making. When technological decisions are linked closely to current developments in science—that is, when the determination of risk involves highly technical information, scientific nomenclature, and what some have called esoteric knowledge—the propensity to encourage citizen participation has been weak, even when the risks to some groups have been clearly ascertained (Krimsky, 1979). The following recommendations are especially relevant for decisions involving such highly complex technical issues.[2]

Public participation must make a real difference   Efforts toward involving citizens in decision making must go beyond the reactive phase. It should take on more than *pro forma* significance. Citizens should obtain access to the decision-making process at points where they can make a difference in the outcome. This will help to reverse the public's disillusionment about the relevance of its input to the setting of policy.

Participation should broaden options—not narrow them   Integrating more diverse interests into the decision-making process should widen the scope of possibilities, by capitalizing on the imagination of many different minds, with their different experiences and perspectives. The options should include fundamental changes, and not simply minor adjustments of preformed policy. On many occasions, citizens severely at risk are not afforded the opportunity to offer input at a point where significant changes might still be made.

Weighted input principle   Those individuals, communities, or regions which are asked to bear the greatest risk from a new technology should have a weighted input into the decision-making process. The risks in question are interpreted as real or potential hazards to the health and well-being of individuals. Where no special consideration is afforded the greatest risk bearers, their interests tend to be overridden by larger numbers of people who accrue benefits but bear little risk. The weighted input principle is advanced to effect greater justice in the deliberation of impacts. The principle has a counterpart in John Rawls's *Theory of Justice*, where it is argued that in a society of unequal distributions, decisions should not make the least advantaged worse off (Rawls, 1971).

How can the weighted input principle be used to guide public policy? First, the population that is particularly vulnerable—in terms of hazards to health and well-being—to the impacts of a technology must be identified. Second, a determination should be made on how the impacted population can have access to the decision-making process, such as whether there are organizations that represent them. If no such organizations exist, other means should be explored to determine how their interests can be represented. Third, the forms of participation should enable citizens to effectively advocate their interests. For technically difficult subject matter, scientific expertise should be available to high-risk groups. Thus, the interests of asbestos workers cannot be fully realized in hearings on exposure levels, unless the workers have scientific personnel at their disposal.

Two forms of participation can be useful in achieving the objectives of the weighted input principle. The prehearing or posthearing creates a more informal atmosphere for citizens to put their case before agency officials. Formal hearings can often inhibit creative exchanges between those in authority and the parties affected by the rule making. For issues requiring extensive analysis and prolonged study, the advisory panel is another way to represent vulnerable populations.

Local options   When a technology selectively impacts a community, such that its residents bear special risks, then maximizing local options for regulation is consistent with the "weighted input principle." Where the issue of federal preemption is being considered, the burden of proof should be on government. Increasingly, cities and towns want to share the decision-making authority with the federal government when differential risks are at stake. Local communities have passed their own ordinances for the transport of hazardous materials through neighborhood streets, despite the fact that federal regulations were issued by the Department of Transportation. Similarly, six cities and towns passed ordinances regulating genetic engineering after federal guidelines were promulgated.

Preconditions for Effective Use of
Citizens on Advisory Boards

If current trends continue we can expect to see a growth in lay member representation on technical-scientific advisory bodies and policy-making boards both at the national and local levels.

Precedents have been mounting for over a decade. Institutional Review Boards (IRBs), initiated by the Public Health Service in 1966, consist of lay members, scientists, and medical personnel who review research protocols involving human subjects (Gray, 1975; 1978). The National Commission for the Protection of Human Subjects of Biomedical and Behavioral Research, established by Congress in 1974, set a new standard for citizen involvement in science policy (Lappe, 1978). Medical experts and lay consumers of health care serve together on Health System Agencies (HSAs) as mandated under the National Health Planning and Resource Development Act of 1974. Also in that year, the Secretary of Health, Education, and Welfare chartered the Recombinant DNA Advisory Committee, which presently consists of twenty-five members, about one-third of whom are nonscientists with backgrounds in law, ethics, and environmental policy.

When scientists and nonscientists serve together on advisory bodies, lay participants face formidable obstacles. How can lay members make reasoned choices when faced with highly specialized, esoteric knowledge? The problems are similar but are expressed differently when the advisory body in question is constituted exclusively of lay members, as in the case of the Cambridge Experimentation Review Board (established by the Cambridge City Council to evaluate the potential public health risks of recombinant DNA research).

It is not easy to achieve effective and meaningful participation by well-informed nonscientists in decisions involving the analysis of scientific information. Although many factors can inhibit a working relationship between scientists and laypersons, there are some conditions which, if satisfied, can reduce the likelihood that participation of lay citizens in technical decisions will become a form of tokenism.

Access to technical knowledge   A scientific liaison advisor (SLA) must be sought for translating technical information and scientific nomenclature for lay members on advisory bodies. Such an advisor must find ways to present technical arguments related to risks. The SLA would be skilled in using special models, analogies, representations, and so forth, to educate the nonspecialist. The goal of the educational process is to demystify scientific arguments, while at the same time raising the technical competence of the nonscientist.

This idea was tested in a limited way by the Cambridge Experimentation Review Board (CERB) during its deliberations on the public health risks of a P3 containment facility for recombinant DNA research. CERB had a technical advisor on its staff who had some expertise in the biological sciences. Unfortunately, no effort was made to set up some educational program for Cambridge citizens prior to their meeting with the scientists. Each CERB member was responsible for his/her own familiarization with the scientific techniques under review. As a result, there were substantial differences in the level of understanding among members of the citizens' committee (Krimsky, 1978a).

Conducive atmosphere for scientific critics   For lay people to effectively participate on advisory bodies that deal with adverse technological impacts, they must have the opportunity to hear opposing arguments. The atmosphere must be suitable for members of the scientific community to express unpopular concerns. If a curtain of fear blocks such expression, then the lay members will be at a considerable disadvantage, for they need scientists to interpret the data and translate the technical vernacular (Holman and Dutton, 1978:1531).

When advisory boards contain a mix of scientists and nonscientists, efforts should be made to select scientists who express diverse views on the subject matter. In this manner, the public members will hear a wide range of ideas and approaches to the problem.

Choice of public members   If the trend of mixing scientific experts and public representatives on advisory bodies continues, greater attention must be given to the choice of public members. To improve the public confidence in such choices, the head of a regulatory agency (or other agency of government) could request nominations of individuals from the important constituencies involved with the issue in question. This can help ensure that the interests of key populations are represented in the policy process—that is, if the agency director actually selects advisors from the list of suggested names.

Special mechanisms for policy input from differentially impacted areas or groups   When federal policy selects out certain target areas as the recipients of technologies with potentially adverse impacts, mechanisms should be available to weigh the impacts and review the safety standards. Local or regional hearings have an advantage over those centered in the nation's capital. Promotion of public debates, educational forums, and local citizen review boards prior to a polarization of views can be useful to all parties.

EPA and FDA have demonstrated that regional hearings can be conducive to broadening citizen input into policy decisions. However, citizen participation cannot be reduced to the hearing process. Where significant hazards are at stake, other measures must work in concert with the public hearing.

Insuring that citizens have a full range of options to address technological impacts   The value of public representation on advisory bodies or technical review boards can be subverted if only a very narrow range of options

is available. Lay representation should broaden the outlook on a technological assessment to include social impacts. But if the process is restricted
to the rules established by society's technocratic sector, then little may be
gained in having lay people represent the broader issues.

When the Recombinant DNA Advisory Committee was expanded to include a greater proportion of public members, the charge to the committee
remained the same. The RAC continued to focus its attention on the issues
of laboratory safety. No provision was made to redraft the original charge.
Thus, even with one-third of its members unaffiliated with scientific research, the RAC has continued to avoid broader issues such as genetic engineering, biohazards associated with nonrecombinant DNA work, or the
industrial exploitation of the new genetic techniques.

If we wish to achieve the full benefit of mixing lay citizens and scientists
on policy boards, then the boundaries of discourse should reflect the concerns of nontechnical participants. Otherwise, lay citizens, following the
lead set by scientific experts, will have little or no opportunity to critically
reexamine the basic problem.

Conclusion

We have examined the transformation that is taking place with regard to
the role of citizen involvement in assessing potentially hazardous technologies. What was once visualized as the exclusive and legitimate responsibility of society's scientific elites is now being viewed along more pluralistic models of decision making. This signals a growing recognition that
risks and benefits cannot be assessed on purely technical grounds because
values are embedded in the process from the very outset. Attempts to di-
vide the functions of analysis into technical and policy components create
a tendency to narrow policy options prior to public review.

Traditional channels of public participation, such as court action, lobbying, and public hearings, although important, are limited in what they
can achieve (Coates, 1975). One way to improve public confidence in decisions involving adverse technological impacts is to establish advisory
bodies to governmental agencies that represent broad societal interests.
The weighted input principle would give special access to those groups
likely to bear the greatest risks from a technology. In this regard, more attention should be given to the intensity and distribution of adverse impacts
and less to the aggregate weighting of risks and benefits. The fact that local
communities are prepared to convene their own panels to study the im-

pacts of major technological innovations is a reflection of a growing dis-trust of large, impersonal bureaucracies, as well as a recognition of the profound impact of technology.

When risk assessment draws upon a highly specialized and complex base of knowledge (the situation illustrated in the recombinant DNA con-troversy), it becomes more difficult for nonspecialists to participate in the decision-making process. However, the involvement of the nonspecialist is integral to that process if we hope to achieve broad public confidence in such decisions. Otherwise, as science and technology become increasingly insulated from the public, the citizenry becomes dependent on expert af-finity groups whose members benefit from the technological instruments that only they can understand. The experiences of both the recombinant DNA affair and the system of institutional review boards for experiments with human subjects show clearly that the public has a legitimate interest in the formation of science and technology policy. As technical decisions behind policy choices become more difficult for the public to comprehend, planners and policy makers must place additional weight on educating and involving the public.

Notes

1 "Participatory technology" refers to the mechanisms by which society can achieve a greater sense of confidence and control over technological decisions (Carroll, 1971).
2 These ideas were presented in embryonic form at the National Conference on Citizen Par-ticipation, held in Washington, D.C., 28 September –1 October 1978 (Langton, 1979).

References

Carroll, James D. 1971. "Participatory Technology." *Science* 171:647–53.

Code of Federal Regulation 45:46.106.

Epstein, Samuel S. 1978. *The Politics of Cancer*. San Francisco: Sierra Club Books.

Gray, Bradford H. 1975. *Human Subjects in Medical Experimentation*. New York: John Wiley and Sons.

———. 1978. "Institutional Review Boards as an Instrument of Assessment: Research In-volving Human Subjects in the U.S." *Science, Technology & Human Values* 25:34–46.

Holman, Halsted R., and Dutton, Diana B. 1978. "A Case for Public Participation in Science Policy Formation and Practice." *Southern California Law Review* 51:1505–34.

Kantrowitz, Arthur. 1975. "Controlling Technology Democratically." *American Scientist* 63:505–9.

————. 1977. "The Science Court Experiment." *Bulletin of the Atomic Scientists* (April): 43–53.

Krimsky, Sheldon. 1978a. "The Role of the Citizen Court in the Recombinant DNA Debate." *Bulletin of the Atomic Scientists* 34:38–43.

————. 1978b. "Politics and Paradigms: The Roots of the Recombinant DNA Controversy." In *Science and the Public Interest: Recombinant DNA Research*, ed. Robert P. Bareikis. Proceedings of a forum held 10–12 November 1977, Indiana University. West Lafayette, Indiana: The Poynter Center.

————. 1979. "Citizen Participation in Scientific and Technological Decision Making." In *Citizen Participation Perspectives*, ed. Stuart Langton. Proceedings of a National Conference on Citizen Participation held 28 September–1 October 1978, Washington, D.C.; Medford, Massachusetts: Lincoln Filene Center, Tufts University.

Langton, Stuart, ed. 1979. *See* Krimsky, 1979.

Lappe, Marc, and Martin, Patricia A. 1978. "The Place of the Public in the Conduct of Science." *Southern California Law Review* 51:1535–54.

Nelkin, Dorothy. 1977. "Thoughts on the Proposed Science Court." *Newsletter on Science, Technology and Human Values* 18:20–31.

Rawls, John. 1971. *A Theory of Justice*. Cambridge, Massachusetts: Harvard University Press.

Suskind, Lawrence E.; Richardson, Lawrence; and Hildebrand, Kathryn. 1978. *Resolving Environmental Disputes*. Environmental Impact Assessment Project, Laboratory of Architecture and Planning, M.I.T. (June).

Yesley, Michael S. 1978. "The Use of an Advisory Commission." *Southern California Law Review* 51:1451–69.

4

Public Participation and Professionalism in Impact Assessment

Frederick A. Rossini and
Alan L. Porter

Introduction

Impact assessment, considered gen-
erically, is the study of the consequences of new or modified technologies, projects, or programs and
the development of policy alternatives for dealing with these consequences. In the United States
impact assessment has been institutionalized in two major areas.

The National Environmental
Policy Act of 1969 (NEPA) required
the preparation of an environmental impact statement (EIS) for
every major federal action affecting
the environment. Although emphasis was placed on the physical
environment, consideration of the
entire human environment was required. Current regulations for EIS
preparation were issued by the U.S.
Council of Environmental Quality
in 1978 (US CEQ, 1978). EIS preparation has become a major activity

involving many federal agencies, their licensees, and contractors. In addition, many states have passed "little NEPAs" with varying requirements for environmental impact assessment.

Technology Assessment (TA) was conceived in the U.S. Congress as a means of providing information about unanticipated consequences of new technologies. Such a development was intended to give Congress its own capability for developing information on technologies, a capability hitherto possessed only by the executive branch. The Congressional Office of Technology Assessment was institutionalized by the Technology Assessment Act of 1972 and has since had a somewhat controversial existence (Porter et al., 1980: ch. 3).

In many other developed countries, impact assessment exists typically as part of the planning process (Hahn, 1977). Industry is gradually becoming more involved in assessment as it becomes a part of the long-range planning process (U.S. House and Senate, 1976).

Impact assessment began without theory or method. What needed to be done was known: how to go about it was another matter. During its first decade (the 1970s), it evolved from a limited activity which emphasized technologies (in the case of TAs) and environmental effects (in EIS preparation), to a more comprehensive effort to understand a broad range of impacts. Yet much was left undone and many problems remain to be addressed in the second decade. One central issue—the subject of this essay—is the relative roles of professionalism and public participation in assessment. Impact assessment began with little thought of public participation beyond routine information gathering. The EIS process introduced the opportunity for public comment, but the assessment itself was to be performed by professionals. The end of the decade saw a vastly expanded role for parties-at-interest in such areas as environmental mediation. The following material will consider alternative roles for professionals and publics in impact assessment. It will suggest some possibilities for interrelating them to strengthen the quality and utility of impact assessments.

The Contributions of the Professional

Research is an activity conducted by credentialed professionals. Impact assessment is a form of research. Therefore, impact assessment is conducted by professionals. This syllogistic argument dominated the earlier days of TA. In its extreme form it became a blind and unreflexive technocratic paean. Likewise, EISs often consisted of lists of undigested impacts with no concern for affected publics.

Yet when all is said and done, the professional researcher has much to contribute to impact assessment. To become a professional requires advanced education and training with its requisite intellectual skills (Coates, 1981). Professionals are committed to keep in contact with new developments in the field. They strive to develop sound judgment and perfect their analytical skills.

As professional researchers, impact assessors are committed to the professional values involved in the scientific search for knowledge. Their values are remarkably homogeneous (Rokeach, 1973). Thus it may be said that they represent one of many competing interest groups. Yet this is a miscategorization of the researchers' mind set. Their commitment to knowledge and their relatively dispassionate way of sifting through a mass of conflicting evidence and opinion may legitimately be argued to give them a privileged position in impact assessment.

Indeed it has been argued that the professional is most qualified to develop information of high quality which may be used to aid in reconciling and balancing competing interests (Coates, 1981). Many issues relating to science and technology are so complex that expertise is a necessity to arrive at any reasonable view of what is happening. Thus, the professional is a requisite. But professionals sometimes offer diametrically opposed interpretations of the same material. They have even served as "hired guns" of the parties-at-interest. Yet these very differences illustrate the complexity of the issues and thereby strengthen the argument that the professional is essential to the conduct of impact assessment.

There is one situation in which the professional is "the only game in town." That is the case when the technology, project, or program studied is in the early development stage and there exist no clearly defined communities of interest. In such cases participation in the usual sense becomes impossible. Thus the professional becomes the early warning system for the impacts of these developments. Indeed it is through the professional that the public may be alerted to potential problems. A TA of the hydrogen energy economy exemplifies this situation (Dickson et al., 1976).

In sum, professionals bring to impact assessment specialized training, analytic skills, and values which make them less biased than other parties-at-interest. They are in the best position to develop high quality information about the development in question. Finally, in the early stages of development where public interest is nebulous or nonexistent, they may be the only ones able to assess the impacts.

Modes of Participation: Contextual Differences

The detached mode of professional analysis can be contraposed to the more visceral public involvement in impact assessment where group and personal interests replace the values of the research community. In considering this prospect, the first issue to be settled is a generic description of the involved public or publics. As noted above, the character of the publics involved as affected groups, public decision makers, proponents, opponents, and so on, depends on the state of the development of the technology, project, or program being assessed. In the case of a development that exists at the level of scientific concept or the beginnings of a prototype, the only public is the collection of R & D personnel involved in the development. This use of assessment as an early warning system relates mainly to technology assessment. At this point the description of the technology is wholly that of the developers, the view of the bench R & D personnel. As the technology develops, other publics enter the picture: the producers of the technology; potential sources of funds for development, including governmental sources; governmental regulators; potential users; and potentially impacted parties. As the alternatives for implementation become more focused, the outlines of the involved publics emerge more clearly. At the point of widespread production and diffusion, the publics perceive the technology and their role much more sharply. Thus, clearly defined publics come to exist as the technology moves from concept to diffusion.

The situation with projects in the environmental impact statement is analogous. There is a significant difference, however; the technologies involved in almost every project assessed are typically not novel or innovative. Such things as highway segments, dams, and buildings require relatively little innovation. The mode of implementation and location of project determine who the publics are. Indeed it is much easier in many cases to identify the publics of a local project than of a technology diffused on an international scale. A program may involve both new technologies and localized situations. Thus the observations already made may be applied to programs as well.

But involvement of generic publics in assessment requires the intermediate steps of determining the important groups involved, and identifying and involving their representatives. When participation dominates, as in the case of mediation, Cormick (1981) argues that all parties should be represented in the process. Invariably the better organized, more articulate, and wealthy groups are more likely to be involved (Freudenberg, 1981; Coates, 1981). If this is the case, then the relationships of power and influence already existing will be maintained. If the involved groups identify themselves, then this will surely be the case. Who will identify the impacted but unorganized and inarticulate groups? One possible candidate is professional assessors. Yet they cannot organize unaware and uncaring individuals into knowledgeable groups. Even with the identification of groups, there remains the problem of identifying and involving representatives of these groups who can speak, at least with a reasonable degree of confidence, for their colleagues. Here too, well-organized, sophisticated, and affluent groups will have relatively less difficulty.

Degree of localization and technological specificity are important considerations in determining the sources and extent of participation. The environmental impact statement process, with its high degree of localization and technical specificity, typically allows relatively easy identification of parties-at-interest. Cases of locating a common technology in a low population density, as a mine near a small town in a barren region (Connor, 1981), present easy opportunities for identifying and involving impacted groups. At the other extreme, a highly sophisticated technology which is not location-specific, such as space colonies, leads to interest only among experts and aficionados, a situation more or less common to early warning TAS.

Participants in assessments can play a broad range of roles, the most basic of which is to supply information. Data used in assessments come from parties-at-interest in many cases. Indeed the developers of a new technology or the proponents of a new project typically possess more technical information about it than do other parties. Other actors in a technological drama are another important source of information. Impact assessment professionals universally recognize this role for involved publics.

Public criticism of impact assessments represents a step toward greater involvement. This is a part of the process of preparing environmental impact statements and is often used in TA under the rubric of technical review or review by users (Ballard and James, 1981). Involvement of interest group representatives on oversight panels is a similar approach which serves to legitimate the study, both process and product, to the interest groups thus represented (Kash, 1977). This active link between professional assessment activities and parties-at-interest is the first step from professionalism to two-way involvement. Yet the involvement of knowledgeable interest group representatives does not necessarily lead to their using the study, in that, from their point of view, it may not add much new knowledge (Berg et al., 1978).

An expanded role for public interest group representatives was attempted during the mid 1970s in a National Science Foundation-sponsored TA on solar energy (Arnstein, 1975). Public interest groups perceived by the assessors as having a stake in solar energy were invited to send their representatives to serve on a public interest panel which would play a substantive role in conducting the assessment along with the professional assessment team from Arthur D. Little, Inc. The first problem arose in getting representatives of the groups to participate. There was considerable suspicion that these representatives would merely serve to legitimate the interests of the "establishment" which was conducting the assessment. Thus those individuals who agreed to participate were viewed with suspicion by the very groups they were supposed to represent. Their interaction with the team of professional researchers conducting the assessment was equally problematic. The researchers' outlook and values were quite homogeneous in their orientation to detailed professional analysis and in their belief that there was no role in the analysis for social values and human interests (in line with the work of Rokeach, 1973). The emphasis on values and interests of the public interest group representatives was seen as hopeless bias by the researchers. Thus the two groups had some difficulties in harmonious collaboration in the course of the assessment. Because the researchers controlled the funds, their views ultimately prevailed.

The concept of an adversary technology assessment involves the preparation of assessments by the various parties-at-interest in a technology (see, for example, Rossini et al., 1976). This explicitly participatory concept has, to our knowledge, never been tried in a full-scale, coordinated manner. Its product is a number of independent assessments which present the strongest possible case for the position of the group performing the assessment. Problems of evaluating the relative merits of these and integrating their analyses are left to the user. No mediation process is involved. Such a process, however, could be added as a final step which would result in a single output.

Finally, there is an approach which reverses the typical roles of professionals and public: environmental mediation (Connor, 1981; Cormick, 1981; Peterson, 1981; Susskind, 1983). Mediation is a voluntary process by which those involved in a dispute jointly explore and reconcile their differences. The mediator has no authority to impose a settlement. His or her strength lies in the ability to help the parties resolve their own differences. The mediated dispute is settled when the parties themselves reach what they consider to be a workable solution (Cormick, 1981). Environmental mediation emphasizes the views of the parties-at-interest as to the actual impacts of a development. The involved parties determine the nature and significance of the impacts. The professional—in this case the mediator— works with the interest groups to achieve a resolution as to the identification, analysis, and evaluation of impacts and appropriate measures of mitigation, if any. The expertise required of the professional in this case is not technical and substantive, but rather mediative. Cormick (1981) notes that significant technical expertise in the area involved is not desirable because in such a situation, the mediator will be likely to favor a particular position and prefer certain mitigation measures, thereby biasing the process for apparently technical reasons, a major reversal of the usual case!

This experience highlights the importance of communication between professional assessors and affected publics. Peterson (1981) notes a case of an agency planning a reservoir involving Indian tribal lands. Agency documents reported and agency personnel honestly believed that they had met with the Indian Tribal Council and had received council support for the proposed project. Interviewing tribal councilmen and inspecting minutes of the Tribal Council failed to indicate any such meeting or express support of the project. On the other hand, the tribal government believed that it had expressed its position at public hearings, a belief not reflected in the agency documents on the hearing in question.

Such occurrences dramatize the importance of mutual understanding by involved groups. We might also suggest in this regard that neither technical language nor bureaucratic procedure should be viewed as somehow neutral.

In considering public participation in impact assessment, it is important to distinguish it carefully from social impact assessment (Freudenberg, 1981; Peterson, 1981). Social impact assessment deals with understanding the impacts of technologies and developments on human beings, groups, and institutions. More so than most other areas of impact assessment, it involves gathering primary data. Typically this includes surveying or interviewing representatives of groups involved with the development being assessed, and, in this sense, with their participation. However, this analysis is under the control of assessment professionals. Participation involves publics in the entire assessment process. In its most developed form, public representatives are the assessors or the determiners of the full range of impacts and approaches to their mitigation. Social impact analysis is part of many assessments; the degree of public involvement is largely independent of the study of social impacts.

In summary, there is a wide range of modes of public participation in impact assessments, extending from minimal information input to total domination of the study. The degree of the physical localization of the development and the stage in the innovation process are factors that affect the type of participation feasible in an assessment. Some of the alternative modes of assessment are mutually exclusive, with each having its own strong and weak points. The section below critically discusses the possible roles for professionalism and participation in impact assessment.

Designs for Involvement

Our first observation is an aphorism: "Professionalism without participation is blind; participation without professionalism is empty." The extreme positions are not worth considering. Parties-at-interest are prime sources of current information, a requisite in any assessment, and, even in the extreme of environmental mediation, a professional mediator plays a major role in the process. Thus our goal should be to identify viable compounds of professionalism and participation in impact assessment.

There are possible designs of three generic types: professional-dominant, partnership, and participant-dominant. Professional-dominant designs are the most common in both EIS and TA. Opportunity for public input and comment is required in the EIS process (US CEQ, 1978). This opportunity is exploited largely by well-organized and high-profile groups; unorganized and diffuse interest groups are relatively unrepresented. Peterson (1981) raises the issue of the researcher going beyond his or her professional role to help organize unorganized, but impacted, publics. Certainly a role for professional-dominated EISs can be argued in the case of generic statements, such as the enrichment of nuclear fuels (U.S. Nuclear Regulatory Commission, 1976), where the assessment subject is nonlocalized and highly technical. Here, understanding the impacts depends on the results of technical analyses, and at least some of the parties-at-interest are geographically dispersed. Likewise, projects where the geographic dispersal of costs and benefits is uneven (for example, concentrated costs with dispersed benefits, or vice versa) usually involve an imbalance of organized parties-at-interest.

In technology assessments, a case can be made for a professional-dominant mode in a wide variety of contexts. In technologies from the conceptual stage up to the point where significant parties-at-interest crystallize, there are literally no nontechnical publics involved, and thus no chance for participation beyond the input of the community of technical experts. Indeed it is arguable that any TA could be performed in a professional-dominant style, if the strategy developed in the University of Oklahoma's Science and Public Policy Program were employed. This strategy (Ballard and James, 1981; see also Kash, 1977) includes:

1 *Early Involvement*   Relationships with sponsors, government agencies, and more general parties-at-interest are established at the earliest possible stages of the project.

2 *On-going Relationships*   Relationships with users are maintained throughout the course of the project in order to understand the dynamics of user needs.

3 *Demand Orientation*   Research issues and tasks must be responsive to the needs of intended audiences. Thus, research agendas are developed in response to socially defined, rather than scientifically defined, objectives.

4 *Integrated R & D*   Knowledge generation must be linked to knowledge application; thus, all phases of research design, development, and utilization are closely linked.

5 *Research Management*   Researchers must recognize their own role in the process of change. This includes developing substantive expertise, understanding how they intrude or affect elements of the social context (especially organizational politics), and understanding the factors (such as political variables) which condition the demand for research.

6 *Active Utilization Role*   Understanding user needs and processes of change are necessary but not sufficient for utilization by such activities as dissemination of findings, increasing awareness and interest in the research, and convincing audiences of its applicability.

Whereas parties-at-interest are actively involved in the assessment and play a major role in forming its product, the professional assessment team is in control throughout and makes all significant decisions.

Although conceptually quite interesting, the partnership mode suffers from internal instabilities, and thus has not emerged as a practical form of assessment, as have the other two modes. The equal involvement of professionals and parties-at-interest pits research values against a range of social values in dominating the study. Thus the potential for a power struggle is great; without a format for resolving disputes, whoever controls the assessment's resources also controls the bottom line. To develop a workable design one issue that must be resolved is whether the professional researchers are themselves one of many interest groups or whether they enter into partnership with each interest group. In the latter case it might be possible for the researchers, if they were relatively unbiased among the parties-at-interest, to offer professional support for the parties-at-interest. This support would have to be given critically, rather than as paid advocates, so that both sides would learn in the process. By critically providing professional support to the assessments of the parties-at-interest, the professionals could serve as glue to bind together the perspectives of the interest groups, now buttressed by analysis. To our knowledge, this design has not been tried. Indeed we have offered the barest outline.

Participant-dominant impact assessment occurs predominantly in the area of environmental impacts where the parties-at-interest determine from their own perspectives what the impacts are and what mitigation strategies are appropriate. The mediator merely facilitates this process procedurally without substantively entering into it. Cormick (1981) notes those questions that should be answered in exploratory discussions among the parties before mediation can begin:

1   Are all parties represented who have a stake in the outcome of the negotiations? Is any party excluded who could prevent an agreement from being carried out?

2   Have all parties reached general agreement on the scope of the issues to be addressed?

3   Are there negotiators for each party who are able to speak for their constituency? Is there reason to believe that if the negotiators reached an agreement, that agreement will be honored by the groups they represent?

4 Have the immediate parties and eventual decision makers committed themselves in good faith to reach a consensual agreement?

5 Has a realistic deadline been set for the negotiations?

6 Are there reasonable assurances that affected governmental agencies will cooperate in carrying out an agreement if one is reached?

7 Does the mediator operate from a base that is independent of both the immediate parties and the decision makers with jurisdiction over the dispute?

8 Do all the parties trust the mediator to carry messages when appropriate and to honor confidential remarks?

In addition to answering these questions, exploratory discussions should address and resolve the sponsorship and commitments necessary to help insure both implementation and the projected form that any agreement will take. Cormick (1981) and Peterson (1981) discuss cases where such an approach has succeeded.

In TA, the adversary TA concept, cited above—which has to our knowledge never been fully implemented—is an example of a participant-dominant mode. Whereas this approach ends with a set of independent assessments, it could be extended to a mediation process in which the assessments confront one another. It is then possible that a total or partial synthesis may emerge. Unlike the results of a successful environmental mediation, this synthesis would be an intellectual document guiding future practice and research, rather than an agreement to be implemented by actions. As in the partnership case, we do not have examples where this has occurred. To succeed, it would require that the issues be formed by a developed technology, and by parties with well-defined interests. Finally, the impacts should not be localized, or mediation would be appropriate.

In sum, the professional-dominant and participant-dominant modes of impact assessment have been used successfully, while the partnership mode has not. It is fair to say that the professional-dominant mode can be used in almost every assessment, provided that any parties-at-interest were involved along the lines suggested above by Ballard and James. In the case of technologies in their early phases of development, and technologies whose effects are varied, broadly spread, and not fully understood, this may be the only viable approach. Where the technology is diffused or the development clearly planned and where there exist well-defined parties, the participant-dominant approach may lead to an agreement among all

Frederick A. Rossini and Alan L. Porter

involved groups if the impacts are local, or to a synthesis of understanding of the consequences and ways to deal with them where they are not. Participant-dominated assessments can lead directly to action, or at least can do so more readily than professional-dominated assessments. The partnership mode, although intriguing, lacks proved designs. Experiments in this mode would require some serious thought and observation on relating professionals and interest groups on an equal basis in assessments.

To conclude, professionalism and participation are both necessary in impact assessment. A number of approaches have functioned usefully, and others are possible. The choice of procedure will depend on the context and parties-at-interest.

References

Arnstein, S. R. 1975. "A Working Model for Public Participation." *Public Administration Review* 35: 70–73.

Ballard, S. C., and James, T. E. 1981. "Ethics, Participation, and Utilization in the Technology Assessment Process." American Association for the Advancement of Science, Annual Meeting, Toronto.

Berg, M.R.; Brudney, J. L.; Fuller, T. D.; Michael, D. N.; and Roth, B. K. 1978. *Factors Affecting Utilization of Technology Assessment Studies in Policy-Making.* Ann Arbor: University of Michigan, Center for Research on Utilization of Scientific Knowledge, Institute for Social Research.

Coates, V. T. 1981. "Professionalism in Impact Assessment." American Association for the Advancement of Science, Annual Meeting, Toronto.

Conner, D. M. 1981. "A Community Approach to Social Impact Assessment." American Association for the Advancement of Science, Annual Meeting, Toronto.

Cormick, G. W. 1981. "Environmental Mediation in the United States: Experience and Future Directions." American Association for the Advancement of Science, Annual Meeting, Toronto.

Dickson, E. M.; Ryan, J. W.; and Smulyan, M. H. 1976. *The Hydrogen Economy: A Preliminary Technology Assessment.* Menlo Park, California: SRI International. Prepared for the National Science Foundation under Grant ERP 73–02706.

Freudenberg, W. R. 1981. "The Promise and Peril of Public Participation in Social Impact Assessment." American Association for the Advancement of Science, Annual Meeting, Toronto.

Hahn, W. 1977. "Technology Assessment: Some Alternative Perceptions and Its Implications Outside the United States." Testimony before the Subcommittee on Science, Research, and Technology of the House Committee on Science and Technology (3 August).

Kash, D. E. 1977. "Observations on Interdisciplinary Studies and Government Roles." In

Adapting Science to Social Needs. Washington, D.C.: American Association for the Advancement of Science, pp. 147–78.

Peterson, J. 1981. "An Anthropological View of Professionalism and Participation in Assessing Human Resources." American Association for the Advancement of Science, Annual Meeting, Toronto.

Porter, A. L.; Rossini, G. A.; Carpenter, S. R.; and Roper, A. T. 1980. *A Guidebook for Technology Assessment and Impact Analysis.* New York: North Holland

Rokeach, M. 1973. *The Nature of Human Values.* New York: Free Press.

Rossini, F. A.; Porter, A. L.; and Zucker, E. 1976. "Multiple Technology Assessments." *Journal of the International Society for Technology Assessment* 2: 21–28.

Susskind, L. 1983. "Uses of Negotiation and Mediation in Environmental Impact Assessment." In *Integrated Impact Assessment*, ed. F. A. Rossini and A. L. Porter. Boulder: Westview.

U.S. Council on Environmental Quality. 1978. "National Environmental Policy Act—Regulations for Implementation of Procedural Provisions." *Federal Register* 36 (November 29), pt. 6, 55978–56007.

U.S. House and Senate. 1976. Office of Technology Assessment. *Technology Assessment Activities in the Industrial, Academic, and Governmental Communities, June 8, 9, 10, 14, Hearings.* Washington, D.C.: Government Printing Office.

U.S. Nuclear Regulatory Commission. 1976. "Final Generic Environmental Statement on the Use of Recycled Plutonium in Mixed Oxide Fuel in Light Water Cooled Reactors." Washington, D.C.: NTIS (PB 256452).

5

Institutionalizing Public Service Science: Its Perils and Promise

Rachelle Hollander

In the mid-1970s, the National Science Foundation became home to a new program that appeared to fit within an expanded vision of the foundation's role in fostering science and engineering research and education. Titled "Science for Citizens," the new program was designed to enable American citizens and citizens' organizations to communicate more effectively with scientists, engineers, and policymakers about science-related policy issues, ranging from the management of asbestos hazards to the treatment of waste.

In 1981 the Science for Citizens program was terminated. This decision reflected the view that the foundation should place lower priority on these kinds of efforts than on those it undertakes in support of basic research, in the physical and natural sciences particularly. It probably also indicated more fundamental disagreements about the value and propriety of federal efforts in this arena.

This article sketches the rise and fall of Science for Citizens and the development of its different parts and describes some of the projects the program supported. Through this examination, I hope to have identified, explicitly and implicitly, some of the perils and promise of institutionalizing public service science.[1]

Science for Citizens' History

The social forces behind the development of the Science for Citizens program were the same as those behind continuing calls for institutional accountability and accessibility. The decades of the 1960s and 1970s saw a proliferation of national, state, and local organizations of citizens concerned about particular issues. These were the years when neighborhoods organized themselves into associations, incorporated, and developed networks. During these years also Congress enacted many laws mandating agencies to insure that citizens participate, somehow, when decisions involving their interests were being made.

A substantial body of federal, state, and local laws and regulations was also enacted during this period in response to problems of environmental hazards, occupational health, and nuclear energy. Such issues have strong scientific and technological aspects, and thus scientists and engineers have been major actors in decisions on these and related issues.

A problem for the public has been that most scientists and engineers work for established institutions—governments, industries, and universities. They provide expert services to "big" government and "big" business. Scientists and engineers also have a strong tradition of public service work, although the reward systems of the institutions in which they work do not strongly encourage these activities.

"Public interest" science has roots in the post-World War II activism of nuclear physicists; in the sixties and seventies, scientists and engineers provided assistance and expert advice on such topics as nutrition, air quality, sewage treatment, and nuclear power to community groups and environmental and consumer organizations. Private nonprofit organizations such as the Center for Science in the Public Interest and the Scientists' Institute for Public Information sprang up. The environmental movement became a more potent social and political force, and some scientists associated themselves with it.

Even in this context, it is very unlikely that the National Science Foundation would have undertaken a Science for Citizens program on its own; NSF priorities are in basic research and training of scientists and engineers. However, calling on the testimony of public interest scientists and its sense of social needs, the Congress directed the foundation to develop a plan for such a program in 1976 and to implement it in 1977. Initially, the relevant committee of the Senate supported the development of the program, while the corresponding committee of the House of Representatives was reluctant to support it, fearing that a venture into activities with political implications might jeopardize the foundation's primary purpose. By the end of 1979, however, the House committee had come to support the program as it had taken shape in the foundation.

Once it became clear that the program would be enacted, NSF developed a rationale for its efforts. The program assumed that federal research and development needed to be sensitive to the social values and needs of American communities if they were to develop in socially useful ways. Therefore, it was appropriate for federal agencies supporting research and development to foster that sensitivity. The program also assumed that American communities needed to understand the implications of scientific and technological developments if they were to make wise social choices. Since these choices had to be made continuously, and involved complicated decisions crossing disciplinary and political boundaries, it was important for communities to institutionalize ways to deal with issues as they arose, and reasonable for a portion of NSF's resources to demonstrate ways to foster institutionalization and feed the results of this experience back into research and development efforts.

Of course, it would not be necessary to spend any money for these purposes if it could be said confidently that scientific and technological research and development only contribute to solving, and never create or exacerbate, social problems. It would not be necessary if we could say confidently that our political and social institutions, at local, state, and federal levels, deal efficaciously with the problems and opportunities that science and technology present. However, scientific and technological advances may alter social and economic systems adversely, inequitably, or in ways that frighten people; they may create environmental hazards as by-products of the improvements they bring; or their potential benefits may be overlooked. Our political and social institutions have not developed concepts and mechanisms to deal with these problems.

Furthermore, scientific and technological contributions occur in changing social contexts which they themselves have helped create. We Americans may expect always to need to modify our public programs and policies in ways that are responsive to changing needs and opportunities. To develop this responsiveness, citizens, scientists, engineers, and officials in local and state governments can use encouragement to explore the options and implications of scientific and technological advances for their communities, while agencies of the federal government can use encouragement to facilitate these efforts and heed the results. Particular policies and programs may vanish but the need for responsive policies and programs will not. It was the ability to respond to these needs, and to recognize their importance, that Science for Citizens attempted to foster.

Science for Citizens' program elements   From its beginnings, the SFC program made awards for public service science residencies and forums, conferences, and workshops. SFC residencies were awards to individual scientists and engineers to undertake applied research and public education projects in association with citizens' groups, units of state and local government, and other nonprofit organizations. These awards could be part-time or full-time; they enabled their recipients to undertake up to a year's work, which could be spread out over two and a half years. They provided a salary stipend, a travel allowance, and a small support allowance to the organizations with which residents associated. Due to lack of funds, no new SFC residencies were supported after fiscal year 1981.

Science for Citizens residents came from the natural and social sciences; they worked with Indian tribes, public interest groups, community action agencies, state and local governments, trade unions, and chambers of commerce. They documented and developed analyses of such diverse problems as urban flooding and run-off, the deinstitutionalization of mental patients, and the effects of pesticides on agricultural workers. Results from their work were published in refereed journals, as well as in more popular media, and cited at neighborhood gatherings, city-wide meetings, and national conferences.

Similar results followed from SFC-supported forums, conferences, and workshops, also terminated after fiscal 1981. These awards went to organizations and were generally of twelve to eighteen months duration. They ranged from $25,000 to $85,000. These projects supported the cooperative efforts of citizens and scientists and engineers to devise programs of information, education, and analysis on particular issues of policy in their communities that involved science and technology. They often focused on matters that were under consideration by local, state, or regional decision-making bodies.

To some degree, these projects challenged government postures. However, they did so by articulating the diverse positions that could reasonably follow from scientific and engineering understanding and its limits, and, often, by suggesting options on which everyone could agree. So several small towns in Illinois developed better water management procedures, and a barrier island community in South Carolina initiated a plan to lessen beach erosion. Scientists and American Indians developed new nutrition initiatives. Scientists, Appalachian citizens, and coal companies clarified areas of agreement and disagreement with respect to the effects of surface mine blasting and the regulations that should govern it. The list can go on and on.

Nineteen eighty marked the initial efforts of Science for Citizens to reach its long-range goals. The program moved from supporting short-term projects giving citizens access to information and analysis about specific community concerns to supporting longer-term projects to set self-sustaining community-based mechanisms in place for that purpose. This new program element, SFC Public Service Science Centers, made three-year awards of a maximum of $100,000 per year. The awards required sponsors to make a matching commitment of 20 percent in the second year and 40 percent in the third year of project activities.

Six centers began their activities in fiscal year 1980; it was hoped that three or four more would begin in 1981, but federal funding cutbacks precluded their support. A later section of this article describes each of the six established by the program.

Science for Citizens' Strategy

From its beginnings in 1977, SFC emphasized the need to incorporate diverse points of view in the projects it supported in order to assure the representation of all groups with substantial interests in project matters. This tightrope act was clearly a response to congressional concerns. The foundation shared many of these concerns and never seriously considered supporting what could be clearly characterized as adversary research—that explicitly directed at making scientific or engineering assistance available to help citizens' organizations bolster a position that they wished to maintain. By no means then could SFC be characterized as a program directed at redistributing social power, nor did a social debate about the appropriate uses of federal funds for this purpose arise.

The foundation desired to support projects in which the discussion of scientific and engineering matters was central, met high standards, and incorporated appropriate scientific and technical perspectives. Adversary science might be less likely to meet these standards. All these emphases and constraints meant that SFC-supported projects were oriented more toward communication than toward action; citizens' groups that wanted to take steps based on what they learned had to do so independently.

The program's emphasis on long-term initiatives grew out of the work of the SFC advisory committee. The legislation that established the program in 1977 required that this committee be formed and provide a report on the program to the director of the foundation and, through him, to Congress. The committee included scientists, engineers, and citizens from diverse backgrounds. They shared a common perception of the need for better communication between citizens, scientists, engineers, and policymakers, and they worked hard to develop a report to Congress that would serve to provide some direction for the program.

In their meetings, committee members and program staff came to agree that short-term projects could not adequately address their fundamental concern. They felt that successful efforts, of whatever sort, would have to be driven by citizens' perceptions of their own needs and priorities. As a result, they recommended that the program support projects to develop long-term, self-sustaining, community-based mechanisms that would involve citizens who normally had little or no access to scientific and technical resources in establishing their priorities, policies, and activities. In their report, the committee recommended the development of citizen-oriented, information-oriented centers, as well as back-up institutes where independent analyses of scientific and technical information germane to policy issues could be undertaken.

In keeping with this orientation, the program's long-range strategy was to develop ways in which to institutionalize citizen-driven public service science. It was an attempt to encourage and manage science and technology in a democratic context. It encouraged nonconfrontational attempts to deal with difficult issues by bringing the best possible scientific and engineering information and analyses to bear in their discussion. It did not support engineering studies to develop one sewage-treatment option or another, nor did it support political initiatives to put bond issues for sewage plants on the ballot. It enabled communities to bring experts and citizens together to discuss the kinds of problems and options they might have, what alternative responses might cost, and how they might affect different groups. It enabled them to develop mechanisms to deal with these kinds of issues in an ongoing fashion, as and where they arose.

There were situations for which Science for Citizens could offer little assistance: where enemies had drawn their battlelines and refused to talk with each other, for instance, or where citizens' groups needed "quick and dirty" scientific or technical assistance to support a legal or political battle. However, there were important goals that Science for Citizens could reach. The program could encourage scientists and citizens to take a look at their problems from broader perspectives than usual. It could encourage analyses of problems that were interdisciplinary or transdisciplinary, and incorporate community perspectives and support from the beginning. It could encourage the diffusion of innovation, after critical appraisal of alternatives. And it could discourage actions taken out of stupidity, ignorance, greed, or carelessness. If half the projects the program supported reached these relatively modest goals, many would say it was wildly successful.

SFC Public Service Science Centers

To meet the committee's recommendation, the Science for Citizens program invited appropriate organizations to apply for grants to plan for ongoing programs for their communities. Fifty organizations applied in June 1978 to conduct these planning studies. Seventeen grants were made: five to universities; one to a science museum; one to a YMCA; five to public interest science organizations; two to consumer health organizations; two to community action agencies; and one to an environmental information center.

Fourteen of the organizations that received planning study awards submitted proposals for the funding of Public Service Science Centers. Six of them received grants for three years (renewable annually after review). The six included two universities, the science museum, and the YMCA, one consumer health organization, and one public interest science organization. They are now coming to the end of the three-year award period, which provides us an opportunity to review their initial accomplishments and difficulties, and draw some lessons from their prospects. The next section of this article provides brief descriptions of the organizational features of these six centers, their accomplishments, and their current status. In the concluding section, there is some discussion of the prospects of the centers and several suggestions about how those prospects might have been improved. However, it is important to recognize that these conclusions and suggestions are premature, because the SFC award period is just drawing to a close. Furthermore, the SFC program's brief duration, unique history, and small number of awards allow only the most tentative conclusions.

Montshire Public Service Science Center   The Montshire Public Service Science Center is part of the Montshire Museum of Science. The museum opened the doors of an attractively converted bowling alley in January 1976, making good the pledge of community leaders to find a home for Dartmouth College's extensive natural history collection. The museum began as an active regional environmental education center committed to working closely with all ages and sectors of the Upper Valley population, 105,000 people living near the Connecticut River in New Hampshire and Vermont. It maintains close ties with Dartmouth and with the Regional Center for Educational Training, a science resource center for the region's public school teachers.

Local citizens see Montshire as a catalyst that provides a neutral forum for working out problems of the region. The museum and the center are meeting grounds for the entire spectrum of the valley's population, and Montshire builds on its educational mandate and the New England history of independent public meetings and community activism to encourage the development of new, voluntary groups to grapple with regional issues.

In 1979, the museum created the "Forum for the Valley's Future." This loose amalgam of people who want to think about what is happening in the region and what these events portend for its future has proved to be a rich source of members for the formation of groups with more specific interests or shared responsibilities. Montshire encourages these groups to evolve and provides staff and scientific and technical assistance for their efforts. So, for instance, staff will identify resources for a variety of meetings on the transportation of radioactive waste. Some sessions will be arranged to draw high school students and an adult public audience; others will be set at Dartmouth seminars or special meetings of the Association of Elected Officials of the Upper Valley and the Regional Commission of Planning Board Members. Montshire played a catalytic role in the formation of both these groups. Although their members had common interests and needs, including the need to know what each other was doing, they had not met together before the groups were formed.

Besides short-term scientific and technical assistance, Montshire has made a commitment to developing a regional data base and analysis service. In so doing, it can generate information that will be useful to various sides in particular disputes, all of whom are people who share an interest in planning a better future for the region. As particular issues arise, Montshire can and does draw all interested parties together for special presentations and discussions where facts and opinions can be aired and questioned.

This positive orientation has enabled the center to enlist financial support from the valley's business, financial, and professional organizations. They are encouraged to join the Montshire Associates. For a yearly fee that goes to support the center generally, they receive special invitations to programs that explore the valley's future and needs. Their advice and involvement in all center activities is solicited.

The Appalachian Technical Association and Institute   Appalachia-Science in the Public Interest (ASPI) incorporated in Kentucky in 1977. Its director, a native Appalachian, helped to found the Center for Science in the Public Interest in 1971. ASPI's goal is to make science and technology responsive to the needs of the rural poor in central Appalachia.

The idea for an Appalachian Technical Association developed from an ASPI conference on surface mine blasting that SFC had supported. ASPI staff realized that Appalachian community groups needed individual and extended assistance in order to make adequate use of scientific and technical resources. Using informal surveys and interviews, ASPI identified some issues of priority—land use, energy alternatives, and transportation—for the citizens in the region, and developed a list of 350 scientists and engineers who agreed to offer *pro bono* services to Appalachian citizens and groups. The listing was called the Appalachian Technical Network. ASPI's solar demonstration center, located on the banks of the Rockcastle River near Livingston, Kentucky, maintained the network's files.

As part of the SFC center's project, ASPI publicized this service and matched citizens and citizens' groups who initiated a written request for help with one or more experts. The citizens had to agree to assist the expert, monitor the results, and become involved in policy-related activities, where necessary.

ASPI is also committed to strengthening and cooperating with Appalachian groups that share their goals for the region. Its goal for the SFC's center project was to create an association of satellite public service science centers that would be relatively autonomous and responsive to local needs in a region where small communities are geographically remote from each other and historically suspicious of outsiders. So ASPI held a competition to select candidate groups for association memberships. The selected groups would receive $10,000 each to enable them to involve citizens in considering issues of public policy with scientific and technical content. Using an advisory panel and criteria known to all the applicants, ASPI selected two groups in Tennessee (Mountain Women's Exchange and Rural Cumberland Resources), and one each in Kentucky (Kentucky New Farms Coalition), North Carolina (Long Branch Environmental Education Center), Virginia (Coalition of American Electric Consumers), and West Virginia (Mountain Stream Monitors). The subcontracts supported a co-ordinator who would undertake specified research, education, and co-operative activities during the award period.

These groups, along with ASPI and the now-independent Rockcastle Resource Center, incorporated in 1982 as the Appalachian Institute. In cooperation with one of the Berea College programs, the institute offers internships, independent study, and summer and short-term courses on alternative technologies, environmental management, and consumer issues. It sponsors research and demonstration projects, and maintains a speakers' bureau and the Appalachian Technical Network listings.

The Appalachian Technical Network has been able to assist community groups with science-related policy problems. For instance, a relocation project for low-income families in heavily flood-damaged Pineville, Kentucky, now includes passive solar design because of a conference of eight architects with housing officials. In McCreary County, blasting experts provided help to residents whose homes were damaged during construction of a coal preparation plant. In the follow-up program, the citizens became interested in water quality preservation, and they are working with state officials to develop a comprehensive stream classification plan.

Boston Neighborhood Network   Boston-area academics initiated the Neighborhood Network. For a number of years, they had sponsored seminar discussions and public events to connect academic resources with local government and neighborhood groups. The informal headquarters for this effort was MIT's Laboratory of Architecture and Planning. After its first year of support from the Science for Citizens' Public Service Science Centers program, the Boston Neighborhood Network emerged from these institutional origins and established an independent office in downtown Boston. It incorporated as a nonprofit organization and its board of advisers, a group of about twenty-five neighborhood leaders, government, business, media, and academic representatives, became a board of directors, with an executive committee and officers. The board and the network still exist; however, the downtown headquarters is closed, and there are currently no funds to support a network coordinator and secretary.

The network's major purpose is still to link the research activities of the area's university scientists and engineers with the research needs of Boston's neighborhoods. While it continues to serve this function, it cannot itself make funds available to support research, outreach, and coordinating activities, as it did with Science for Citizens' money. So the board and former staff are struggling to decide whether the network should continue as a separate organization or merge with one or another of the groups with which they have worked successfully to achieve network purposes.

Through subcontracts with research organizations and university-based researchers, BNN provided technical assistance to numerous neighborhood groups. It concentrated on community energy planning, banking and community credit, neighborhood change, neighborhoods and environmental impacts, and patterns in the locations of community residences.

In community energy planning, network involvement sparked the first courses on the subject at MIT and Tufts University. Energy internships enabled students to work on projects in the cities of Somerville and Cambridge, part of the inner core of the metropolitan Boston area. Network researchers, working with the Somerville Citizen Energy Advisory Committee, completed a city energy profile and eight energy action pamphlets. Other energy-related projects provided assistance on specific problems and on opportunities to community groups and community development corporations.

Through a subcontract with the Massachusetts Urban Reinvestment Advisory Group (MURAG), the network sponsored community banking forums, where local bankers and representatives of community groups could discuss with each other the results of research on bank lending patterns, and their implications. Besides providing direct training to community groups, MURAG also developed the "Community Reinvestment Training Manual," a tool for training community groups on how to document bank lending patterns in their neighborhoods.

Science for Citizens' Center of Southwestern Michigan   A "Citizens' Policy Council," with its membership drawn from and representative of the population in the fifteen counties surrounding Kalamazoo, directs this center. A group of consulting associates, made up primarily of representatives from science faculties at colleges and universities throughout the region, advises the council. The center is a self-governing part of Western Michigan University (WMU); the small core of staff are university faculty and support personnel. The economic crunch in Michigan has adversely affected the staff support WMU can allow the center; however, a good working relationship exists between the center's staff and the university administration, who assist the center in its fund-raising endeavors.

A set of bylaws and policy documents govern council policies. Proposals for center projects and activities come from or through council members, as well as from inquiries to center staff. The staff works in helping people who have made inquiries that seem suitable to develop a proposal for a project. The council considers all proposals for projects and votes on whether or not to conduct the project. Many projects have financial or in-kind support from other groups, agencies, and individuals. Staff and consulting associates look for appropriate scientists and engineers, and the center maintains a list of such researchers and evaluations of completed projects. Over its first two and a half years, the center has supported more than forty projects. Staff can authorize small-scale services independently of the procedure outlined here; many small-scale scientific consultations have been undertaken, and numerous referrals have been made to other sources of assistance.

Most of the projects the center has supported fall into two categories: those of special interest to minorities and disadvantaged populations and those concerning environmental issues. In the former category, the largest project was the Career-Oriented Science Education Program for Minorities. The program, which includes summer and after-school sessions for elementary school minority youngsters, has secured external funding to continue in one of the three communities where it was initiated. A fourth community initiated a related program for high school students, and is working to begin a program for elementary school youngsters. Because of its success in this area, the center is becoming involved in some state-wide initiatives on science education, working in cooperation with relevant agencies and groups.

Center support for a number of other projects has enabled them to develop the credibility to receive continued funding from state or local agencies. One area where the center hopes to receive funding to continue is in its work with groundwater quality. Because of citizens' concerns, the center sponsored a number of projects involving questions of groundwater contamination and solid waste disposal; the reports coming out of these projects have been well received. Now the center would like to develop, over a five-year period, a baseline quality analysis of the groundwater in many of the counties in its service area. The U.S. Geological Survey has offered to provide technical support to this activity; four counties have joined the project and submitted their $1,000 participation fee; five more are actively considering whether to join. This project requires substantial additional funds to get underway, and the center is soliciting support from private and public sources.

Consumer Health Information and Resource Center   This center began as an activity of the Consumer Commission for the Accreditation of Health Services, Inc., a nonprofit organization in New York City. The commission's goal is to educate the public at large about current issues in health care from a consumer perspective. Its name is an ironic take-off on the Joint Commission for the Accreditation of Hospital Services, Inc.

With SFC funds, CHIRC undertook a series of community-needs assessment surveys. It used this information to plan public seminars and to encourage community groups with health interests to develop requests for scientific and technical assistance projects. Summaries of the seminars and projects are published in the commission's newsletter, *Consumer Health Perspectives*. The center also provides referral and networking services.

A board of directors supervises the center's activities. Several board members are also members of the board of the Consumer Commission; others come from university faculty, health agencies and hospitals, and community and consumer groups. During the course of the project, the commission and the center did not always agree about center priorities, and some members of the commission's board and staff felt that the commission's activities should be limited to working with unionized labor. Recognizing the need to build on their successful history of consumer health advocacy, however, the commission's board finally voted unanimously to accept the center as an ongoing program within the commission. The commission accepted responsibility for fund-raising to maintain a minimal level of assistance projects and seminars beyond the expiration of NSF funding.

The center has worked very successfully with community boards and consumer groups to develop requests for technical assistance, find adequate consultants to undertake the studies, and develop reports that can be understood by the clientele. These reports have provided groups with the technical documentation and information necessary to initiate actions and ground requests for relief. Of ten initial projects, six produced positive action; in three cases action is pending; in one case, the report was unsatisfactory. At least one of these projects helped a client document the need for and utility of its services, which resulted in a major government grant. Reports range over such subjects as the operational status of a particular sewage-treatment plant and alternatives for its improvement; construction of a better survey to determine transportation needs of disabled persons; and the need for bilingual communicaton in adequate medical care, with suggestions of how to meet that need. Summaries of many reports have been published in *Consumer Health Perspectives*, as have excerpts from seminar presentations and discussions on questions of occupational hazards, and hospital codes and standards.

Scientists/Citizens Organized on Policy Issues Metrocenter, the city-center branch of the YMCA, helps Seattle's citizens address significant urban problems by sponsoring a wide variety of educational, recreational, and social assistance programs. Working with the People Power Coalition and the Social Management of Technology program at the University of Washington, Metrocenter developed an SFC Center project, called "Scientists/Citizens Organized on Policy Issues," or the SCOPI Project.

Seattle is a city with strong neighborhood associations and activist minority communities. Like all such groups, they often need scientific and technical assistance to understand and evaluate their problems. SCOPI was designed to provide those services, especially to lower-income groups.

A nine or ten member executive board sets SCOPI policy and has the authority to hire and fire the SCOPI director. Members include the directors of Metrocenter Y and the People Power Coalition, which is a coalition of community organizations, media groups, educational institutions, and governmental agencies that coordinates media and information programs on public issues. Also represented on the board are University of Washington faculty, community organizations, educational organizations, government agencies, and industry. There is a looser and larger advisory panel of scientists, engineers, environmentalists, and community leaders to which SCOPI staff and the board turn for project ideas, recommendations, and technical assistance. SCOPI has also developed a long list of scientists and engineers willing to offer *pro bono* or lower-rate services to SCOPI clients. The project publishes two newsletters. *Newswatch* keeps people informed about SCOPI activities and their results, while *Issuewatch* provides up-to-date information on the policy-related aspects of regional issues involving science and technology.

SCOPI offers scientific and technical assistance on issues involving housing, energy, and health. The project has carefully given priority to issues that clearly interest and affect low-income and minority groups and that concern policy or program responsibilities of local units of government or service agencies. Like ASPI, Consumer Health Information and Resource Center, and Science for Citizens Center of Southwestern Michigan, SCOPI staff work closely with citizen groups and scientists to tailor a request so that scientific help will be valuable to the clients and in the decision-making process. By keying its assistance to the timetable that local authorities have set for making decisions, SCOPI has been able to provide useful research products to citizen groups concerned about downtown land-use plans, about disposal of waste water plant effluent, and about the environmental impact of transit terminals and a mall proposed for downtown Seattle. Many research projects have been supplemented with funds from other sources, and some referrals have resulted in useful assistance without the need for any SCOPI outlays.

Working with the United Indians of All Tribes Foundation and University of Washington social work faculty, SCOPI coordinated a comprehensive survey of Seattle Indian street youth that has proved of great benefit. It generated a large amount of descriptive data about that population, enabling the foundation to document need and design better programs. It also increased the foundation's knowledge and experience in needs assessment, identified new consultant resources, and enhanced interagency cooperation and public knowledge about this problem.

Besides benefiting their direct clients, SCOPI-supported studies have benefited units of local government. The work they have done on renter weatherization and energy conservation options has been very useful to Seattle City Light Company. Reviewing the results of the projects they have sponsored, SCOPI has decided to consider reorienting its activities to the provision of technical assistance to local government and private service agencies for a fee. Right now it does not appear likely that the SCOPI director/coordinator's position will find financial support, but the success of a recent community conference on AIDS, which SCOPI convened, has added to its credibility and given it the potential to exploit this option.

Ethics and the Science for Citizens' Centers

One of the aspects of bureaucratic history worth noting in describing the SFC centers and their prospects is the NSF source for third-year support for five of them. This source has clearly affected the work of three of those five centers. In spring 1981, it became known that Science for Citizens would not be able to make any awards in the federal fiscal year 1982. The program had made second-year funding available to the centers from its 1981 appropriation; it had no money left to make third-year awards. Science for Citizens approached the program on Ethics and Values in Science and Technology (EVIST) at NSF to determine whether some of its funds might go to supporting the third-year efforts if they would incorporate research and dissemination about ethical and value components of local or regional issues that involved science and technology. EVIST and SFC were able to make satisfactory arrangements with Montshire, ASPI, BNN, the SFC Center of Southwestern Michigan, and CHIRC to do this; and SFC had enough money left to make most of the originally planned third-year incremental award to SCOPI.

The effect of this intervention can be seen most clearly in structural changes and reports from three centers. The Science for Citizens Center of Southwestern Michigan set up an Ethics and Human Values Advisory Council. This group has selected special activities to support, and provides suggestions and assistance in incorporating attention to ethical issues in other center activities and publications. One notable effort resulted in the contribution "Value Perspectives in the Control of EEE" to the publication *Eastern Equine Encephalomyelitis (EEE) and Public Health in Southwestern Michigan*. Since EEE is a rare, often fatal mosquito-carried viral disease, the decision to spray widely or not becomes a morally difficult one; the issues involved are discussed carefully in that publication.

The Consumer Health Information and Resource Center set up an Ethics Advisory Committee; this group incorporated discussion of ethical issues into the technical assistance projects and seminars. One issue of *Consumer Health Perspectives* was devoted to the topic of bioethics; its author, who was a member of the committee, has become a member of the center's board of directors.

Appalachia-Science in the Public Interest used an adviser to develop the capabilities of the satellite centers to reflect on the ethical dimensions of their activities under the grant. The groups sponsored a conference, "Land Ethics in Appalachia," at which citizens and specialists in ethics and social values discussed American land attitudes and the attitudes of decision makers, issues of eminent domain, land and toxic waste disposal, and the ethical implications of citizens' actions. The conference proceedings are available from ASPI.

Prospects

The successful activities of Science for Citizens' centers demonstrate at least that there is much community interest in the scientific and technical components of policy issues. In addition, center staffs have demonstrated energy, creativity, and flexibility in setting up their programs. They have provided policy-oriented research and educational services that interested and attracted broad participation in their communities, created new networks, and revised policies and practices.

Clearly, SFC-supported activities and centers have had positive impacts on individual careers and institutional decisions. Many SFC-supported people are still working on their original activities or are working on related projects. Projects demonstrated that lay groups can develop the capability to design effective programs and participate responsibly in resolving policy issues with scientific and technical components. The feasibility and utility of this approach has been proven.

It will be much more difficult to judge comparative or long-term success. It is not clear whether any of the centers will survive. Policy changes are slow to form and slower to solidify; to determine these would necessitate tracking the centers over a long period. The public service science center concept would need several three-year cycles to provide a comparative basis for meaningful lessons about the effectiveness of different models.

This section will discuss some of the problems inherent in trying to assess the centers' viability and will advance some funding criteria that might provide further assurance of survival, should efforts like this be considered in the future. It will be apparent that, to some extent, those problems will make the significance and justification for the criteria very questionable.

As conceived by NSF staff and advisers, an important test of the centers' concept comes after the scheduled three-year funding ends. Once this happens, it should be possible to determine what, if any, aspects of the centers survive. Continued operation does not provide a good measure of the utility of the activities the centers undertook; there are other, independent measures for that. But continued operation, by definition, measures viability, and NSF staff and advisers believed independent viability was essential if the SFC goal of institutionalizing public service science was to be met.

It may not be easy to determine what constitutes continued operation, however. Some unique and important features that centers shared may disappear without allowing us to justify the conclusion that the centers themselves have disappeared. For instance, all centers were able to use small amounts of funds set aside in their budgets to provide scientific and engineering consultant services, of varying duration and expense, to citizen groups. It may prove difficult to persuade other funding sources to allow this flexible use of money.

Without this capability, centers may well remain viable, but less able to meet an important need of the constituencies they were designed to serve. Future endeavors of this sort might do well to consider how to persuade their clientele or potential clientele to commit some small but regular yearly amount to a center so that this capacity would be retained.

Furthermore, if they continue to exist at all, the centers may be pulled away from their original purposes. Often the demands and needs of citizens are for direct services rather than for those related to policy analysis or development that were the central purposes of the Science for Citizens program. So far, the centers have dealt effectively with this potential problem, by linking the provision of such services to the development and testing of programs that are then expected to survive independently, or by using self-help programs to develop citizens' interest in working on the related policy issues.

Related to this problem is that of the tension created by emphasizing responsiveness to the needs of less-affluent citizens in the centers' mandates. The primary constituencies that are concerned about environmental or development issues are affluent and white. There is a tension between the priorities of these constituencies and those of the less affluent, who are often concerned with service and cost issues. Where this tension exists, it has been a very healthy one for centers.

There is also tension between the more specific technical assistance efforts centers undertake and their broader educational mandate. The former, while certainly the most distinctive and directly helpful service centers provide, can, in their development, implementation, and outcomes, raise questions about whether centers are stepping beyond technical assistance into advocacy activities. And the catalytic role required of centers' staff, in order to bring citizens and scientists into a public policy decision-making arena, can be very time-consuming. Besides placing centers in a position where their objectivity may be questioned, this role may leave little time for the development of more general information programs for diverse public audiences. In turn, this can contribute to undermining centers' broadbased social support. In the end, a downward spiral can result. On the other hand, concentration on programs of general public education would lose sight of the SFC objectives, as would concentration solely on the kinds of data collection and analysis activities appropriate to regional planning councils.

Finally, the search for funds for survival may persuade centers that their scientific and technical services must be offered to those groups that can provide regular sources of income. State and local government officials and agencies come to mind. This does not mean necessarily that projects are not useful or beneficial to citizens and citizens' organizations. However, the initiative for their selection comes from elsewhere; citizens' priorities might not be the same; even their definition of the problem may be different.

These reflections provide grounds for the position that viability is not a sufficient measure of success in meeting SFC objectives. Nonetheless, viability was a fundamental measure of success for the SFC program, and it may be worth presenting two criteria that, based on the program's experience, appear potentially important in this regard. With the advantage of hindsight, they appear obvious, but they may not be true even so. Meeting these criteria may help their ability to survive, but their impact on meeting SFC goals is unknown.

It is best to start with a center director who is committed to a personal investment of time and effort in the project over the long haul, whose salary and support for continued involvement does not depend on the federal investment. Thus, it is important for the director to have, or have time to develop, strong institutional support for the program beyond the federal period of award. If this criterion cannot be met, the support of the sponsoring organization or organizations for the project should be demonstrated, say by providing the coordinator's salary. Once funds for a salary have been found, they are easier to keep; the hardest part of the quest is over.

The implicit requirement for each center to have a board of directors or advisers should be rethought. If there is a board of directors for the project, and the members represent other organizations, it is best that these organizations demonstrate a financial commitment to the project. This could be done by organizational recognition that this activity is part of their employees' job functions, so that working hours will be devoted to it each week. If this kind of support is lacking, the utility of the board to the project is questionable. A board may provide a project credibility or be a useful source of balance nonetheless. But staff time and effort spent cultivating such a board may be spent better in other ways, so its costs and benefits need careful consideration.

A third requirement that might have helped to assure viability is an increased emphasis on developing and exploring funding initiatives and support systems independent of the federal government. Of course, requiring this without providing increased funds or technical assistance for it would create difficulties, but it might have helped to ask applicants to present funding development plans in their proposals and to identify staff and resources that would be used to implement those plans. Perhaps these initiatives would be less likely to conflict with the initial impetuses and priorities for a center.

In Conclusion

Science for Citizens has ended. The first centers may succeed despite being cut adrift, but they will remain isolated success stories. Their numbers are too small to permit any significant generalizations. This result is not unusual in federal initiatives, however. It speaks to a need in our society to assure long-term federal commitments. It also emphasizes the necessity for community-based efforts to tap multiple sources of support—federal, state, and local; public and private. But this is an old lesson, one that the SFC, with its emphasis on independent viability, recognized and attempted to teach. Sadly, the program expired before it could devise and test a lesson plan.

Notes

1   Rachelle D. Hollander is Program Director, Ethics and Values in Science and Technology, NSF. She was formerly Program Manager, Science for Citizens. Judith G. Stoloff, Project Manager, Cornerstone Development Company, Seattle, and former Program Associate, SFC, was the co-author of an earlier version of this paper, which presents their personal views and does not necessarily reflect the views of the National Science Foundation.

References

Berry, Jeffrey M. 1980. "Public Interest vs. Party System." *Society* (May/June):42–48.

Brooks, Harvey. 1976. "Technology Assessment in Retrospect." *Newsletter on Science, Technology and Human Values* 17:17–24.

Carroll, James D. 1971. "Participatory Technology." *Science* 171:647–53.

Hollander, Rachelle. 1980. "The Science for Citizens Program and the Folly Island Workshop on Erosion Abatement." *Environmental Impact Assessment Review* 1:306–11.

National Academy of Sciences. 1969. *Technology: Processes of Assessment and Choice.* Washington, D.C.: Government Printing Office.

Nelkin, Dorothy, ed. 1979. *Controversy: Politics of Technical Decisions.* Beverly Hills: Sage Publications.

Organization for Economic Cooperation and Development. 1979. Committee for Scientific and Technological Policy. Chairman James Mullin. *Technology on Trial, Public Participation in Decision-Making Related to Science and Technology,* written by K. Guild Nichols, Paris.

Petersen, James C. 1983. "Science for Citizens: Death at an Early Age." Paper presented at the Conference on Citizen Participation and Technocracy in Public Decision Making, Cleveland.

Pitts, James P. 1975. "The Community Service Voucher Program: An Experiment in Community Access to University Resources." Research and Policy Papers, Center for Urban Affairs, Northwestern University (January).

Primack, Joel, and von Hippel, Frank. 1974. *Advice and Dissent: Scientists in the Political Arena.* New York: Basic Books.

Woody, Bette; Walters, Ronald W.; and Brown, Diane R. 1980. "Neighborhoods as a Power Factor." *Society* (May/June):49–55.

6

The Legitimacy of People's Participation in the Formulation of Science and Technology Policy: Some Lessons from the Indian Experience

Jayanta Bandyopadhyay
and Vandana Shiva

The Concept of Science and Technology Policy

The concept of science policy is of rather recent origin.[1] Its rise can be identified with government intervention for the purposeful orientation of science and technology contributions to the war efforts in the Second World War. Since then, most industrially advanced countries, and some countries of the third world, have had science policies as an integral part of their policy framework for national development. These science policies, however, until recently have been based on some naive and innocent views on the relationship of science, technology, and development. One commonly held view has been that of technological determinism according to which the growth of science and technology would directly result in the overall socioeconomic growth and development in the country. Further, in this view, the healthy growth of science and technology is a matter to be left entirely to the professionals, who alone are seen as having the expertise that is considered to be the prerequisite for a legitimate role in formulating science policies. Recently, however, these views are facing stiff opposition. The thesis of technological determinism is being challenged by a record of unfulfilled expectations in countries like India.[2] The view that science policy is an exclusive domain of professional experts is being challenged by social movements through which people all over the world are trying to establish the legitimacy of their role in the making of science policy.[3]

The idea of technological determinism had emerged with a particular interpretation of the history of the postindustrial revolution period in the Western world, which saw the drastic improvements in the standards of living of these countries as a direct consequence of the advancements made in science and technology. This historical interpretation was then used as a model for planned development in third-world countries like India. Conscious efforts were made to build a large science and technology establishment that was expected to lead to rapid industrialization and consequently to improvements in the standard of living of the Indian people, roughly half of whom exist below the poverty line. However, though a giant scientific establishment (third largest in the whole world in terms of manpower) was created, it did not set off the linear impacts on industry or society that had been anticipated. While the modern industrial sector grew (slowly, at the rate of 7 percent), its base was not in domestic research and development, but it repeatedly depended on direct importation of technology from the West. Further, the growth of this sector had no significant impact on the improvement of the quality of life of the people. A linear model of development in which science and technology led to positive social change had therefore to be replaced by a less deterministic approach to the relationship of science, technology, and development which recognized that human problems of development do not have solely technical solutions. As the problems of technological determinism became clear, the incompleteness of the holistic knowledge and social awareness of the experts also came to be recognized. This recognition, however, did not originate with the experts or policy makers themselves. It came into existence through the destructive and unexpected impacts of technological development on the people in general and the poor people of rural areas in particular. These impacts generated popular movements in various parts of India around attempts to safeguard resources that were the material base for survival from destructive impacts of official science policy. This essay discusses a recent trend in which the people of rural India are becoming involved in such movements and are asserting their right for a place in the formulation of science policy and management of the local natural resources. Movements have erupted in the tribal areas of Central India, in the Silent Valley and Bedthi areas of South India, in the entire coastal areas of the peninsula, and in the Himalayan areas of the north.[4] The philosophical and material roots of these movements will first be analyzed and the movement in the Himalayan areas, popularly known as "Chipko Audolan" ("Hug the Trees Movement")—a movement directed at saving the fast-depleting forest resources of the region—will be discussed in some detail.

The Roots of the Ecological Movements in India

There is a popular argument, still very commonly used, that ecology is a luxury poor countries cannot afford. Proponents of this argument see concern for ecology as a pastime and indulgence of rich countries and of rich people in poor countries. However, a number of movements that have the active participation of agricultural and rural communities are indicating that ecology is more important for the poor than it is usually perceived to be by the not so poor. The whole life-style of the rural poor is closely interlinked with the local ecosystem, and dangers to that ecosystem are often first sensed by these communities as they recognize the threat to the material base of their existence. The more privileged and urban sections of the population are removed from the resource base that satisfies their needs through indirect technological chains. Since most professional planners and bureaucrats fall into this category, their strategies for development are at best ignorant of the importance of a stable ecology in satisfying the needs of the rural population. At worst they consciously contribute to the transferring of resources from the rural poor to the urban rich. In either case, their development plans, based on technological determinism, consciously support and encourage the development and use of technologies that tend to destroy the local ecology, and, hence, the sustenance of the material base for survival. The traditional technologies, on which the life-style of threatened communities is based, consequently get overtaken by

Jayanta Bandyopadhyay and Vandana Shiva

ecologically unstable and socially irresponsible modern technologies. Lewis Mumford was probably addressing himself to these distinctive technologies when he wrote: "from late neolithic times in the Near East, right down to our own day, two technologies have recurrently existed side by side: one authoritarian, the other democratic, the first system-centered, immensely powerful, but inherently unstable, the other man-centered, relatively weak, but resourceful and durable" (quoted in Winner, 1980). The weaker but ecologically stable technologies are, however, systematically threatened by the more powerful ecologically reckless technologies that are presented as being more efficient and productive in some absolute sense. Traditional technologies are identified as unproductive and are given, at most, a marginal role in the development plans. In the process, the knowledge and skills of local communities are also rendered invisible. Professionals are the only ones viewed as having reliable knowledge. Their role in policy making, therefore, gets more and more entrenched until an ecological crisis threatens the livelihood of vast rural populations and sets off organized opposition to development and science policy.

The case of the exploitation of the forestry resources may be taken as an illustration of the conflict of interests and knowledge systems of professionally accepted experts and the traditional communities whose lives are very closely linked with forest products. The professionals are scientists in the forest research institutes and bureaucrats who manage reserved forests, demarcated areas that originated during British rule. The silvicultural practices of the foresters have been largely restricted to developing species that are commercially valuable. Encouragement of such species is interpreted as scientific forestry. Species that are not commercially valuable but are, nevertheless, materially valuable for local populations as sources of fuel, of building materials, of fodder, and for soil and water conservation are ignored and depleted. Forestry experts neither know much about such species (since the training of foresters does not expose them fully to the role of forests), nor do they recognize that local populations have knowledge about these species. Thus, there have been recent attempts by the forest department in the State of Madhya Pradesh to plant commercially valuable teak and pine by destroying the traditional Sal forests that, in the forester's view, are unproductive. The local tribal population has responded with a movement against this policy of the forest department because Sal trees have played a central role in their economy and culture. They use the seeds for oil, the leaves for fodder, the flowers as food and drink, and the bark for medicinal purposes. (Diabetic patients are treated by drinking water kept in a pot made of Sal wood.) The teak and pine have thus become the embodiment of a political and technological structure that takes resources away from local populations while the Sal is the embodiment of a structure that allows the local population to survive with local resources and local control. Trees and forests have been an integral part of rural living in India and they continue to be so. Ninty percent of the poor population of the world still uses firewood as fuel, and no affordable alternative is available to them as yet. Most rural housing is still based on locally available forest products. Finally, but most important, village communities do not see trees in terms of their dead product, timber, but as dynamic living systems that conserve water and soil and provide soil nutrients. In other words, it is the ecological role of forests that is significant to rural people, and this role has been decreasing as the forest resources get depleted through commercial exploitation.

The ecological role of forests is specially crucial in the hill areas where forests rejuvenate springs and feed the rivers of India. They bind the soil and contribute to its fertility, thus preventing landslides and preventing the decline of agricultural productivity. In recent years, however, these forests have been fast disappearing—and their disappearance has created severe ecological crises. In one landslide alone in 1980, 150 inhabitants of a Himalayan village were buried alive. Earlier major landslides had occurred in Tawaghat and Chamoli in the Uttar Pradesh hill regions. In August 1978, the river Ganges was blocked by a landslide and formed a two-mile lake at an elevation of over 6,000 feet. This later burst and caused one of the worst floods in India's history with flooding all the way to Calcutta in Bengal. Over 66,000 villages were inundated, more than 2,000 people drowned, and 40,000 cattle were swept away. Two states, West Bengal and Uttar Pradesh, lost a total of $750 million in crops. On a superficial level, this was just one more natural disaster, and this is the analysis used by officials to explain the occurrence of such floods. However, the increasing frequency of floods and the extent of damage caused by them suggests that they are not purely accidental. Their occurrence is closely associated with land-use management and forestry practices in the watershed areas in the hills. In the words of Erik Eckholm,

> Decades of research have proved, for example, that the deforestation of watersheds can increase the severity of flooding, reduce stream-flows and lead to the desiccation of springs during dry seasons, and increase the load of sediment entering waterways. Yet most efforts to

combat such problems have entailed engineering measures—dams, embankments, dredging—that address their symptoms but not their causes. The exact contribution of deforestation to flood trends is probably impossible to pinpoint, but as flooding worsens in country after country, new attention must be given to land-use practices in watershed areas. [Eckholm, 1979:31]

Short-sighted utilization of resources and misplaced remedies have accentuated the social and ecological manifestations of the crisis in terms of spreading firewood and timber scarcity, deepening soil erosion, declining soil fertility, and record floods caused by denudation of forest cover. The problems are most severely felt in the Himalayan areas, the source of water for the entire northern plains, where, within living memory, streams have become seasonal, springs have dried up, subsoil water has gone down, and agricultural productivity has suffered. The people's movement in this region is primarily a response to this ecological crisis. We will now turn to a more detailed discussion of how the crisis emerged, and how the Chipko movement emerged as a response.

Chipko: The People's Response to Ecological Crisis

The Chipko movement is a grassroots movement that started in 1974 as a response to the anarchy of planned development in the hill regions that had led to the rapid denudation of forests. It started in the Tehri-Garwhal region of Uttar Pradesh where 75.5 percent of the total area comes under the management of the state forest department and where only 11.3 percent is left for community use. The ecological crisis had been building up as the forest areas were completely denuded through the sale of timber to private contractors and as the local broad-leaved species were systematically replaced by pine monoculture. The ecological crisis led to a social crisis when in March 1973 villagers in the Chamoli district would not allow a sports-goods manufacturing firm of Allahabad to cut the ash trees auctioned to them by the Uttar Pradesh government. It is interesting that just before this incident the villagers were not allowed to fell the trees for making yokes for their ploughs, on the ground that it was not feasible from the silvicultural point of view. Naturally, the villagers protested that the trees that they had nurtured were not made available to them for their day-to-day needs, but were sold to contractors for the manufacture of sports goods. The villagers made their dissatisfaction known in a novel way. They clung to the trees that were marked for felling, so that the contractor's men would have had to hurt them in order to fell the trees. This is how the movement came to be called "Chipko"—which in the local language means to cling or embrace. The Chipko action does not merely provide resistance to tree-cutting; it also acts as a symbol of protection for a resource that provides the hill people, directly or indirectly, with all their basic needs. In the Menval Valley, another area of Chipko activity, the women pledged to protect the trees ear-marked for felling by tying "rakhis" (a thread that is a symbol of protection) to the trees. They created slogans that replaced the myopic vision of forests as dead products with an ecological assessment of forests as living systems central to the hill economy. They parodied the forest department's view "What are the benefits of forests? Timber, resin, and profits"—with their own approach that they expressed in the song—"What are the benefits of the forests? Soil, water, and oxygen, which are the basis of sustenance." In the Henwal Valley, when efforts of the interested parties to induce the laborers to fell the Advani forest failed, the forest officers and contractors resorted to calling a unit of armed policemen on February 1, 1973, to defend the hired axemen and to terrorize the women. But the women fearlessly clung to the trees and the police force was helpless. Forests were saved through Chipko in many other areas through other ways conceived by the village women to protect their forest resources. In many villages a community watchman, "Van Rakshak," has been employed to protect the few trees that are left. These ecological movements have also exposed the paradoxes in state development policy. On World Environment Day in 1979, women from far-away villages collected in the district headquarters at Thri to demonstrate against water scarcity which they symbolized with empty water pots. They ridiculed the government for laying costly water pipes without ensuring that the water source from which these were to be fed was secure.

At Ranichauri, which is the site of the hill campus of an agricultural university, an attempt was initially made to clear a large area of oak forests for the campus. The women from fifty villages in the vicinity that were dependent on these forests as the only nearby source of fodder, firewood, and water came and held demonstrations. Later, large pipes were laid to pump water from the Henval River in the valley for the irrigation of the experimental farms. The villagers were very disturbed about this because they were convinced that it would leave very little water in the small river for the irrigation of the village fields. Moreover, on the basis of these well-irrigated experimental plots, the villagers may be told to change their cultivation patterns to ecologically unstable and financially unaffordable ones. If they do not change their practices, they will be called unprogressive and unscientific. The implication is that villagers are irrational because they do not do "scientific farming." Villagers, however, believe that chemical fertilizers are undesirable—first, because of the absence of irrigation facilities; second, because of their costs; and third, because they result, in the long run, in decline in soil fertility. Karl Marx had predicted this when he wrote that "every advance in capitalist agriculture is an advance in the art, not only of robbing the worker, but also of robbing the soil; every advance in the fertility of the soil for a given period of time, is simultaneously an advance towards the ruin of the permanent sources of this fertility" (quoted in Govevitch, 1966). This holistic analysis of "productivity increase" is found to be completely absent in professional experts who practice and propagate "scientific farming" and yet it is implicitly understood by illiterate village peasants who lack the power to articulate their knowledge and understanding. A village woman expressed it as follows: "We might not be educated, but we do know what is good for us. The educated are often very ignorant."

The villagers have deep knowledge of the making of organic compost to revitalize their fields, and for this they depend a lot on green manure from forests. Organic manure is the only viable alternative for farms that depend completely on rain. Even in lower lying fields where irrigation channels can be used, dependence on chemical fertilizer makes the agriculture more vulnerable, because the irrigation networks built in recent years are under the control of irrigation departments and contractors, and this collusion of bureaucracy and private interest often works against the local people. Earlier the villagers used to have mud canals that they built themselves. These were replaced by the more "efficient" cemented canals. However, according to the villagers, their community-built and community-managed canals were far more efficient. If they were damaged at sowing time, the whole village would work together to repair them. Now the canals have been taken over by the government and it assigns repairs to private contractors. Contractors make money first by saving cement and later by repairing the broken canal (and breakdowns are frequent). In the bargain, villagers are often left with no irrigation facilities when they need them most.

"Chipko" and the related movements in the hills are therefore attacks on the development politics and science policies advocated by the government. Technologies that support these development efforts are not the most efficient in an absolute sense. They are efficient for certain interest groups, permitting them to exert control over some resources and their outputs. Thus forestry practices that are projected as "scientific" may actually be ways for the state bureaucracy to control the community's forest resources and make them available to the traders and the industrialists who own the pulp and rayon mills. This system, though ecologically unstable, is immensely powerful and draws part of its power from its "scientific" status. The weaker, ecologically stable system of the villager is slowly rendered unstable because of state intervention in the control of resources. These two systems can be symbolically represented in the forest species they try to protect and propagate. The state and industry encourage pine, which gives resin and good softwood for pulp and rayon but which has no soil-building or water-conservation capacity. The villagers instead want the oak tree, whose leaves provide fertilizer and fodder, whose wood provides agricultural equipment, and whose roots rejuvenate the water in the springs. In an important sense in the Himalayas, the choice between growing pine or oak is a political one. Nature for the privileged and powerful is one thing, it is another for the weak and oppressed. The Chipko movement basically demands that people, their knowledge, and their organizations be included in formulating science policy if science and technology are really going to contribute to the basic needs of the people and are going to grow in ecologically sound and stable ways that ensure sustained development.

In the words of one of the leading Chipko activists:

The main contention of this movement is that the main gift of the Himalayas to the nation is water and its function is to produce, maintain and improve soil structure. Hence felling of green trees for commercial purposes should be stopped forthwith at least for 10 to 15 years, until green coverage of at least 60% of the area is restored as professed in the National Forest Policy of 1952. Mass plantation of trees with capability of holding soil and water conservation should be taken up on war footing to enable the villagers to be self-reliant for their inevitable basic needs of food and clothings. Five "F" trees, i.e., trees providing Food (nuts, fruits, oilseeds, honey, etc.), Fodder, Fuel, Fertilizers and Fibre should be planted. Such trees should be planted all over the sloppy agricultural land and forest areas. The local population would automatically take interest in the plantation of these trees and would protect them too. The main reason for the forest devastation is the destruction of natural forests by planting of such species which would be profit-making. Naturally local people had no interest in this. Another thing responsible for the crisis is the plantation of pine, deodar and other coniferous varieties in the hills and eucalyptus, etc., in the foothills. All this has robbed the land of its fertility. India is an agricultural country and here forestry should be in support of agriculture. We have the example of China which faced the problem of floods due to the most terrible forest devastation and yet emerged out of this catastrophe by making forestry the basis of agriculture. Forest management and protection requires people's active participation. [Bahuguna, 1979]

The people's participation in development planning and management can be justified on a number of grounds. First, it is the poor people who know best what their basic needs are, and hence their input for identifying objectives for development is essential if development is to touch their lives positively. Second, local people are the best agents for assessing the social and ecological impacts of technological change since the impacts are most directly felt by them. Finally, local people have informal, traditional knowledge about their resources and about ways to raise them in ecologically sound ways. There are good reasons to believe that the traditional knowledge of the local population is by itself a complete and reliable system.[5] It is ecologically sensitive because the livelihood of these people depends on the stability of the ecosystem, in contrast to the exploitation of resources for profits by businessmen and bureaucrats sitting in distant urban areas. The analytic sophistication of traditional knowledge might not compare with that of professionals, but its holistic insights become indispensable in development planning for long-term economic growth through ecological stability. This traditional knowledge has never had a legitimate place in science policy so far. Its inclusion, however, seems unavoidable if ecologically sound and economically stable science policies are to be formulated. The issue about whether or not people can participate in formulation of science policy is no longer an academic pastime. Popular movements throughout the country are ensuring that people's participation can no longer be ignored.

Notes

1 For the sake of convenience, the term "science policy" will be used to subsume both science and technology policy. A discussion of the evolution of science policy has been presented by Salomon (1977).

2 See Layton (1977) for arguments against technological determinism.

3 Some of the movements in the West are discussed in Nelkin (1977).

4 Details on these movements can be obtained from *The Silent Valley Project* and other publications of Kerala Sashtra Sahitya Parishad, Trivandrum; Madhav Gadgil's works on the Bedthi Project, published by the Institute of Science, Bangalore; Xavier Institute of Social Service, Ranchi, for literature on tribal movements in central India; John Kurien of Centre of Development Studies, Trivandrum, for fishermen movements in Kerala; and C. Fonseca, M. Saldanha of Goa. Chipko information is available from Chipko Information Centre, Parvatiya Navjeevan Mandal, P.O.: Silyara, Tehri-Garhwal, U.P.

5 For arguments that traditional knowledge is relevant to human development, see the special issue of the *Bulletin of the Institute of Development Studies* (January 1979).

References

Bahuguna, Sunderlal. 1979. *Chipko: A Novel Movement for Establishment of Cordial Relationship between Man and Nature.* Silyara: Parvatiya Navjivan Mandal.

Eckholm, E. 1979. "Planning for the Future: Forestry for Human Needs." *World Watch Paper* no. 26.

Govevitch, Alexander. 1966. *Technological Change and Employment.* New York: Augustus Kelley.

Layton, E. 1977. "Conditions of Technological Development." In *Science, Technology and Society*, ed. Ina Spiegel-Rosing and Derek de Solla Price. London: Sage.

Nelkin, Dorothy. 1977. "Technology and Public Policy." In *Science, Technology and Society*, ed. Ina Spiegel-Rosing and Derek de Solla Price. London: Sage.

Salomon, J. J. 1977. "Science Policy Studies and the Development of Science Policy." In *Science, Technology and Society*, ed. Ina Spiegel-Rosing and Derek de Solla Price. London: Sage.

Winner, Langdon. 1980. "Do Artifacts Have Politics?" *Daedalus* 109:121–36.

III

Case Studies

7

Research Missions and the Public: Over-Selling and Buying the U.S. War on Cancer

Daryl Chubin

Public criticism of current health policy has not sprung full-blown upon an unsuspecting scientific enterprise. It began years ago, and has steadily increased in intensity. Perhaps because of its extraordinary success in attracting sustained congressional support for health science research during the past few decades, the scientific community has paid little attention to this growing criticism.
Peter Barton Hutt (1978:157)

Introduction

Although characterizations of scientists' indifference to public criticism such as that offered by attorney Hutt accurately state the general case, the 1970s were an exceptional decade for an exceptional disease. The public, rather than being ignored, was manipulated. Its hopes and expectations for a cancer cure were raised and dashed time and again. Such manipulation, even when it is neither carefully orchestrated nor consciously misleading, provokes anger and cynicism. You can sell an idea for only so long; then the most vigilant trusting public begins to suspect that their short-term investment included some hidden clauses assuring a long-term costly purchase. When you've promised a "cure," it's hard to convince the investors that progress to date means larger and more effectively applied "band-aids."

Such research progress may be appreciated by scientists and physicians. The subtleties of health-care delivery and reduced mortality rates, however, may be lost on a public that remembers only the promise of cure. But this essay is not about "truth in health-care advertising"; it does concern the selling of a bill of goods called the "war on cancer" and how the public, though given no real choice, came to buy it and inevitably feel fleeced by doing so. Again, the process through which this occurred was unplanned; yet it was predicted by many at its origins. The U.S. war on cancer was oversold.

The Context

Cancer is a categorical dread disease whose elimination, prevention, treatment, control, and/or cure was originally mandated by the U.S. government in 1937 with the creation of the National Cancer Institute (Strickland, 1972). With the debate over the National Cancer Act of 1971 the war on cancer became a public mission, scientists a sympathetic but reluctant army. The mission was noble, the strategy for its realization dubious. Research funding is usually welcome, but not when the tactics for conducting the research—i.e., utilizing the money—raise expectations for success on a politically determined timetable: a cure by the time of the Bicentennial of the Republic (Rettig, 1977).

What is muted by talk of a cancer war is evidence that the mission was a long-evolving one, that the National Cancer Institute (NCI) had concentrated research monies years before the Cancer Act of 1971 became political fodder, that indeed, biomedical scientists had learned how to manipulate institutional, cognitive, and rhetorical norms to serve their interests, bolster their ideologies, and perpetuate their research support (Chubin and Studer, 1978; Studer and Chubin, 1979: chs. 1, 3).

Thus, the visibility and urgency of the cancer war is more typical than one might imagine. This war encompasses many of the tensions experienced by other sciences in their quest to justify and capitalize on specific science policies. Moreover, it reminds us that technical expertise plays a political role in science (Nelkin, 1975), including the selling and buying of research missions. The missions and experts may change, but the questions remain very much the same:

1 How should research be organized to maximize the production of applied knowledge?
2 What should be the role of the scientist in the establishment of priorities and organization of research?
3 How do scientists assess the success of science policies, and moreover, explain those assessments to nonscientific audiences?

In what follows, these questions are addressed in the context of the war on cancer and perhaps its principal post-1971 Cancer Act mission: funding of research on the hypothesized link between RNA viruses and cancer. The discovery of an enzyme in 1970—a discovery that intellectually altered the disciplines of genetics, virology, microbiology, and biochemistry —also lent credibility to the viral etiology hypothesis (Chubin and Studer, 1979). It was this latter effect that propelled "reverse transcriptase" into the cancer war and which I examined both through the primary biomedical and policy literatures and in face-to-face interviews with fifteen bench scientists and administrators at NCI and various academic and private laboratories (Chubin, 1978). Reverse transcriptase was merely a pawn in the mission; through it, however, we can reconstruct how the cancer war, over the objections of many scientists, was oversold to the American public.

The Research Mission

The concept of the "research mission" has had a checkered history. It can be traced back to the pre-World War II Marxist concern for relating science to social needs. As articulated by Hessen (1931) and Bernal (1939), science was seen as an instrument of and a service to the state. Hence we are all familiar with the synonyms that emphasized "planned" research: applied, policy-oriented, targeted. Those terms for which definitive references can be supplied include "goal-directed" (Johnston and Jagtenberg, 1978), "politically directed" (van den Daele et al., 1977), and "public interest" (von Hippel and Primack, 1972) science. Each of these terms contains a rhetorical commitment to persuade the public and its surrogates —e.g., Congress—that the scientific community, through its rational devices, has identified a problem that requires immediate attention and the blessing of federal research dollars. By recognizing the problem and authorizing dollars for its resolution, the government agency, itself blessed with congressional committee approval, has defined a mission. Its pursuit becomes public knowledge, a matter of priority both within the scientific community (or more accurately, within segments of a research specialty) and without.

This initial justification—the blessing of the mission—signals the onset of several processes. For example, a monitoring of progress begins, while scrutiny by congressional committees (Culliton, 1976) and science journalists (Hixson, 1976) intensifies. The public interest must be served (e.g., as alleged in the recombinant DNA debate, see Culliton, 1978; Nelkin, 1978). If your "tax dollars are at work," it's your right to know whether that work is coming to fruition. Such "public participation" in science seems intrinsic to democratic societies where accountability and government intervention in controversial research and its applications go hand in hand (Nelkin, 1979; 1980).

To accommodate the demands of accountability, scientists vary their "vocabularies of justification" (Mulkay, 1976a:654) to suit the audience they must address, impress, reassure, and so on. The rhetoric changes as the purpose or situation dictates. Perhaps the best example—illustrated both by public testimony before the Kennedy and Rogers health subcommittees in hearings on the conquest of cancer bills (U.S. Senate, 1971), and by private responses of scientists and administrators to queries posed by Rettig (1977) and Chubin (1978)—was the fact of "overpromising" research progress to lay audiences—be it politicians, journalists, or citizen groups. This was done to ensure an allocation of research funds exemplary of a national health mission.

Once the research priorities are set, and the missions defined, a public commitment to a course of action exists.[1] The determination of that course, and the organizational apparatus created or invoked to achieve policy goals, is far more crucial than any declaration of "mission accomplished." One may indeed question the imposition of organizational structures intended to hasten the discovery through laboratory research of mechanisms which, for example, regulate processes of cell transformation in humans, and therefore, represent a key to cancer causation. Some cancer researchers resisted such an imposition, but to no avail; the politics of the cancer mission, as it were, prevailed.

Daryl Chubin

Mission-Making:
Experts at Work, the Public at Bay?

It is from the relations between science and politics that research missions emerge. We may regard these relations as unholy alliances, but they are a fact of scientific life. In Lakoff's (1977:377) words: "The scientific process is not insulated against the full force of political controversy and its normal outcomes; the involvement of scientists in decision making can have harmful repercussions on the research process, and it may at times compromise the scientists who enter it."

Fortunately, some science administrators who have come to straddle the worlds of science and politics have reflected on their experience. Without claiming the representativeness of their views, I shall present a select sample of critically astute observations on the science-politics relationship of which I have become enamored (in part or whole). These observations, I contend, apply not only to research policy formulation in general, but to mission-making in particular.

Whereas the practice of science advising has arguably *not* advanced to a high art, the role of expert advisor has. Whether or not this role is "mediating," as some have claimed (Mulkay, 1976b), it is surely indicative of the government patron availing itself of the scientific community's resources (Ezrahi, 1971; Nelkin, 1975; Hadden, 1977), indeed of an elite segment of that community (Groeneveld et al., 1975). The willingness to enter the "corridors of power" and play the role of advisor "does away with any pretensions to political neutrality on the part of scientists" (Salomon, 1977:58). In this era of Big Science (Weinberg, 1961), scientists' "complex multiplicity of roles and the consequent ambiguity of self-consciousness are now essential structural features of science" (Ravetz, 1977:85).

Research missions underscore the partisanship of scientists who, in the name of public welfare, argue for their urgency and the investment in them. That investment is tantamount to a placing of bets. Consequently, the mission-maker and -manager, recruited from the scientific community, must reckon with the double-edged sword of control and responsibility: he or she exercises little control over setting research priorities and mobilizing programs in the name of the mission, but bears responsibility for lending scientific credibility to mission strategy, its tactical plan, and ultimately, even the public's perception of its success or failure. Full cooptation means, in Salomon's (1972:32) words, "the powers that be place their criteria on the level of utility to *themselves*; science is one of their objectives only in so far as it is a means towards their ends." Taking the inevitable step toward demolishing the pretense of privilege[2] which science advisor *cum* mission-makers evoke, Salomon states:

> It is within the competence of scientists to define utility not because they have a greater mastery than other people over the measuring instruments on which it depends but because they themselves as citizens, on par with their nonscientific fellows, desire to see it defined in a certain way. They can change the orientation of the research effort and make it more rational and more in line with the universal intentions of scientific discourse, not by influencing the research system as a means at the service of the state, but by influencing the ends of the state themselves.

Missions, of course, by definition, are·"ends"-oriented. Once defined, advice is solicited with respect to their achievement only, not with respect to the other candidate missions, i.e., those deemed of lesser priority. Salomon's expectation is thus a lofty one; few scientists, including the presidential science advisor, can actually influence ends. Ends are born in the political sphere unto politicians who can shrewdly enlist members of the scientific community to justify most any mission. The scientist mission-makers are quick to learn the language of the state; their value as "experts" and "opinion leaders" should not be underestimated. They *can* buffer and soothe a restive public as well as an incredulous scientific community.[3] Some scientists play this role so well that their transition into the political sphere, say, as a career civil servant-science administrator, is relatively swift, painless, and permanent. For these scientists, the internal-external, science-politics, and pure-applied dichotomies are empty of meaning. Allegiances shift as alliances form. The origins of priorities and criteria of choice pale; what matters is decisive action, a commission of resources that will render measurable results—not necessarily "targeted" results, but tangible policy-oriented findings. In other words, research missions are premised on, and must generate, knowledge claims (van den Daele and Weingart, 1976).

As seen below in the case of viral cancer research, a mission validates the science policy which spawned it—duly crediting the foresight of political and scientific leadership. But the claims are usually just that: provocative notions and plausible hypotheses which contain a modicum of empirical support and a surfeit of optimism.

NCI and the Virus Cancer Mission

The problem with concentrating massive funding in areas of "promising" claims is that other claims, especially under conditions of scarce resources, are virtually ignored. Hypotheses based on comparably tenuous data are singled out for different treatments. The one is programmed, packaged, and sold to scientists and the public as the next site of anticipated break-throughs; the other suffers the stigma of neglect—little growth in research budget, implied rejection of the knowledge claim. A classic "have versus have-not" situation arises. Funding, manpower, and publicity accrue to the targeted "haves"; these resources recede from the disfavored "have-nots." Negligible intellectual endowments are amplified into substantial differences.

The Virus Cancer Program and mission money In 1964, NCI authorized the Special Virus Leukemia Program (now Virus Cancer Program) with a $10 million budget "to expand and intensify research on viruses and leukemia and other related diseases, making NCI the first institute to engage in any large-scale contracting programming at NIH" (Kalberer, 1975:475). This was a quiet mission which nonetheless linked, in an unprecedented way, categorical disease research as performed under the Public Health Service or American Cancer Society aegis to the tactic of contracting for knowledge (for a concise history, see Bruno, 1974:7–11; fuller treatment is found in Strickland, 1972). For the first time, *the* federal health research agency had targeted one long-suspected causal agent, viruses, for special support (Studer and Chubin, 1980:chap. 1). The science of viral oncology had not suddenly come of age, of course, but its status among the family of (100 plus) diseases represented by cancer had been elevated. The government's blessing had been bestowed; the biomedical research community—more specifically, its virological component—was invited to receive the blessing and act on it.[4]

With the passage of the National Cancer Act of 1971, the mission was no longer quiet. A comprehensive national plan to prevent, detect, and treat cancer—aimed at the public, Congress, and the biomedical community—had been in the making since late 1970. According to NCI Associate Director for Program Planning and Analysis Louis Carrese (1974:24), the assemblage of 250 scientists to formulate a comprehensive national program plan for cancer was a unique event in the history of biology and medicine in this country.[5]

As Carrese (1978) explained further:

Our major problem here was to convince people that first, in addition to the traditional support of many bench investigators, we should try other things. The cancer problem is certainly large enough to accommodate more than one approach . . . and these would not supplant or replace things . . . but would be complementary and supplementary . . . on how best to distribute and invest the total resources we've got across a whole spectrum of activities.

Interestingly, with the passage of the act in 1971, total federal obligations to NCI tripled. Currently, it amounts to an annual billion dollar obligation. However, at no time have contract programs received more than 50 percent of NCI's extramural research support (Kalberer, 1975; Gustafson, 1975), as directed by the National Cancer Advisory Board. As one academic defender (Amos, 1977:263) of NCI policy stated:

No one involved in policy decisions in the Cancer Program would deny that the problem of the support of basic research in the total Health Program remains unresolved. In my opinion, solutions involve increased funding allotments in the total Health Program for *untargeted* research. The current state of our ignorance of fundamental human biological processes should make evident that this reality cannot be denied. . . . The basic sciences [including immunology, virology, cell biology, and biochemistry] have been and are still being asked to play a focal role in the Program and in advising all segments of the Program.[6]

Perhaps the loudest reassurance of the biomedical research community came in the fifth report of the director of the President's National Panel of Consultants on Cancer. Benno Schmidt (quoted in Rettig, 1977:319), in a rhetoric-tempered message, observed that,

just as the past five years have brought a greatly enlarged science base, they have also brought important improvements in the clinic in dealing with cancer, but here again our progress only serves to emphasize how far we have to go. . . . [We] cannot afford not to support basic research . . . for we are, in truth, profoundly ignorant about the real nature of cancer.

This tone, of course, contrasts glaringly with the rhetoric both preceding and following passage of the act. For this, some (e.g., Epstein, 1978) blame the Lasker-inspired American Cancer Society;[7] most however, blame NCI and its privileged status at NIH, at the Office of Management and Budget, and with Congress. Dr. Frank Rauscher, a luminary of the cancer establishment, does not deny that rhetoric and privilege are important allies. In discussing the significance of discovering reverse transcriptase (RT), he admitted (Rauscher, 1978) that RT

> fit very comfortably into their [the congressional committees formulating the cancer legislation] idea that there was new progress in cancer research that was exploitable. . . . It was certainly, then, used politically a lot. There is no question. And, in a sense, appropriately because it did represent the first opportunity to deal with a class of viruses that everybody knew was important, and no one knew how to deal with. . . . [J]ust by providing a tool . . . it changed [overnight] the whole ability of handling these viruses. And since Huebner had imbued everybody with the belief that these were the key to cancer, there was no question that this was an enormous political, as well as scientific, breakthrough. The tough thing is to really say to what extent it mattered.

It mattered plenty—*strategically* to the other institutes whose allocations suffered relative to the budgetary boosts given NCI (Chubin and Studer, 1978), and *tactically* to cancer researchers eligible only for large contract funds (private labs) or intramural support (NCI labs). Academic-medical school virus researchers were at a competitive disadvantage (Chubin and Studer, 1979) and nonvirus cancer researchers were disenfranchised intellectually, so to speak, by funding of research on the viral etiology hypothesis.

Indeed, the discovery of RT was made simultaneously at two academic labs—one, an MIT researcher supported by National Institute for Allergy and Infectious Diseases funds, the other a recipient of an NIH "institutional grant" to the McArdle Laboratory, University of Wisconsin. The exploitation occurred largely *within* NCI and quasi-governmental, greater Bethesda-area labs stocked with intramural mission money and contracts from the John Maloney/Robert Huebner-directed Virus Cancer Program. The irony is the false impression of credit that NCI garnered. To be sure, this institute capitalized on the discovery; it hastened confirmation of its experimental implications, but was hardly responsible for its occurrence.

The claim of a viral etiology, then, helped to create the mission. The mission was politically viable given the social climate: numerous public opinion polls showed that in the United States cancer was the most feared of the dread diseases (Rauscher, 1974)—though more Americans succumbed to heart disease—and the Virus Cancer Program became the tactical vehicle for pursuing the mission. Congress had coopted the Cancer Institute. NCI, in turn, coopted segments of the cancer research community. Expectations rose as federal obligations grew, but a cure for cancer by the Bicentennial of the Republic was not forthcoming. Nor has there occurred a momentous breakthrough in viral oncology since reverse transcriptase. The public may have grown more restive since 1976, but the biomedical community was not so patient.

A scapegoat for mission impossible?   In March 1973, NCI Director Rauscher, on behalf of the National Cancer Board, appointed an ad hoc committee to review the Virus Cancer Program. Composed of basic scientists outside the virus cancer community and with known doubts about contract research, the 10-person Zinder committee, named for its head, Norton Zinder of Rockefeller University, issued a predictably harsh report.[8] As Benno Schmidt (Culliton, 1974:143–44) remarked:

> You can get any kind of advice from the scientific community that you want. If we had wanted to hear about all of the things that are right about the Virus Cancer Program [VCP], and there are many, we'd have appointed one sort of committee. But we needed to know what was wrong with it. So, we appointed a committee that would tell us that.

Though the bulk of the committee's criticisms related to administration of the VCP, its basic objection was to the knowledge claims upon which the program was established:

> It was the assumptions that were wrong. There did not, nor does there exist, sufficient knowledge to mount such a narrowly targeted program. Basic ignorance of the mechanism involved in the cancer process, even in animals where a viral etiology is definitively established, is so profound that it is difficult to be certain where to begin, much less organize a focused attack. . . . We agree with the goal of identifying human cancer viruses and evaluating their role in the etiology of cancer but reject the concept that this holds sufficient promise for a short term solution to the cancer problem to justify compromising basic research in this and other areas. The search for cancer viruses is an essential and feasible part of the long range attack on cancer, but must be viewed as a high risk, high payoff gamble in terms of short range

benefits. Even a restructured *SVCP should be an "in-addition-to" rather than an "instead-of" program.* [Pp. 10–12]

Aside from its intellectual premises, the VCP became an organization which concentrated enormous power in the hands of its various program segments, e.g., Breast Cancer, Biohazard Control, and Solid Tumor Viruses. About six segment chairmen were identified as diluting peer review and overseeing disbursements of program funds as extensions of intramural activities to be performed in private sector labs. The gravity of this situation was that in the early 1970s the VCP disbursed 10–12 percent of NCI's total budget of $500–600 million (Culliton, 1974:143–44). In the words of the Zinder committee report:

Administratively its [the VCP's] procedures lack vigor, are apparently attuned to the benefit of staff personnel and are full of conflicts of interest.... [A]lthough the available funds for the program continued to grow, the program seems to have become an end in itself, its experience justifying its further existence. In doing so, it is eroding what is good in both the grant and contract mechanisms, a fact which may account for the widespread antipathy to SVCP in the scientific community. [P. 21]

By June 1974, a National Cancer Advisory Board Subcommittee presented its response to the Zinder report. It proposed a "review committee" structure to monitor the activities of VCP segments, but moreover, signaled the promise of organizational reform throughout the National Cancer Institute (Rettig, 1977:301).

Stripped of its rhetoric, the viral oncology mission was seen to be flawed —in both its execution and its intellectual premises. The perception of flaws above, however, can negate no knowledge claims. Rather, it can retrospectively render as dubious the use of those claims for launching and sustaining a research mission. As standard-bearer of the NCI promise to ascertain a viral etiology of cancer in humans, the VCP became a scapegoat and an anomaly in its science policy—in short, a "mission impossible."

Old Missions Never Die, They Are Superseded

That the "viral mission" has faded as a rhetorical weapon in the cancer war arsenal is beyond dispute. In my conversations with NCI interviewees in early 1978, I was assured that the VCP would slowly be dismantled while another mission would come to the fore. The "new" mission (or redefined "old" one) would reflect the leadership of the new NCI director Arthur Upton (Culliton, 1977).[9] It would not mean, however, the demise of viral oncology research. Rather such research would be replaced in the public's eye by a fresher, more marketable mission, a visible shifting of priorities.[10] As the NCI scientist-administrators with whom I talked prophesied:

> There is a lot of pressure from Congress, and probably the public, with "What are you doing to protect me from getting exposed to this?" and "How can I eat this?" and "Why don't you test all these things?" So there is a lot of pressure on the Cancer Institute . . . to get more involved in those kinds of new testing programs and environmental carcinogenesis. [Todaro, 1978]

> For the last year, I've been mainly pushing not treatment or cure, but diagnostics. And the reason for that is that if you look at what's going on in clinical oncology in the last 20 years, you find that the real advances that have been made in curing the disease have always been accompanied by a better diagnostic procedure. Even with the methods that we have now, if you have an early signal, and a systematic one, you could handle 90 percent of the cancers that occur. By handling, I mean really cope with them. So while a diagnostic is certainly a more modest goal to accept than cure, I think it's more realizable. [Spiegelman, 1978]

> There's no doubt about the fact that the environment out there will continue to be contaminated for some time. We're not going to do away with the automobile, the asbestos in its brake linings, very quickly. So it's good to try and talk about cleaning up the environment, cutting down on emission, and so forth. . . . We've got to look for some common denominator ways of preventing cancer despite the fact that we're going to continue to be exposed to carcinogens for our bad habits. [Rauscher, 1978]

To the surprise of few, then, the shift to environmental carcinogenesis became public policy in the FY '80 budget. Soon thereafter, HEW Secretary Califano announced the establishment of a National Toxicology Program (NTP). This program would pool resources from four HEW agencies—NCI, the National Institute of Environmental Health Sciences, the National Institute of Occupational Safety and Health, and the Food and Drug Administration—but NCI would contribute (for testing carcinogens) over half of the NTP's first year budget totaling $41 million (Carter, 1979:525).

Speaking to the NCI's National Cancer Advisory Board on 17 January, Andrew Maguire (D–N.J.), the principal sponsor of the 1978 cancer act amendments,[11] said that their passage "mandate[s] a generally increased emphasis on programs for preventing cancer from occupational or environmental causes [and] 'reflected a feeling in Congress that [NCI] has tended to neglect the original concern of Congress with achieving, as rapidly as possible, some beneficial impact on public health' " (Carter, 1979: 525). In preparing a list of carcinogens for regulatory purposes, NCI was, for the first time, expected to decide which chemicals are carcinogenic or anticipated as such, a role destined to keep it in the center of controversy. NCI was also made to curtail "some part of the effort devoted to basic cellular research on cancer" so that "the bio-assay program's formidable backlog of suspect but untested or inadequately tested compounds" can be reduced (Carter, 1979:527). Finally:

> Coming from a heavily industrialized area in northern New Jersey that figures prominently on NCI's cancer map [Rep.] Maguire had made cancer prevention and research a major focus of his first two terms in the House.... Moreover, as an influential member of the House Health and Environment Subcommittee, Maguire can either reward or chastise the HEW agencies, as in supporting or taking issue with the balance struck by NCI between cancer prevention programs and basic cellular research (which, incidentally, Maguire says deserves continued support). [Carter, 1979:528]

As implied, old research missions never die, but they do live precariously. NCI respondents were unanimous in stating that the basic unit at NIH has always been the laboratory. Research programs come and go, and are more flexible, as a visible means of carrying out specific parts of the mission. This is the strength, I was told, of programmed research:

> People will tell you there was a lot of wasted money. I see it from both sides. Now I see it from the NCI or government point of view, and I saw it from the other point of view when I was working at Columbia. We could never have done what we did if there wasn't such a thing as a Virus Cancer Program or programmed research. It would have taken us, what we did in three months, maybe four years. [Schlom, 1978]

Concluding Thoughts and Postscript

For a decade, the U.S. war on cancer has manipulated knowledge and institutions in pursuit of a nobly targeted mission.[12] The "failure" of the mission to pinpoint a viral mechanism that regulates the transformation of human cellular material in ways we call cancer, some would insist, could be construed as a cultural warrant for the evolving policy emphasis on environmental carcinogens. Some of the testimony presented above belies this claim. At the same time, much of this testimony can be labeled self-justifying rhetoric.

But research missions are far more complicated. They demand a configuration of events and institutional responses that include:

1 *A cultural need for scientific and technological innovation.* Whether proclaimed by the president in broad strokes[13] or in the public's clamor for investigation of risks, benefits, and costs,[14] the pursuit of applied knowledge is taken as an axiomatic responsibility of contemporary democratic cultures. The "need," in other words, has been elevated to the status of self-evident truth. The rhetoric of the mission is thus oriented to the issue of "how" a mobilization of effort to fulfill the need must proceed.

2 *A national research policy that condones action.* Once the bandwagon is rolling, a centralization of effort is apt to follow. An agency of the federal governnment will "respond" to the clamor of a vast (if largely unseen) constituency. Missions are defined, scientific wars declared, a policy for effecting a mobilization of talent to match the government's priority allocation advanced. At this juncture, "means and ends" becomes a chief rhetorical device.

3 *A scientific community that sanctions the mission.* By adapting the foci of its research, a scientific community can ensure the selective support of that research under the mission rubric. According to Mulkay (1979), "In order to make basic science 'work,' it has to be radically reinterpreted in accordance with the requirements of the social context of practical application."

It may be the rhetoric of need, policy, and sanction by experts that carries the mission forward—even in the absence of consensus and certainty within a scientific community (Bazelon, 1979:278). Nonetheless, a segment of that community has been coopted to legitimate the mission, its originating policy, and the institutional architects of both. The public does not ordinarily witness the process of cooptation. Instead of the making and selling of missions it sees illusions of progress—a cancer research policy that, unwittingly or not, cannot help but oversell its promises of cure and underdeliver to its investors. A vigilant public continues to buy the war on cancer; it has no choice. The issue is not *whether* the war on cancer should be waged, but *how*. What are the research priorities within the mission and how do we know when they have been fulfilled? The public is at best an anxious bystander to this process. It can no more witness the negotiation of priorities than comprehend the cyclical politics of cancer.

As we reflect on the cancer research policy of the 1970s, a 1980s postscript has already emerged. In the wake of election year discontinuities, the U.S. Congress includes a new alignment of committees, subcommittees, and architects of health policy. A noteworthy example is the abolishment of the subcommittee on health and scientific research which under Senator Edward Kennedy, "dominated health care politics for more than a decade" (Sun, 1981:684). A substitute subcommittee under Orrin Hatch's Senate Committee on Labor and Human Resources has been formed with freshman Senator Paula Hawkins at the helm. And the announced subject of her first inquiry: why the National Cancer Institute, and for that matter other parts of the cancer establishment such as the American Cancer Society, has not been more successful in finding a cure for cancer.

For those who have traced the politics of the U.S. war on cancer, such news sounds all too familiar; it smacks more of politicians' rhetoric than responsible analysis. One can only hope, therefore, that after this rhetoric filters—once again—into the public consciousness, the mission-making of the seventies will yield to more modest expectations for success in cancer treatment and cure. If such expectations do not prevail, the cancer establishment and the architects of health policy in Congress will have no one to blame, or nurture, but themselves.[15]

Notes

1   According to Weingart (1977:61) the scientific community, or some part of it, "has an initiating function in the process of issue formation and is, at the same time, subject to a bandwagon effect as the issue crystallizes in the public and political sectors."

2   Privileged knowledge—that which is produced, understood, and/or applied by scientific communities—is a pivotal issue in the science-society debate. If scientific knowledge has no claim to special status in the belief system of the wider culture, then it is merely a self-

serving ideology, like any other, promulgated to protect the interests of scientists *qua* professional workers. The history of science, right or wrong, has accorded to scientific knowledge a special status, and only recently has this privilege been challenged (e.g., by an antiscience literature) and deemed a suitable problem for investigation in the history, philosophy, and sociology of science (Barnes, 1977; Millstone, 1978; Overington, 1979; Mulkay, 1979).

3   Mission-making, or the impression of such, often entails "activating" appropriate segments of the scientific community while keeping the public at bay, and vice versa. A noteworthy example is the Laetrile controversy in the United States (see Markle et al., 1978; Petersen and Markle, 1979) where a sizable social movement composed of pro-Laetrile advocates have adopted a populist ideology of medicine. Their alienation from the political and medical establishment is evident in the latter's tactic of attacking the professional credentials of the Laetrile movement's leadership. This attempt by the American Medical Association, the American Cancer Society, and the National Cancer Institute to discredit the pro-Laetrile leaders, however, has been weathered to the extent that the medical establishment has now changed its tone: "Once it [Laetrile] was a 'cruel fraud' and a 'hoax'; now it is just another rather unpromising, minimally active, substance. This new strategy, which seeks the participation, and perhaps even the cooptation, of advocates is a striking shift in the behavior of authorities" (Markle and Petersen, 1979:18).

4   A comparable chemotherapy program soon followed, on what was then a trial basis (Carrese and Baker, 1967).

5   In Rettig's (1977:300) view, "the [national cancer] plan, though the object of much concern and criticism, has proved useful in explaining the cancer program to the Congress and the public and in providing general directions for NCI. It has not been used to any significant degree in governing the actual day-to-day management of various NCI programs."

6   Representative statements of the belief are contained in Comroe (1978) and Thomas (1977). Evidence of the basic science investigations that were crucial to "ten important clinical advances," a sort of biomedical TRACES study, is reported in Comroe and Dripps (1976).

7   Not surprisingly, Frank Rauscher (1978), former director of NCI and now a vice-president of the American Cancer Society, offers a different perspective:

I think the American Cancer Society was a powerful force in lobbying, but not enough. . . . The way the game is played you have people go around and try to provide information upon which a Congressman can make a decision beneficial to what you want done. But . . . if somebody didn't do it, if we didn't have a Cancer Program now, if Mary Lasker had not done what she did, if the Society had not talked to Ann Landers, I think we could definitely say that there would be more Americans dead of cancer now than there would have been had this not been done.

8   This *Report of the Ad Hoc Committee of the Virus Cancer Program* is an elusive document that was apparently never *accepted* by the board. Although Rettig (1977:369) cites it as "submitted," it was not catalogued in the National Library of Medicine as late as February 1978. Dr. Rauscher's office at ACS graciously provided us with mimeo ver-

Daryl Chubin

sions of the draft and final reports dated November 1973 and March 1974, respectively. It is the latter whose page numbers are referenced in the excerpts presented below.

9 Rauscher resigned in 1977 to join the American Cancer Society. Upton resigned in late 1979 to return to New York University Medical School, declaring that cancer had become a "social disease" due to habits of life style, especially smoking and industrial pollution. Vincent T. DeVita, Jr., an expert in chemotherapy, is the current director of NCI.

10 Van den Daele et al. (1977) term this shift a "relabeling" phenomenon, a repackaging of knowledge claims to justify an increase in research support. Also see Weingart (1977: 56–61) on the dialectic of "issue formation."

11 A reauthorization, in 1974 and 1978, of the National Cancer Act of 1971 was mandated as part of the original law. Hence the 1978 hearings and resultant amendments.

12 The cancer mission in the United Kingdom, spurred by the Rothchild report and concern for the "clinical relevance" of esoteric scientific work, has apparently not differed significantly from the U.S. cancer war (Whitley, 1978:438–39), though the use of experts to defuse controversy, as in the case of determining the pesticides Aldrin and Dieldrin noncarcinogenic (Gillespie et al., 1979), is decidedly cooptive. Scientific expertise in U.S. cancer controversies has not consistently been aligned with the federal government's position (Chubin, 1981).

13 To quote from President Carter's Science and Technology Message to Congress on 27 March 1979: "We look to the fruits of science and technology to improve our health by curing illness and preventing disease and disability. . . . We expect science and technology to find new sources of energy, to feed the world's growing population, to provide new tools for our national security, and to prevent unwise applications of science and technology" (quoted in Staats, 1979:18).

14 As noted earlier in the Laetrile controversy (n. 3), society (as embodied by various public interest groups) is "no longer content to delegate the assessment of and response to risk to so-called disinterested scientists. Indeed, the very concept of objectivity embodied in the word disinterested is now discredited" (Bazelon, 1979:277; Markle and Petersen, 1980).

15 A longer version of this paper was presented at the Annual Meeting, International Studies/Southwestern Social Science Association, Fort Worth, Texas, 28–31 March 1979 and revised in September 1979. Support for the interviews reported herein was provided by NSF Grant No. SOC77–11593. The views expressed do not reflect those of the National Science Foundation. The comments of the following colleagues are gratefully acknowledged: William Blanpied, Timothy Hall, Gerald Markle, Everett Mendelsohn, Dorothy Nelkin, James Petersen, and Peter Weingart.

References

Amos, Harold. 1977. "Basic Science and Public Policy." *Yale Journal of Biology and Medicine* 50:261–64.

Barnes, Barry. 1977. *Interests and the Growth of Knowledge*. London: Routledge Direct Editions.

Bazelon, David L. 1979. "Risk and Responsibility." *Science* 205:277–80.

Bernal, J. D. 1939. *The Social Function of Science*. London: Routledge.

Bruno, A. M. 1974. "National Cancer Institute: An Overview with Historic Footnotes; A Report on the U.S.–U.S.S.R. Health Agreement." *National Cancer Institute Monograph* 40:7–20.

Carrese, Louis M. 1974. "The National Planning Effort: The Need for a Comprehensive National Plan, Its Organization and Implementation." *National Cancer Institute Monograph* 40:21–24.

———. 1978. Personal interview (24 February).

Carrese, Louis M., and Baker, C. G. 1967. "The Convergence Technique: A Method for the Planning and Programming of Research Efforts." *Management Science* 13:420–38.

Carter, Luther J. 1979. "Yearly Report on Carcinogens Could Be a Potent Weapon in the War on Cancer." *Science* 203:525–28.

Chubin, Daryl E. 1978. "Intellectual Mobility, Mentorship, and Confluence in Biomedical Problem Domains: The Case of Reverse Transcriptase." Final Technical Report on Grant No. SOC 77–11593 to the National Science Foundation (November).

———. 1981. "Values, Controversy, and the Sociology of Science." *Bulletin of Science, Technology, and Society* 1:427–36.

Chubin, Daryl E., and Studer, K. E. 1978. "The Politics of Cancer." *Theory and Society* 6:55–74.

———. 1979. "Knowledge and Structures of Scientific Growth: Measurement of a Cancer Problem Domain." *Scientometrics* 1:171–93.

Comroe, Julius H. 1978. "The Road from Research to New Diagnosis and Therapy." *Science* 200:931–37.

Comroe, J. H., and Dripps, R. D. 1976. "Scientific Basis for the Support of Biomedical Science." *Science* 192:105–11.

Culliton, B. J. 1974. "Virus Cancer Program: Review Panel Stands by Criticism." *Science* 184:143–45.

———. 1976. "Kennedy Hearings: Year-Long Probe of Biomedical Research Begins." *Science* 193:32–33, 35.

———. 1977. "Arthur Canfield Upton: New Director of the NCI." *Science* 197:737–39.

———. 1978. "Science's Restive Public." *Daedalus* 107:147–56.

Epstein, Samuel S. 1978. *The Politics of Cancer*. San Francisco: Sierra Club Books.

Ezrahi, Y. 1971. "The Political Resources of American Science." *Science Studies* 1:117–33.

Gillespie, Brendan; Eva, Dave; and Johnston, Ron. 1979. "Carcinogenic Risk Assessment in the United States and Great Britain: The Case of Aldrin/Dieldrin." *Social Studies of Science* 9:265–301.

Groeneveld, L.; Koller, N.; and Mullins, N. 1975. "The Advisors of the U.S. National Science Foundation." *Social Studies of Science* 5:343–54.

Gustafson, Thane. 1975. "The Controversy over Peer Review." *Science* 190:1060–66.

Hadden, S. G. 1977. "Technical Advice in Policy Making: A Propositional Inventory." In *Science and Technology Policy*, ed. J. Haberer. Lexington, Massachusetts: Lexington Books (Health), pp. 81–98.

Hessen, Boris. 1931. "The Social and Economic Roots of Newton's *Principia*." In *Science at the Crossroads*, ed. N. Bukharin et al. London: Kniga (reprint, Frank Cass, 1971), pp. 151–212.

Hixson, Joseph. 1976. *The Patchwork Mouse*. Garden City, New Jersey: Anchor Doubleday.

Hutt, Peter Barton. 1978. "Public Criticism of Health Science Policy." *Daedalus* 197: 157–69.

Johnston, Ron, and Jagtenberg, Tom. 1978. "Goal Direction of Scientific Research." In *Sociology of the Sciences*, vol. II, *The Dynamics of Science and Technology: Social Values, Technical Norms and Scientific Criteria in the Development of Knowledge*, ed. W. Krohn, E. Kayton, and P. Weingart. Boston: Reidel, pp. 29–58.

Kalberer, J. T. 1975. "Impact of the National Cancer Act on Grant Support." *Cancer Research* 35:473–81.

Lakoff, S. A. 1977. "Scientists, Technologists and Political Power." In *Science, Technology and Society: A Cross-Disciplinary Perspective*, ed. I. Spiegel-Rosing and D. deS. Price. London: Sage, pp. 355–91.

Markle, Gerald E., and Petersen, James C. 1979. "Resolution of the Laetrile Controversy: Past Attempts and Future Prospects." Presented at the Hastings Center, New York (16 June).

———. 1980. *Politics, Science, and Cancer: The Laetrile Phenomenon*. Boulder, Colorado: Westview.

Markle, G. E.; Petersen, J. C.; and Wagenfeld, M. O. 1978. "Notes from the Cancer Underground: Participation in the Laetrile Movement." *Social Science and Medicine* 12:31–37.

Millstone, Erik. 1978. "A Framework for the Sociology of Knowledge." *Social Studies of Science* 8:111–25.

Mulkay, M. J. 1976a. "Norms and Ideology in Science." *Social Science Information* 15: 637–56.

———. 1976b. "The Mediating Role of the Scientific Elite." *Social Studies of Science* 6: 445–70.

———. 1979. "Knowledge and Utility: Implications for the Sociology of Knowledge." *Social Studies of Science* 9:63–80.

Nelkin, Dorothy. 1975. "The Political Impact of Technical Expertise." *Social Studies of Science* 5:35–54.

———. 1978. "Threats and Promises: Negotiating the Control of Research." *Daedalus* 107: 191–209.

———. 1979. "Science, Technology, and Political Conflict: Analyzing the Issues." In *Controversy: Politics of Technical Decisions*, ed. Dorothy Nelkin. Beverly Hills: Sage Publications, pp. 9–22.

128
Case Studies

———. 1980. "Science and Technology Policy and the Democratic Process." In *The Five-Year Outlook: Problems, Opportunities, and Constraints in Science and Technology.* vol. 2, pp. 483–92. Washington, D.C.: National Science Foundation.

Overington, Michael A. 1979. "Doing the What Comes Rationally: Some Developments in Metatheory." *American Sociologist* 14:2–12.

Petersen, James C., and Markle, Gerald E. 1979. "The Laetrile Controversy," in *Controversy: Politics of Technical Decisions*, ed. D. Nelkin. Beverly Hills: Sage Publications.

Rauscher, Frank. 1974. "Budget and the National Cancer Program." *Science* 184:871–75.

———. 1978. Personal interview (21 March).

Ravetz, J. R. 1977. "Criticisms of Science." In *Science, Technology and Society: A Cross-Disciplinary Perspective*, ed. I. Spiegel-Rosing and D. deS. Price. London: Sage, pp. 71–89.

Rettig, Richard A. 1977. *Cancer Crusade: The Story of the National Cancer Act of 1971.* Princeton: Princeton University Press.

Salomon, J. J. 1972. "Science Policy and Its Myths: The Allocation of Resources." *Public Policy* 20:1–33.

———. 1977. "Science Policy Studies and the Development of Science Policy." In *Science, Technology and Society: A Cross-Disciplinary Perspective*, ed. I. Spiegel-Rosing and D. deS. Price. London: Sage, pp. 43–70.

Schlom, Jeffrey. 1978. Personal interview (28 February).

Spiegelman, Sol. 1978. Personal interview (21 March).

Staats, Elmer B. 1979. "Federal Research Grants." *Science* 205:18–20.

Strickland, Stephen. 1972. *Politics, Science, and Dread Disease.* Cambridge, Massachusetts: Harvard University Press.

Studer, Kenneth E., and Chubin, Daryl E. 1980. *The Cancer Mission: Social Contexts of Biomedical Research.* Beverly Hills: Sage Publications.

Sun, Marjorie. 1981. "Hatch Takes Over Senate Labor Committee." *Science* 211:684–85.

Thomas, Lewis. 1977. "Biomedical Science and Human Health: The Long-Range Prospect." *Daedalus* 106:163–71.

Todaro, George. 1978. Personal interview (23 February).

U.S. Senate. 1971. Committee on Labor and Public Welfare, Subcommittee on Health. *Conquest of Cancer Act, Hearing*, 92d Congress; Washington, D.C.: Government Printing Office.

van den Daele, W.; Krohn, W.; and Weingart, P. 1977. "The Political Direction of Scientific Development." In *Perspectives on the Emergence of Scientific Disciplines*, ed. E. Mendelsohn et al. Chicago: Aldine, pp. 247–75.

von Hippel, F., and Primack, J. 1972. "Public Interest Science." *Science* 177:1166–71.

Weinberg, A. M. 1961. "Impact of Large-Scale Science on the United States." *Science* 134:164.

Weingart, Peter. 1977. "Science Policy and the Development of Science." In *Perspectives in the Sociology of Science*, ed. S. S. Blume. Chichester: Wiley, pp. 51–70.

Whitley, Richard. 1978. "Types of Science, Organizational Strategies and Patterns of Work in Research Laboratories in Different Scientific Fields." *Social Science Information* 17: 427–47.

8

Consumers and Health Planning: Issues and Opportunities

Barry Checkoway

P.L. 93–641, the National Health Planning and Resources Development Act of 1974, created a national network of Health Systems Agencies (HSAs) and emphasized consumer participation in health planning, a field long dominated by medical providers and hospitals. Not only were consumers to have a majority on each HSA governing board, but they were also to be "broadly representative of the social, economic, linguistic, and racial populations, geographic areas of the health service area, and major purchasers of health care," and were deemed "essential to the effective performance of an agency's function" (Federal Register, 1976). The regulations also required public notice and open meetings, public hearings on plans, and a public record of proceedings. Moreover, each HSA was authorized to formulate health plans and priorities, to review and approve or disapprove of proposals for federal funding, to assess the appropriateness of services provided by hospitals and other health institutions, and to help develop neighborhood health centers, health maintenance organizations, and health education programs. The new agencies were mandated not only to gather data, develop plans, and provide technical assistance, but also to make decisions about needs for institutional health services, major medical equipment, and capital expenditures and projects. In short, the agencies promised a powerful force in determining the direction of local health planning.

After five years, the record of health planning is uneven. On the one hand, the program's success has been limited and considerable dissatisfaction with the program has been expressed from various quarters (Kotelchuck, 1979; McClure, 1979; Salkever and Bice, 1979; Glenn, 1980; Government Accounting Office, 1980). Analyses of consumer participation under P.L. 93–641 focusing on social characteristics of consumer board members have found that such members are not always representative of the area's population (Hyman, 1976; Clark, 1977; Orkand Corporation, 1977; Sypniewski and Semmel, 1977; Tannen, 1977; Darling and Poole, 1980). There is even evidence to suggest that HSAs may themselves be contributing to the further concentration of power among selected provider groups identified with traditional medical practice (Checkoway, O'Rourke, and Macrina, 1981). Although some agencies have fervently sought citizen participation (Checkoway, 1980), the record is uneven and many problems of participation remain.

On the other hand, health consumer groups concerned with planning appear to be increasing in number and capacity. National organizations have influenced federal legislation and administrative regulations; state organizations have developed statewide coalitions and communications networks; and local organizations have achieved agency reforms and have elected candidates to governing boards (U.S. House, 1978). Legal Services attorneys have worked to expand access for low-income clients; Public Citizen's Health Research Group has disclosed and drawn attention to the costs of unnecessary construction of local facilities and the need for responsible planning; and the Consumer Coalition for Health has built a national alliance of groups dedicated to greater consumer control over the health care system.

This essay will examine the major issues with which health consumer groups have been concerned, and the opportunities and resources which have helped make group formation possible. Although there are no systematic data on the scope of the movement, it is possible to identify selected groups and examine their issues as a basis upon which to characterize the status of the consumer movement in relation to health planning today.[1]

Issues

Health consumer groups have addressed a wide variety of issues, but most are tied to the development of health planning itself.[2] Specifically, they have concentrated on consumer representation, access to health services, and cost containment.

Representation The issue of representation frequently cropped up during the Health Systems Agency (HSA) application and designation process. For example, in suburban Cook and DuPage counties in Illinois, an HSA application was submitted by a group of consumers, local officials, and allied medical professionals (Chinn, 1980). They sought the input and representation of low-income and minority consumers, called for an open public membership, showed a willingness to oppose unnecessary hospital construction, and gained the endorsement of the governor of Illinois. Another application, submitted by a group representing medical societies, hospitals, physicians, and provider-backed consumers, prohibited general membership of public voting rights. Public Citizen's Health Research Group threatened litigation and press coverage if the provider-dominated application were chosen, and the Department of Health, Education, and Welfare (HEW) finally designated the consumer-oriented group. This group subsequently provided the basis for a caucus of governing board members who meet regularly to exchange ideas, discuss consumer viewpoints, and formulate strategies. Consumer caucus members have been instrumental in agency opposition to expansion proposals made by local hospitals and have organized the Illinois Association of Health Planning Consumers which aims to strengthen consumer participation in HSAs throughout the state. Consumer groups have organized around HSA designation in Connecticut, Mississippi, Tennessee, Oklahoma, and elsewhere. It appears as if health planning gave birth to these groups.

Concern for issues of representation also followed from several studies showing that consumer majorities on health planning boards did not always represent their area populations. A study of HSA governing boards in HEW Region II found that female, elderly, and low-income consumers were insufficiently represented to ensure influence in planning (Hyman, 1976). A study of twenty-eight HSAs in eleven southern states found that low-income individuals, blacks, women, and other minority groups were inadequately represented on governing boards and staffs (Clark, 1977). A national study for the Bureau of Health Planning found that HSA governing boards were comprised predominantly of professional, technical, and managerial workers (Orkand Corporation, 1977). Other studies produced similar findings in California, Texas, Kentucky, New York, and elsewhere.

The Center for Law and Social Policy, a Washington-based public-interest law firm, was among the first of several groups to challenge the under-representation of low-income consumers on HSA governing boards. In an important case, *Texas ACORN* v. *Texas Area 5 Health Systems Agency, Inc.*, the center won a district court judgment holding that low-income consumers must be represented by persons of the same income group in numbers roughly proportionate to their presence in the area's population (Sypniewski and Semmel, 1977). The Fifth Circuit Court rejected this view on appeal, but only after it required HEW to promulgate regulations regarding governing body composition. Publicity over Texas ACORN helped stimulate further litigation and organization around issues of representation.

The center has also provided leadership and counsel in organizing the Consumer Coalition for Health. This coalition arose out of a consumer conference sponsored by the center and attended by representatives of national and local consumer groups concerned about health planning. Since its formation, the consumer coalition has grown into a national alliance which includes national organizations, local groups, HSAs, and individual members. On the national level, the consumer coalition has sought to represent consumer viewpoints in health planning legislation and administration. It was influential in securing the ban on self-perpetuating boards as reflected in the 1979 health planning amendments to P.L. 93–641, and in voicing complaints to federal agencies about state and local consumer participation practices (Kleiman, 1979). On the local level, the coalition has provided technical assistance, political support, and lobbying aid to consumer groups seeking to influence health policy. Overall, the coalition has tried to unite consumers and consumer groups working in health planning, and to provide a national network of information exchange and advocacy.

Consumer representation has also engendered controversy at the local level. A study of the HSA in east-central Illinois found that of the thirty sub-area council members selected for analysis, only one was from the lowest income residential area. No low-income, minority, or rural area was actively represented (Community Planning Workshop, 1977). In response, large numbers of local consumers decided to join the HSA, to increase their involvement on its governing boards and committees, and to speak up and argue their viewpoints at hearings and meetings. Since then, the Champaign County Health Care Consumers (CCHCC) has grown into a strong organization concerned with improving health care through consumer participation in planning (Checkoway and Doyle, 1980). Their community forums have educated the public on consumer health issues; their leadership training workshops have provided HSA consumer board members with information and skills to carry out their responsibilities; and their newsletter now goes to thousands of consumers. They have also presented testimony to legislative bodies at all levels of government.

Since its formation, CCHCC has encouraged large numbers of people to join the local HSA and participate in local health planning elections, has circulated a questionnaire to find candidates who can represent consumer viewpoints, and has endorsed those concerned with responsible health planning and consumer participation. In 1977, despite inexperience and meager resources, the consumer group generated an unprecedented turnout and elected seven of its twelve endorsed candidates. In 1978, following a vigorous voter registration drive and publicity campaign, consumers elected an entire consumer slate by a 2 to 1 margin. Among those elected were low-income and minority consumers, a labor union official, an elected township supervisor, a legal services attorney, and a provider concerned with preventive medicine.

Then in 1979 the local medical society and area hospitals joined together in a campaign to elect their own candidates to the board (O'Rourke, 1980). Physicians and hospital employees were bused to the polls during working hours to vote for the medical slate. Hospital administrators and physicians stood at open voting tables and were able to watch over the voters. The medical slate won by a 2 to 1 margin. It did not represent the area population and was closely tied to hospitals coming up for review. Consumer leaders wrote to federal officials warning of the pitfalls of elections and calling for new standards to assure fair representation practice. They also decided that it would be a strategic mistake for local consumers to focus exclusively on health planning when providers could easily mobilize resources to defeat consumer participation.

Other consumer groups have also sought reforms in HSA representational methods. Georgia Legal Services investigated all HSAs in Georgia and found a pattern of self-perpetuating governing bodies and underrepresentation of the poor (U.S. House, 1978). As a result an Atlanta Consumer Health and Monitoring Project (CHAMP) was formed out of concern that the North-Central Georgia HSA governing body was self-perpetuating—members were selected from among a single slate of nominees chosen by a nominating committee appointed by the HSA president. CHAMP efforts to reform the local HSA became a symbol of health consumerism in Georgia.

In *Rakestraw* v. *Califano*, Georgia Legal Services challenged the selection methods and board composition of each HSA in Georgia, citing HEW Secretary Califano in particular for designating agencies that underrepresented low-income individuals, handicapped groups, and women, and for failing to "propose and promulgate regulations dealing with the composition . . . and selection process." The federal court was asked to require HEW to devise a method of selecting consumer representatives that would render them accountable to the public. Working closely with the Consumer Coalition for Health, Georgia Legal Services attorneys and clients also traveled to Washington to engage in legislative advocacy and to testify on behalf of new methods of representation before hearings of the Subcommittee on Health and the Environment, which was considering amendments to P.L. 93–641 (U.S. House, 1978). In the 1979 health planning amendments, Congress reaffirmed the idea of broad representation and mandated new methods to ban self-perpetuation and assure accountability.

The North-Central Georgia HSA developed new methods of board selection with the participation of the very groups whose advocacy had been instrumental in changing the law (Blackburn, 1980). Acting through a series of agency working papers, committee reports, and formal hearings, Georgia Legal Services and CHAMP helped mobilize local groups to caucus, select, and hold accountable their own representatives to the governing body (Lowe, 1980). This innovation promises to stimulate further community organization around health planning in Georgia.

Access Legal services attorneys have been at the forefront of efforts to expand access for low-income, minority, and other consumers in the health care system. Although legal services involvement in health planning is relatively new, Chavkin and Runner (1980) report that over twenty-five lawsuits have been filed challenging health planning implementation on behalf of consumers. Among the first cases were those brought on behalf of low-income plaintiffs to expand their representation on HSA governing boards. More recently, however, legal services attorneys have recognized the statutory and regulatory structure of health planning agencies as a vehicle to raise questions on behalf of clients. Chavkin and Runner report several cases in which project reviews have allowed attorneys to ask such questions as: Will a project increase access to health services? Does a facility take its fair share of Medicaid patients? Is there evidence of racial discrimination?

For example, a hospital's request for HSA approval for an equipment purchase was opposed on the grounds that the facility was unresponsive to community needs; it was approved only on condition of closer cooperation with community groups. Shortly thereafter, the first low-income consumer was elected to the hospital's board. In other cases, legal services attorneys have enabled low-income residents to participate in the local review of a planned land purchase for future hospital relocation; forced a nursing home to admit Medicaid patients as a condition of agency approval for expansion; blocked designation of a state health planning body whose proposed membership was all white males; secured an HEW ruling that a state planning agency must deny a construction application to a hospital ordered to a hearing on civil rights violations; and negotiated free service compliance under Hill-Burton as a condition of facility expansion approval (Chavkin and Runner, 1980).

Legal services and other attorneys have also worked to strengthen the statutory and regulatory structure of health planning through national legislative and administrative advocacy. The National Health Law Program (NHeLP), a specialized litigation and support center of the Legal Services Corporation, has established a branch office in Washington to facilitate national advocacy on behalf of clients. NHeLP advocates and clients have testified before congressional committees, commented on proposed regulations and guidelines, and submitted administrative complaints about state and local planning agencies. NHeLP, in addition to Georgia Legal Services and the Consumer Coalition for Health, claims victory for the ban on self-perpetuating boards in the 1979 health planning amendments (Chavkin and Runner, 1980).

Local consumer groups themselves have also used health planning as a way to address access issues. On Cape Cod, for example, a coalition of consumers, hospital workers, and community groups organized to take charge of the local HSA subarea council. They recruited 300 new HSA members, enlisted twenty-four consumer and provider candidates to run for the board, conducted a vigorous election campaign, and finally claimed a majority of seats on the board. The new HSA board voted to investigate low-income discrimination under Medicaid, and an HSA hearing produced consumer testimony of widespread violations. One case, concerning an infant whose eye emergency was untreated because of Medicaid status, led to an inquiry by the state Medical Licensing Board, and action by the state's Secretary of Consumer Affairs.

Today the Cape Cod Health Care Coalition consists of more than thirty community and social service organizations led by Local 880 of the Massachusetts Hospital Workers Union and the Community Action Committee of Cape Cod and the Islands, a low-income advocacy group. Since its original actions, the coalition has gone on to demand that Cape Cod Hospital require physicians to accept Medicaid patients in exchange for staff privileges, open an out-patient department, print and distribute a Patients' Rights Handbook, open a Women's Health Clinic, end the use of liens and sheriff sales as a means of collecting unpaid hospital bills, provide a more aggressive program to inform patients of the Hill-Burton program, and post a sign above its door: "This hospital will refuse no patient needing care because of inability to pay."

Cost containment   The third area in which consumer groups have used health planning is in the area of cost containment. Public Citizen's Health Research Group (HRG), a national leader in this movement, has published several reports on the excess of hospital beds, overproduction of medical equipment, and unnecessary construction of health facilities. In 1975 HRG published *The $8 Billion Hospital Bed Overrun: A Consumers' Guide to Stopping Wasteful Construction*. The report suggested that there was a substantial national surplus of hospital beds, constituting a major source of waste in the health care system (Ensminger, 1975). It argued that surplus beds cost $5 billion to build and another $2 billion each year to maintain, warned that excessive hospital construction and dangerous overuse would cost another $6 billion, and called for health planning agencies to declare moratoriums on new construction. HRG's 1976 publication, *CAT Scanners: Is Fancier Technology Worth a Billion Dollars of Health Consumers' Money?*, called for health planning agencies to declare a moratorium on the purchase of additional CAT scanners until there was evidence that their purchase and maintenance would be offset by cost savings and medical benefits to patients (Wolfe, 1976). That same year, HRG published

Trimming the Fat Off Health Care Costs: A Consumers' Guide to Taking Over Health Planning. It summarized earlier investigative work, urged consumers to participate in health planning as a method to contain costs, and provided practical suggestions for consumer involvement and community organization (Bogue and Wolfe, 1976). HRG staff have become familiar advocates of these positions in congressional hearings (Bogue, 1978). In 1976 HRG began publishing the *Consumer Health Action Network Newsletter* (CHAN) to inform and activate consumers concerned about health planning. Since then, CHAN has grown into a major monthly medium of exchange among consumer activists.

Cost containment issues raised by HRG have effected changes in several communities. Health planning agencies in Honolulu, Atlanta, Dayton, San Francisco, and Baltimore were among those declaring moratoriums on hospital bed construction. The Arizona Center for the Public Interest intervened in several HSA review hearings to oppose cases of hospital construction. The Health Care Coalition of Cleveland was formed in response to proposed hospital expansion, and testified on behalf of a more cost-conscious health systems plan. The Colorado Health Research Coalition contested proposed CAT scanners in HSA review hearings across the state and presented extensive testimony against a proposed scanner purchase in the Central-Northeast Colorado HSA; the purchase was ultimately defeated.

Opportunities

The number of health consumer groups has increased in response to the development of health planning itself. But they also have been strongly influenced by the expansion of opportunities and resources making possible further group formation. These opportunities include funding support, staff development, and support networks.

Funding support   The successful development of a health consumer group depends in large part on its ability to obtain funding.[3] Provider organizations have long paid the price of participation in health politics. The American Medical Association leads all other interest groups in the amount of money it gives to political campaigns. Some state medical societies employ full-time staffs to aid physicians on local health planning boards and to run political campaigns for board candidates. In comparison, consumers have entered health planning with little financial support to hire staff, publish newsletters, or otherwise build organizations that can operate in imbalanced health political arenas. Despite a slow beginning, recent years have witnessed an increase in the availability of institutional resources for consumer activity (McCarthy and Zald, 1973). Although it is difficult to calculate the full scope of support, established institutions have become an important factor in the funding of consumer activity.

All major types of foundations provide funding for community problem-solving projects. Several have increased their funding support for consumer groups committed to social change at the same time as consumer staff and leaders have developed the skills to write winning proposals. Directories include lists of numerous change-oriented foundations and describe publications, resource centers, and training workshops designed to help consumers win foundation support. The Ford Foundation, National Science Foundation, and the Campaign for Human Development are among the foundations which have funded consumer proposals.

Government also has supported health consumer activity. The *Catalog of Federal Domestic Assistance* lists details on over 1,000 categorical grants for state and local governments as well as nonprofit groups. The Legal Services Corporation and Volunteers in Service to America (VISTA) have indirectly funded health consumer staffs by making health care a priority. The Health Resources Administration, Community Services Administration, and several state health departments have supported such projects as a feasibility study for a national health consumer network, health consumer bulletins, and training conferences. Selected HSAs have also provided funding to consumer groups proposing to undertake projects related to planning objectives. Other local consumer groups have raised some or all of their operating budgets through voluntary donations or "grass roots" fund-raising projects such as membership drives, bake sales, bingo games, and door-to-door solicitation. Although these combined resources comprise no more than a fraction of what is available to the AMA and other provider organizations, they have at least allowed some consumer groups to develop.

Staff development   Funding support has increased the possibility of part-time, temporary, or full-time career opportunities in health consumerism. For example, VISTA volunteers have been assigned to health consumer groups in California, Georgia, Illinois, Massachusetts, New York, and other states. Funding has also created opportunities for professional community organizers to work for health consumer groups. The lead organizer of the Cape Cod Health Care Coalition, for example, was trained by Saul Alinsky and previously had organized for the Massachusetts Welfare Rights Organization and Massachusetts Hospital Workers Association. In summer 1978 the coalition staff peaked at twenty-one part-time or temporary workers.

Institutional resources have allowed a growing number of professionals to earn an income by committing themselves full time to activities related to health consumerism. McCarthy and Zald (1973) have noted the emergence of several professions that support commitments to social change in modern America. In the area of law, for example, the Legal Services Corporation, with a budget of $300 million for fiscal year 1980, supported more than 5,000 staff attorneys, 2,500 paralegals, and thousands of student personnel in 335 independent legal services programs. The Western Center on Law and Poverty in Los Angeles, Georgia Legal Services in Atlanta, and Community Action for Legal Services in New York employ full-time staff for health consumer advocacy and community organization.

Government has also supported health consumer professionalization. In recent years, federal agencies have increased the number of citizen participation and consumer affairs programs, and these activities have become part of most major domestic programs. Executive Order 12160 ordered federal agencies to institutionalize consumerism by creating consumer affairs staffs at various levels of government. The 1979 health planning amendments also required each HSA to provide staff aid to governing board members and particularly to consumer members. These actions further fuel the possibility of health consumer professionalization. Indeed, HSA staffs with a consumer orientation have recently formed their own "progressive caucus" within the American Health Planning Association.

Support networks The growth of support networks for health consumer groups is an indicator of, and contributor to, increased health consumer professionalization. The Consumer Commission on the Accreditation of Health Services presented the case for such a support network in a 1977 position paper (Consumer Commission on the Accreditation of Health Services). Formed in 1972 to provide information on the quality and cost of health services in New York City, the commission soon broadened its work to include reports on health issues of national significance. Under contract to the Health Resources Administration, the commission surveyed consumers and consumer groups to determine alternative forms of support needed to create an organized consumer health constituency. The completed report called for new initiatives to provide technical and educational assistance to consumers, create regional resource centers, establish a national newsletter, and organize and support local health consumer groups. The commission concluded that "to become responsible and responsive representatives, consumers need the technical and political support of an organized consumer health constituency."

Several consumer groups have transformed elements of the proposed consumer support network into consumer handbooks and other publications. Legal Services Corporation, in cooperation with the Appalachian Research and Defense Fund, published three guides that received widespread circulation among health consumer advocates: *The American Health System* contains an analysis of key factors in the health system (Madison, 1978a); *The People's Guide to Good Health* gives information on consumer rights (Madison, 1978b); and *Organizing for Better Health Care Planning* contains basic information on health planning and consumer group formation (Association of Health Care Consumers, 1978). Another publication, *Stop the System—We Want To Get On*, is a manual instructing consumer advocates on how to evaluate an HSA's commitment to consumerism (Philadelphia Health Management Corporation, 1978). And *Planning, Politics and Power* is a collection of many works from the consumer health planning literature (Glenn, 1980).

Several groups have also sought to facilitate information exchange and mutual consumer support through newsletters and other publications. These include the *Health PAC Bulletin*, which publishes analyses of the American health care system and collects these in periodic anthologies; the *Health Law Project Library Bulletin*, which includes articles on health consumer planning issues and lists of health publications and resources; *Health Perspectives*, published by the Consumer Commission on the Accreditation of Health Services, which treats a particular policy problem in each issue; and *CHAN*, published jointly by the Health Research Group and Consumer Coalition for Health, which reports on local consumer health initiatives.

Other consumer groups have developed education and training projects designed to increase the knowledge and capacity of consumers regarding health planning. The California Public Interest Research Group (calPIRG) monitored HSA meetings in the San Diego area and found that consumer board members often lacked knowledge of health planning, influence in health policy decisions, and accountability to constituency groups (Glenn, 1980). In response, calPIRG applied to the National Science Foundation for funding to support a Community Health Advocacy Training Project, at the heart of which was a series of consumer training workshops on health planning issues. Participants were drawn from representatives of medically underserved populations and others not traditionally involved in health planning. Among the outgrowths of the project was a decision by participants to form a Health Action Coalition (HAC) to work for reform of the health care system. HAC membership today includes representatives of low-income, minority, labor, senior, rural, student, and social service groups. HAC members have pressured the local HSA to expand staff time and resources for community outreach, and have worked to facilitate appointment of consumers to the governing board, subarea councils, and local committees.

Citizen Action in Perspective

Consumer groups in the health planning field appear to be increasing in number and capacity, and the issues they address are generally tied to the development of health planning itself. There are no systematic data as yet on the number and scope of these groups, nor on their impact on health planning and community systems. Nonetheless, given the traditional obstacles to consumer organizing around health issues, the very formation of these groups might in itself be taken as a significant change.

It is important to emphasize that these groups have largely taken for granted the stated aims and institutional context of health planning and have sought compliance and change within that context. They have viewed health planning as a legitimate vehicle for local health action and have organized to influence and improve the process. They have embraced the prevailing ideal of democratic pluralism and have sought to create the needed countervailing power. In other words, they have been "good citizens" with a reformist, not radical, orientation.

An exception to the reform pattern is the Health Policy Advisory Center (Health PAC), a New York-based group of policy analysts that provides information to health activists while "serving the larger movement for radical social change in America, by making health a 'case study' in the need for democratic restructuring of American institutions" (Ehrenreich, 1970). Since 1967, Health PAC has published a succession of reports critical of consumer organizing around health planning for tending to support the dominance of the medical industry. *The American Health Empire: Power, Profits, and Politics* argues that "the American health system is not in business for people's health," but instead "quite efficiently pursues its own priorities of profits, research, and education" (Ehrenreich, 1970:vii). *Prognosis Negative: Crisis in the Health Care System* views government intervention as a vehicle to contain and rationalize further expansion and corporatization (Kotelchuck, 1976).

It is also important to emphasize that the apparent increase in health consumer groups interested in health planning is related to funding support and staff development. Traditional studies of social movements assigned primary importance to what Leites and Wolf (1970) call the "hearts and minds of the people." According to this approach, group consciousness and widespread grievances give rise to the formation of social movement organizations, which then appoint leaders or hire staff to carry out ameliorative actions. In contrast, studies of health consumer groups assign primary importance to resource mobilization and professionalization. According to these latter studies, institutional resources have helped create career opportunities and support-networks among activists and professionals, who, in turn, seek to identify issues and build organizations where consumers have typically lacked such consciousness and grievances. This does not mean that grievances about health care do not exist—instead, emphasis is placed on the importance of other factors that facilitate the development of these groups.

The same forces that stimulate the growth of health consumer groups—especially health planning issues, resource mobilization, and professionalization—could also jeopardize the development of this movement. If key health planning issues or mechanisms were to disappear, then groups lacking multiple issues or independent agendas might be unable to adapt. The community organization literature is filled with cases of single-issue organizations that faded after the issue was either won or lost. Likewise, if institutional resources were no longer available, some groups might cease to exist. If activists and professionals are unable to build a broad base for their work, some groups might be unable to survive either major changes in leadership or sustained attacks by political opponents. The future of this movement, then, may depend in part on the capacity of health consumer groups to increase both their numbers and the issues they advocate, to stabilize their resources and funding support, and to strengthen their leadership and political base.

Consumer participation in health planning is changing in America. Traditionally, consumers have accepted the notion of provider control over health care delivery, with a resultant show of little support for public intervention. Patients have often been socialized into a subservient orientation in which acceptance of the medical monopoly in treatment is transferred to planning and administration. It is as if consumer participation in health planning were equated with amateur interference in medical treatment matters. Now, however, federal legislation has provided a basis for consumer groups to increase public awareness, develop leadership, form alliances and support networks, and challenge mainstream medicine. Whatever the fate of current health planning, these groups have helped define an action agenda for the eighties.

Notes

1   This paper is based on work commissioned by the Institute of Medicine of the National Academy of Sciences. Earlier versions are reported in Checkoway (1981a; 1981b).
2   This section focuses on consumer groups working in the health planning field. Other groups not treated here include those concerned with alternative health institutions, self-help or preventive issues, environmental health, occupational safety and health, or Laetrile and other marginal medical movements.
3   My debt to the work of McCarthy and Zald (1973) is obvious in this and the following section.

References

Alford, R. R. 1975. *Health Care Politics: Ideology and Interest Group Barriers to Reform.* Chicago: University of Chicago Press.

Association of Health Care Consumers. 1978. *Consumer Guide to Local Health Care Planning.* Chicago: Association of Health Care Consumers.

Blackburn, S. H. 1980. *HSA Board Elections: A Case for a Combination of Methods.* Atlanta: North Central Georgia Health Systems Agency.

Bogue, T. 1978. "Consumer Issues around HSAs: Amending the National Health Planning Act—Will Consumers Benefit?" *Health Law Project Library Bulletin* 3:19–25.

Bogue, T., and Wolfe, S. M. 1976. *Trimming the Fat Off Health Care Costs: A Consumer's Guide to Taking over Health Planning.* Washington, D.C.: Health Research Group.

Burlage, R. 1979. "Part of the Way with HSAs." *Health PAC Bulletin* 2:1–2, 14.

Chavkin, D., and Runner, M. 1980. "An Advocate's Guide to Health Planning." *Clearinghouse Review* 13:831–47.

Checkoway, B. 1979. "Citizens on Local Health Planning Boards: What Are the Obstacles?" *Journal of the Community Development Society* 10:101–16.

———. 1981a. "Consumer Movements in Health Planning." In Institute of Medicine, *Health Planning in the United States: Selected Policy Issues.* Washington, D.C.: National Academy of Sciences.

————. 1981b. "Citizen Action in Health Planning." In *Citizens and Health Care*, ed. Barry Checkoway. New York: Pergamon Press.

Checkoway, B., and Doyle, M. 1980. "Community Organizing Lessons for Health Care Consumers." *Journal of Health Politics, Policy and Law* 5:213–26.

Checkoway, B.; O'Rourke, T.; and Macrina, D. 1981. "Representation of Providers on Health Planning Boards." *International Journal of Health Services* 2:573–81.

Chinn, P. 1980. "The Struggle for Consumer Control." Paper presented at the Symposium on Citizen Participation in Health Planning. West Springfield, Massachusetts.

Clark, W. 1977. *Placebo or Cure: State and Local Health Planning Agencies in the South.* Atlanta: Southern Regional Council.

Community Planning Workshop. 1977. *Power, Participation, and Health: The Case of the Health Systems Agency in East Central Illinois.* Urbana: University of Illinois.

Consumer Commission on the Accreditation of Health Services. 1977. "The Development of a Consumer Health Network." *Health Perspectives Special Issue* 4.

Darling, H., and Poole, D. 1980. *A Selected Statistical Review of Consumers on HSA Governing Bodies.* Washington, D.C.: Institute of Medicine, National Academy of Sciences.

Ehrenreich, B., and Ehrenreich, J., eds. 1970. *The American Health Enterprise: Power, Profits and Politics.* New York: Vintage Books.

Ensminger, B. 1975. *The $8 Billion Hospital Bed Overrun: A Consumer's Guide to Stopping Wasteful Construction.* Washington, D.C.: Health Research Group.

Federal Register. 1976. 41 (60), Sec. 122. Friday, March 26, 1976.

Glenn, K. 1980. *Planning, Politics, and Power: A User's Guide to Taming the Health Care System.* Washington, D.C.: Consumer Coalition for Health.

Government Accounting Office. 1980. *Unreliability of the American Health Planning Association's Savings Estimate for the Health Planning Program.* Washington, D.C.: Government Accounting Office.

Hyman, H. H. 1976. *HSA Governing Body Composition: Analysis of Region II.* New York: Public Health Service, Department of Health, Education, and Welfare, Region II.

Kleiman, M. 1979. "What's in It for Us? Consumer Analysis of the 1979 Health Planning Act Amendments." *Health Law Project Library Bulletin* 328:332–36.

Kotelchuck, D., ed. 1976. *Prognosis Negative: Crisis in the Health Care System.* New York: Vintage Books.

Kotelchuck, R. 1979. "HSAs and Cost Control." *Health PAC Bulletin* 83, 84, 85 (triple issue):1–2, 34–41.

Leites, N., and Wolf, C. 1970. *Rebellion and Authority.* Chicago: Markham.

Lipsky, M., and Lounds, M. 1976. "Citizen Participation and Health Care: Problems of Government Induced Participation." *Journal of Health Politics, Policy and Law* 1:85–111.

Lowe, L. 1980. "Models for Accountability in Health Planning." Paper presented at the Symposium on Citizen Participation in Health Planning. West Springfield, Massachusetts.

Madison, T. M. 1978a. *The American Health System: A Consumer Information and Action*

Guide. Chicago: Legal Services Corporation and Appalachian Research and Defense Fund.

―――. 1978b. *The People's Right to Good Health*. Chicago: Legal Services Corporation and Appalachian Research and Defense Fund.

―――. 1978c. *Organizing for Better Health: Strategies for Consumer Health Groups*. Chicago: Legal Services Corporation and Appalachian Research and Defense Fund.

McCarthy, J., and Zald, M. 1973. *The Trend of Social Movements in America: Professionalization and Resource Mobilization*. Morristown, New Jersey: General Learning Press.

McClure, W. 1979. *Comprehensive Market and Regulatory Strategies for Medical Care*. Excelsior, Minnesota: Interstudy.

Orkand Corporation. 1977. *Assessment of Representation and Parity of HSAs and SHPDAs*. Rockville, Maryland: Orkand Corporation for the Bureau of Health Planning and Resources Development.

O'Rourke, T. 1980. "Elections Are Not Enough." *Health Planning Newsletter* 7:7.

Philadelphia Health Management Corporation. 1978. *Stop the System, We Want To Get On: A Reference Manual for Consumer Health Advocates*. Philadelphia: Philadelphia Health Management Corporation.

Salkever, D. S., and Bice, T. W. 1979. *Hospital Certificate-of-Need Controls: Impact on Investment, Costs, and Use*. Washington, D.C.: American Enterprise Institute.

Sypniewski, B. P., and Semmel, H. 1977. "From Little Acorns . . . Representation on Health Systems Agencies." *Health Law Project Library Bulletin* 335:1–6.

Tannen, L. N. 1977. "Consumer Issues around HSAs: The Eastern Kentucky HSA." *Health Law Project Library Bulletin* 333:19–22.

U.S. House. 1978. Subcommittee on Health and the Environment. *Hearings on H. R. 10460*. Washington, D.C.: Government Printing Office.

Wolfe, S. M. 1976. *CAT Scanners: Is Fancier Technology Worth a Billion Dollars of Health Consumers' Money?* Washington, D.C.: Health Research Group.

9

The Impact of Public Participation in Biomedical Policy: Evidence from Four Case Studies

Diana Dutton

When the Cambridge City Council met on 5 January 1977, there were klieg lights, TV cameras, and scores of newspaper reporters. This was no ordinary meeting. It was when Dan Hayes would present the report of the Cambridge Experimentation Review Board (CERB)—a citizens' panel charged with reviewing the risks of recombinant DNA research—of which he was chairman. Not only would the panel's report determine the future of recombinant DNA research at two of the world's leading universities, it would also reveal how well a group composed entirely of nonscientists had been able to deal with a complex and highly charged scientific controversy. Such a twist in science policymaking was as unprecedented as the research itself (Knox, 1977a, 1977b).

The citizens' panel had been appointed by the Cambridge city manager the previous summer, at the height of public alarm about the potential hazards of the research. Its seven members were carefully chosen to be broadly representative but, in order to avoid "scientific elitism," included no practicing scientists. Chairman Hayes ran an area oil company, and the other members included a nurse, two physicians, a nun, a community activist, an engineer, and a professor of urban policy. Most of the members knew nothing about recombinant DNA research when they began meeting in August, so their sessions were a combined inquiry and crash course in molecular biology. To this end, they received a stack of background materials some three feet high to read, heard testimony from more than thirty-five experts, engaged in countless hours of discussion, and even conducted a mock trial with eminent witnesses presenting different views.

All the work paid off. The group produced a document that even a critic such as Harvard Professor George Wald, a Nobel Prize winner and prominent opponent of the research at the time, called "a very thoughtful, sober, conscientious report." Although the panel basically allowed the research to proceed—adding only minor restrictions to existing federal requirements—it was very proud of the report, according to Chairman Hayes. He pointed out that all of the recommendations—including some sophisticated measures either overlooked or avoided by NIH officials and advisors—came from members of the citizens' group itself, not from its scientific advisors. Over the course of its work, the group had gained both technical competence and self-confidence. Some members who couldn't even formulate a question in the beginning learned not only to ask questions, but also to pursue unsatisfying responses with a series of follow-up inquiries. According to Hayes, a few could even spot instances where a witness was quoting someone out of context.

Whatever one thinks of the panel's final verdict or the process by which it was reached—and both have been criticized (Goodell, 1979)—one thing seems clear: the Cambridge Experimentation Review Board showed that a broadly representative group of nonscientists could tackle a monumentally complex science policy issue and arrive at a solution widely regarded as intelligent and responsible.

Four years later, another public controversy involving recombinant DNA research erupted in and around Cambridge. As in other towns near major universities, fledgling genetic engineering companies were sprouting up rapidly. Their presence forced city councils to decide for themselves what, if any, conditions to place on the research—inasmuch as mandatory federal guidelines do not apply to private companies. Boston and other cities have passed regulatory legislation extending NIH guidelines to private industry and adding further requirements such as formal medical surveillance (*Business Week*, 1981).

Now the choices are harder than ever, however, for they involve both public and private wealth as well as public health. Communities have to weigh the medical and environmental risks of inadequate safety precautions against the economic and social risks of overly strict provisions which could drive companies away and lose needed tax revenue. And despite lack of harmful evidence, many long-term health hazards are still unknown. Who should make the very difficult decisions about risks and benefits—and how?

Recombinant DNA research, of course, merely exemplifies a more general dilemma facing society: how to assure the general public a meaningful voice in directing and controlling developments in modern science and medicine, some of which may profoundly affect the nature of life as we know it. Democratic principles promise citizens a voice in such matters, but traditional governmental institutions fail to provide it. Polls indicate that the public wants more control, especially over technology (La Porte and Metlay, 1975). For several decades, direct citizen influence has been a persistent theme in various social arenas—from the civil rights, antiwar, and women's movements of the 1960s, to the consumer and antinuclear movements of the 1970s, to Reagan's rhetoric about the "New Federalism" in the 1980s. Increasingly, many political theorists are advocating direct participation as a way to combat the apathy and alienation characteristic of postindustrial society (Pateman, 1970; Carnoy and Shearer, 1980).

Yet serious questions remain. Is participatory democracy possible in the modern context of mass organization and technological interdependence? Is it realistic to expect people to participate in long-range decisions about biomedical policy when personal matters may be more pressing? And, most important from a practical standpoint, in the present society do ordinary people—people from all walks of life—really have anything useful to say about technical issues whose intricacies defy even the experts?

This essay addresses these questions based on evidence from four controversial medical innovations. One, recombinant DNA research, is still unfolding, while three—the nationwide swine flu immunization program of 1976; the government-funded research effort to develop an artificial heart; and DES (diethylstilbestrol), a synthetic hormone used prenatally to prevent miscarriages and also as a "morning-after pill" contraceptive—have had, on balance, disappointing or harmful results. Each case is examined below in terms of both various public efforts to influence policy, and—in light of subsequent events—the actual or potential effects of such efforts.

The following material focuses primarily on different forms of direct intervention in the policy process by citizens or outside experts, rather than on the conventional functions of representative government. Whereas the latter have certainly been important, it is the less traditional forms of direct involvement that seem most likely to offer citizens a greater sense of control over policy decisions. Direct involvement can occur both within the formal political system (in public hearings, for example) and outside it (through the creation of grassroots citizen groups). Specific forms of involvement include participation on advisory panels of task forces, organized public interest groups, individual "whistleblowers" (employees who "go public" with grievances), and citizen review boards with delegated responsibility for particular issues.

By the "public," we mean lay citizens, professionals in fields unrelated to the innovation under consideration, and representatives of public interest organizations—anyone, essentially, who does not have a professional, political, or pecuniary interest in the issues in question. This excludes employees of industries that would benefit financially from the innovation's development, as well as most scientists and government employees who would benefit professionally—unless these individuals were clearly *not* acting in their own immediate organizational or career interests, as in the case of "whistleblowers" and "dissident scientists." Whether such dissenting experts are considered part of the public under these circumstances, in fact they do form symbiotic alliances with public groups by providing valuable technical expertise, while the public groups add political pressure.

We are as interested in the nature of public efforts to intervene as in their ultimate success in bringing about change, through government policy or otherwise. To judge public contributions by their degree of impact would be to ignore the very real disadvantages most public groups face with regard to resources, information, experience, and authority. (And it would only reinforce the prevailing view that the public has nothing worthwhile to offer to science policy.) Thus, we focus mainly on the kinds of public interventions attempted in the four cases, returning briefly at the end of the chapter to consider the question of why some efforts failed while others were successful.

Diana Dutton

The Nature of Public Concerns

Medical innovations usually come to public attention only after an important breakthrough has occurred. Prior work and decision making are controlled almost exclusively by medical and scientific experts—people whose professional lives are devoted to a given area of investigation. It was heart surgeons and cardiac researchers who proposed the artificial heart program, molecular biologists who developed the new recombinant DNA technique, biochemists who first synthesized DES, medical researchers who initiated the experimental use of DES as a morning-after pill, and virologists and epidemiologists who conceived and promoted the swine flu immunization program.

The very beginning of an innovation is a particularly critical period, for it tends to shape the agenda for later deliberations. Because of the central role of experts initially, issues are often interpreted and boundaries of discussion set in a way that renders public concerns irrelevant and builds the dominance of experts into the very framework of debate. Furthermore, once an initial commitment is made, jobs and professional prestige come to depend on continuing momentum, thus generating further resistance to concerns that might threaten the innovation's development. Such impediments were apparent during the early years of the artificial heart program. Although it rapidly became clear that the initial plans contained major miscalculations, National Heart Institute (NHI) officials refused to allow a largely nonmedical panel appointed in 1973 (the Artificial Heart Assessment Panel) to include in its evaluation such basic issues as the need for the device and its technical feasibility (Jonsen and Katz, 1980).[1] The program never received more than ritual attention from Congress, nor did many probing questions come from the NHI Advisory Council—ostensibly a vehicle for public review, but in fact heavily dominated (especially during the early years) by cardiac researchers and others in the medical community.

Yet, despite similar limitations in all of the cases, each witnessed various forms of direct public participation. Efforts by outside groups to influence policy decisions on DES and recombinant DNA research were relatively broad and publicly visible, whereas in the swine flu and artificial heart programs they were much more limited and largely restricted to professionals from other fields. Three themes recur in all these efforts: (1) reassessing risks and benefits; (2) broadening and humanizing the perspective taken on issues; and (3) trying to assure sound and legitimate decisions through a more democratic decision process. The following sections describe how these themes were played out in each of the case studies.

Reassessing Risks and Benefits

Because powerful economic and professional interests tout the *benefits* of many technologies, a common role for public participation has been to highlight possible *risks*. In all four cases, consumer advocates, outside experts, and a handful of dissenting scientists have pressed for more attention to known and potential risks while questioning optimistic assessments of benefits. In the swine flu program, many Americans expressed their own concern about risks by deciding not to roll up their sleeves. The danger of radiation hazards led the Artificial Heart Assessment Panel, composed of outside professionals, to oppose further development of the nuclear-powered heart. Concern about risks has been a continuing theme in the controversies over both recombinant DNA research and DES.

When Dr. Arthur Herbst and his colleagues at the Massachusetts General Hospital reported in 1971 that DES was associated with a rare form of vaginal cancer in daughters of women who had taken the drug during pregnancy (Herbst et al., 1971), the first priority for most women's organizations was to identify and aid DES daughters, for whom risk had become tragic reality. This discovery also reinforced the longstanding concerns of environmentalists and consumer groups about the use of DES as a growth stimulant in cattle feed.[2] And finally it provided grim confirmation of the fears of feminist health critics, who had repeatedly decried the use of synthetic hormones for birth control and during menopause as a classic example of exploitation by the male-dominated medical care establishment (see, for instance, Barbara Seaman's *Women and the Crisis in Sex Hormones*).

Women's groups and health activists also became alarmed about the growing use of DES and other estrogens as postcoital contraceptives, a medical "experiment" that was quickly becoming routine practice in the early 1970s. Their basic objection was that, inasmuch as estrogens were known carcinogens, the morning-after pill exposed women to unnecessary health risks. As Belita Cowan, representing a network of women's health groups, pointed out in 1975 congressional hearings on DES, very few women became pregnant from a single unprotected sexual encounter—even at midcycle (roughly 10 percent). She argued that risks would be less if, rather than taking the morning-after pill, women waited for the results of pregnancy tests. Then, only the 10 percent who turned out to be pregnant would, if they chose, be exposed to the risks of therapeutic abortion (Cowan, 1975:50).[3]

Information gathered and publicized by health activists indicated that DES use as a morning-after pill was widespread during the early 1970s, even though it was supposedly restricted to emergency situations and was never approved by the FDA for marketing as a contraceptive. By 1973, according to an NIH consultant cited by the Health Research Group (a Nader spinoff), about two million women had received DES or another estrogen as a morning-after pill (Johnson and Wolfe, 1973).[4] At the University of Michigan, research by health activists (notably Kathleen Weiss and Belita Cowan) revealed other disturbing findings: few women who had been given postcoital DES reported being asked about factors that might contraindicate this use (such as prior DES exposure); few were told of its experimental status and carcinogenicity; few were informed that debilitating side effects (mainly nausea) were common, with the result that many women failed to complete the full regimen of pills; and medical follow-up to verify the treatment's success was apparently rare (Weiss, 1973). Weiss released these results at a press conference in December 1972, and they were the subject of an ABC News documentary.

DES activists also challenged the actual—as opposed to theoretical— effectiveness of the morning-after pill. At the 1975 congressional hearings, Cowan debunked the much-heralded Kuchera study purporting to show 100 percent efficacy, pointing out major methodological problems, such as lack of a control group and sloppy follow-up (Kuchera, 1971:562).[5] (Kuchera later admitted that some pregnancies did occur among subjects excluded from the study [1973:1038; 1974]). And a study of the routine prescription of DES to rape victims in an Atlanta municipal hospital showed that the failure rate in that setting was at least 6 percent, and that many of the women who received DES were not even at risk of pregnancy (Jones, 1978).

By investigating actual settings, DES activists found risks that were not revealed in research situations. To ignore such problems, they argued, could be not only misleading but also dangerous. For example, the assumption that DES was 100 percent effective and that patients would always complete the full regimen might lead doctors to pay less attention to informing patients of the dangers of DES and to verifying the treatment's success—thereby increasing the chance that some women might unwittingly give birth to DES-exposed babies.

Another risk that health activists helped publicize was the higher rate of breast cancer among DES mothers. In 1977, the Health Research Group obtained, through the Freedom of Information Act, a copy of preliminary data from a study led by Arthur Herbst, the physician who had first discovered the DES-cancer link. According to Herbst, the data did "not show increased risk of breast cancer among DES-exposed women in comparison to those unexposed" (1978).[6] Dr. Sidney Wolfe, the Health Research Group's director, thought otherwise, claiming the data showed "a substantial increase in breast cancer and other hormone-related cancer" among the DES mothers (1978). They disagreed not about the incidence *level* of breast cancer, which was clearly higher for the DES-exposed women than for the unexposed (4.6 percent vs. 3.1 percent, respectively), but about whether this difference was statistically *significant*. Wolfe argued that it was, in that—in light of animal studies linking DES to breast cancer and of suggestive evidence in humans—"significance" should be judged by a looser standard. Choosing the proper standard is a highly technical and ultimately subjective matter about which statisticians often disagree. But Wolfe found strong support for his position from Dr. Adrian Gross of the FDA's Bureau of Drugs, who called the Herbst team's conclusion "nothing short of absolute nonsense" (Wolfe, 1978).[7]

Wolfe reported his findings to HEW Secretary Califano in a letter he released to the press, and presented them at the January 1978 meeting of the FDA's Fertility Drugs and Maternal Health Advisory Committee. After much wrangling, this committee finally agreed that the data did provide "evidence for concern," and urged the FDA to inform physicians and the public of the findings.

The data caused quite a stir. Lobbying by DES activists had put mounting pressure on the government to "do something" about DES, and when the breast cancer controversy broke, Secretary Califano appointed a national task force to study all aspects of DES exposure and advise HEW. Different attitudes toward risks again emerged between many of the experts on the task force and the four "public" members (appointed as consultants at the insistence of consumers' and women's groups). For example, despite the lack of conclusive scientific evidence and opposition from some of the medical experts, the public members played a key role in convincing the task force to recommend "that oral contraceptives and other estrogens should be avoided" by DES-exposed women (Adess, 1978).

A similar split developed between experts and nonexperts over the nature and magnitude of potential risks involved in recombinant DNA research. Scientists tended to focus on specific biological hazards of the research and so devised elaborate laboratory "containment procedures" for protection and a series of "risk assessment" experiments to clarify the toxicity and survival capacity of particular organisms.[8] What worried many nonscientists, on the other hand, were social, ethical, and ecological risks which might not be manifest immediately and which most laboratory experiments would never address. These ranged from the moral dilemmas of human genetic engineering to the danger of disturbing the "infinitely complex and delicate balance among living things" (Coalition for Responsible Genetic Research, undated); and, with heavy commercial involvement, from the unknown hazards of mass production to the implications of corporate control for product development and academic science. A key issue underlying such concerns was the unique power of recombinant DNA methods to create new life forms with potentially irreversible consequences. As Erwin Chargaff, a prominent biochemist and outspoken critic put it: "You can stop splitting the atom; you can stop visiting the moon; you can stop using aerosols; you may even decide not to kill entire populations by the use of a few bombs. But you cannot recall a new form of life" (1976:938).

Given these stakes and the admitted scientific uncertainties, many groups representing public interests argued for caution. In 1977 congressional hearings on proposed federal regulatory legislation, several environmental and labor groups called for an immediate moratorium on the research pending further investigation. Representing the Oil, Chemical, and Atomic Workers Union (OCAW), Anthony Mazzochi charged that to continue the research would allow "industry and academic institutions to play roulette with the lives of this particular generation and those of generations to come" (1977a:467). A few well-known intellectuals, such as anthropologist Margaret Mead, also pleaded for restraint while the uncertainties were being explored.[9]

Most of the research community took a very different position. Dismayed by the degree of public concern and criticism, many scientists found the results of early risk assessment experiments reassuring. Thus began an effort to convince the public that the risks—as scientists defined them—

were far less than originally feared. By 1977, leading investigators were backpedaling hard. Testifying in congressional hearings, James Watson, a Nobel Laureate biologist, compared the risks of recombinant DNA research to those of "being licked by a dog." And he stated flatly: "Science is good for society" (Wade, 1978:33). Others questioned the intelligence and training of anyone concerned about risks. The president of the American Society of Microbiology called them "uninformed laymen and scientists who . . . have little understanding of the mechanisms of spread of infectious agents" (Halvorson, 1977:140). More colorfully, Watson called them "kooks, shits and incompetents" (Watson, 1977:26). Such attacks, in addition to more subtle forms of censure, took a heavy toll on many scientist-critics (Wade, 1977b).

Most scientists testifying against regulation spoke little of the broader risks that concerned many public groups, and when they did it was mainly to discount them. For example, Dr. Oliver Smithies, a noted molecular geneticist, predicted in the 1977 hearings that human genetic engineering was scientifically remote. (Three years later, its beginnings were well underway.) "But," Smithies added with supreme confidence, "even if the chances were good, I would not be concerned. Why should rational individuals want to create monsters? They would not" (1977:248).

What accounts for these divergent views of risk? First, as in the case of DES, the scope of concerns varied markedly, with experts focusing primarily on technical and scientific matters. The context within which risks were interpreted was also different, with nonexperts tending to judge risks on the basis of actual experiences. OCAW's Mazzochi, for example, viewed the containment of recombinant DNA organisms against a long history of occupational hazards, and concluded: "We know of no situation where any toxic substance has been successfully contained in any industrial establishment. . . . What is in will out" (1977a).

Experts and nonexperts also seemed to have different attitudes toward uncertainty. To many nonexperts, unknown risks justified considerable caution. This response is consistent with psychological research which has shown that most people prefer to avoid present or future harms than to take risks in the hope of benefits (Tversky and Kahneman, 1981). Experts, in contrast, tended to be more optimistic about benefits and less concerned about unknown risks. Greater optimism among experts has also been observed in other studies, and has been attributed to overconfidence in current scientific knowledge, inadequate appreciation of the overall function of complex systems, and insensitivity to human errors (Slovic et al., 1980).

In the recombinant DNA controversy, human fallibility was one of the key points stressed by those who advocated caution. As Ethan Signer, a prominent critic, warned:

> Just what are the dangers? We know so much about genes that we forget how much more we don't know. These are totally new hybrids, that is exactly why they are interesting. . . . We will slowly move from high level containment to low level containment to large scale production to buying the hybrids at the local drugstore. At each stage we will get a little cockier, a little surer we know all the possibilities. . . . And then one day we will learn that the hybrid can also do something we hadn't thought to look for. [1977a:79]

Finally, divergent views of risks may stem from underlying value differences. Perceptions of risks probably reflect more than merely the perceived likelihood of adverse events. They may also incorporate the *values* people attach to these events. If so, public attitudes toward risks do not express "irrational" perceptions of past experience, so much as they reveal hopes and preferences for the future.

Soft Issues and Hard Choices: Broadening and Humanizing Biomedical Policy

Costs, risks, and benefits are key concepts in today's "rational" policy discussions. But not all issues fit neatly into this framework. How should the emotional anguish of a DES mother be translated into dollar costs? How should one balance possible social and ethical risks by recombinant DNA research against its predicted economic benefits? Answers to such questions are fraught with uncertainty and depend on widely varying personal and social values. They are, inevitably, "soft." Yet in many ways, these choices are the most crucial of all, for they reflect basic notions of justice and humanity. Calling attention to these choices—the "soft" sides of policy decisions—has been another important function of public participation.

For example, at congressional hearings in 1975, two DES mothers and a DES daughter recounted their personal tragedies and called for a total ban on DES. Their testimony was dramatic and poignant; it reached millions of Americans on national news. Consumer representatives on the 1978 task force, including DES mothers and daughters, likewise drew attention to the emotional and psychological problems of the DES-exposed, as well as to practical issues such as contraceptive usage, fertility, and effects on the next generation. According to one physician member of the task force, the presence of individuals who had been personally affected helped to remind the group that it was "discussing a *human*, not an academic problem" (Fishbane, 1979). Although there are no easy ways to factor the emotional dimensions of problems into decisions, simply making them visible—and evocative—helps counteract the tendency for abstract policy discussions to "anesthetize moral feelings" (Tribe, 1972).

Wider involvement of professionals in humanistic or ethically oriented disciplines also tends to promote awareness of these "soft" issues. In the artificial heart program it was not until the broadly based Artificial Heart Assessment Panel issued its report in 1973 that underlying moral and social problems received serious consideration. The panel stressed the need for ongoing public monitoring of the program, and raised ethical concerns about human experimentation, informed consent, criteria for patient selection, and quality of life for recipients. Recalling the bitter experience of rationing life-and-death medical care during the early days of kidney dialysis, the panel urged that access to the artificial heart be based on medical criteria alone, excluding any consideration of patients' "social worth" or ability to pay.

Social and ethical issues have been prominent in the controversy over recombinant DNA research, due largely to the efforts of religious groups, public interest organizations, and a few outspoken scientists. Many warned of the consequences of scientists "playing God" and the perils of using genetic engineering methods on humans. Others foresaw a whole new set of moral dilemmas for which society was unprepared—choices which would ultimately affect "our understanding of ourselves and of our relation to nature" (Bishops Committee, 1977:8).[10] Organized religion has become increasingly involved. The National Council of Churches, representing the major Protestant denominations, has sponsored meetings and symposia and appointed a special panel to review the emerging theological, ethical, and policy implications of the new technology. In 1980, after the Supreme Court's decision allowing patents on new life forms, the general secretaries of Protestant, Jewish, and Catholic national organizations called for the government to launch a thorough investigation of the issues raised by genetic engineering and to "provide a way for representatives of a broad spectrum of our society to consider these matters and advise the government on its necessary role" (General Secretaries, 1980). Such concerns have generally not been allayed by changing scientific attitudes toward risks. Indeed, some have been intensified by the technique's rapid proliferation.

To some observers, the most fundamental ethical issue was how the new technology would be used. Critics argued that jazzy "genetic fixes," which themselves posed potential risks, should not be used as "band-aid" solutions to problems whose roots were economic and political. Thus, the potential uses of recombinant DNA technology raised larger questions about alternative forms of social change. Ethan Signer pointed to the past failures of technology in solving problems due to the structure of society:

> Look at the last technological miracle, the Green Revolution. It hasn't relieved hunger in Asia, it's only made the rich richer and the poor even poorer. The problem is political, not technological, and it's going to be with us until there's a political solution. People are hungry, but it's not for lack of recombinant DNA research. [1977b:232]

The National Conference of Catholic Bishops was more circumspect, but also implied that other forms of progress might sometimes be preferable to the new genetic techniques.[11]

Such arguments took the recombinant DNA debate out of the narrow framework of health and safety and placed it in the broader context of appropriate technology. Not only might the new recombinant techniques be used inappropriately—warned groups such as Science for the People—but they also might be positively harmful if substituted for preventive or nontechnological measures: a handy "bug" that can clean up oil spills would do little to promote more stringent efforts at prevention, while ready supplies of insulin and other genetically engineered drugs might discourage the use of nonpharmaceutical methods of prevention and cure.[12] Such fears were not unwarranted. This exact bias toward chemical technology over natural prevention was evident in an article by Rudman and colleagues in the *New England Journal of Medicine*, reporting the successful treatment of short children using genetically produced human growth hormone. An accompanying editorial noted that although "commercial DNA technologists will applaud" these findings, the study had virtually ignored the role of nutrition—the major influence on growth—as either cause or possible cure (Crawford, 1981).

The controversy over recombinant DNA research also raised basic questions about the nature of contemporary science and medicine. Critics claimed that a more "popular" approach to scientific investigation, one involving lay people directly, might yield more socially useful knowledge.

Although (or perhaps because) this vision remained rather abstract, it enjoyed passing popularity, even among the scientific community.[13] Far more contentious was the question of whether some knowledge might ultimately be too dangerous to pursue. This was a troubling reminder of the role of American research in developing the atomic bomb, and a number of scientists held that perhaps certain types of knowledge should *not* be sought.[14] But this argument shook the very foundations of the scientific establishment and it reacted accordingly: the rallying cry was freedom of scientific inquiry, and stories of Galileo and Lysenko were resurrected.

The concerns of religious organizations, public interest groups, and dissident scientists have expanded the boundaries of policy discussions, amplified the human and spiritual side of policy problems and, by focusing on "the big picture," have linked technical issues to the larger social, political, and economic context. Yet, policymakers frequently ignored the issues and options raised, especially those which conflicted with prevailing professional and economic interests. And outsiders were often helpless to prevent this. Thus, not surprisingly, changing the *process* of decision making was another recurrent goal of public groups in their efforts to affect policy.

Democratizing Decisions

Most of these efforts were directed toward making decision making more open, accountable, and democratic. On one level, such changes may be viewed as purely procedural. They offered public groups the hope of greater access to policy decisions and were typically justified in terms of public rights. Yet these proposals also had important substantive implications: some "procedural" changes would virtually guarantee different outcomes. Moreover, many choices simply could not be evaluated in terms of results; the issues involved were so complex, uncertain, and disputed that the only measure of confidence possible was a sound decision process. A persuasive proponent of this view has been U.S. Appeals Court Judge David Bazelon, drawing on extensive experience with federal regulatory decisions. Bazelon advocates public scrutiny, discussion, and criticism to encourage the fullest possible consideration of relevant data and viewpoints, which in his view constitutes the essential basis for good decisions (1979). On this more substantive level, then, open and democratic policymaking could also be justified in terms of *improved decisions*.

In the four cases, proposed changes were most often based on an appeal to public rights. For example, the Artificial Heart Assessment Panel, citing the notion of "societal informed consent," maintained that at a minimum: (1) the public has a right to reject a biomedical innovation if it conflicts with important social values; (2) researchers have an obligation to disclose the risks involved in any development; and (3) it is desirable for society to evaluate new technologies carefully before they are put into use. To implement these goals, the panel recommended the creation of "permanent, broadly interdisciplinary, and representative groups of public members" that would monitor and help direct the program (Adess, 1973:2, 197).[15]

In the debate over recombinant DNA research, support for the public's right to participate in policymaking came from a wide range of sources. To some, it was the paramount issue, transcending concerns about risks and benefits. As David Clem, a member of the Cambridge City Council, stated at a 1977 Senate hearing: "The real issue before us is not recombinant DNA research. The basic issue is the right of the public to know and the right of the public to decide" (p. 173).

This right was taken quite literally in Cambridge and in the handful of other towns and states which also passed ordinances regulating the research.[16] And, for a time, it had strong support in Congress, most notably from Senator Edward Kennedy. Kennedy told a 1977 Senate hearing: "The assessment of risk and the judgment of how to balance risk against benefit of recombinant DNA research are responsibilities that clearly rest in the public domain. And it follows that these issues must be decided through public processes" (p. 2). The *New York Times* (1977) declared bluntly: "Regulation is too important to be left to the scientists."

Various forms of national regulatory legislation were submitted to Congress during the winter and spring of 1977, but the bill proposed by Kennedy included the most far-reaching role for the public: a freestanding commission including a majority of nonscientists was to make regulatory decisions and also to consider broader, long-term policy implications. The public would thus participate in the crucial step of identifying issues to be decided as well as in the decisions themselves.

In the political arena, however, the struggle over public rights quickly became a struggle over power. The scientific community was watching all of these developments with growing alarm. The prospect of national legislation was distasteful, but even more threatening was the spectre of Cambridge and the possibility of a hodgepodge of regulations varying from one town to the next. To head off such a possibility, scientists organized a lobbying effort in Washington to represent a broad coalition of scientific organizations and professional societies. After consulting with professional lobbyists for advice on strategy and tactics, coalition leaders agreed on nine target principles.[17] High among these was preventing local communities from setting their own research standards—a goal that was also strongly endorsed by the burgeoning biotechnology industry.[18] In explaining the involvement of the once-pristine professional societies in the dirty world of politics, the president of the American Society of Microbiology cited the need for "scientific expertise" in evaluating the issues (Halvorson, 1977a:141). Critics charged it was merely a self-serving attempt to protect professional autonomy.

Whatever the motives, the science lobby had a powerful impact on Congress. Legislators were deeply disturbed by the ominous warnings they heard from scientists forecasting the loss of valuable health, medical, and economic benefits. In vain, public interest groups defended the need for legislation, arguing that local initiative was vital in promoting wider understanding and acceptance of the new technology, and that the Cambridge experience had shown that public decision making could be intelligent and responsible. Support for federal legislation of any sort eroded rapidly under the influence of the science lobby combined with the impact of new data suggesting fewer research risks. Finally, even Kennedy withdrew his support for legislation, citing scientists' fears of overly restrictive regulation (Cohen, 1977; Culliton, 1978).

With legislation doomed, public interest groups redirected their energies toward the NIH guidelines governing the research, then undergoing major revision. Concerns about democratic decision making again figured prominently. Environmentalists, labor representatives, and dissident scientists all criticized the draft revisions on numerous counts, including their vague provisions for public participation. Several critics also reiterated their by-then-familiar objection to the potential conflict of interest in having NIH, the major *sponsor* of the research, draft guidelines intended to *regulate* the research. The final revisions, issued after Christmas 1978, responded to many of these concerns. Although containment levels were lowered, the new guidelines went farther than any previous draft in providing for more accountable policymaking. Most notably, they mandated broader representation in both federal and local policymaking, requiring 20 percent of the NIH's Recombinant DNA Advisory Committee (RAC) members to have legal, social, environmental, or occupational health backgrounds, and 20 percent of each local institution's biosafety committee to be drawn from outside the institution. And to the surprise of some, a few known critics were also appointed to the RAC.

This was a gratifying—if ultimately somewhat hollow—victory for public interest advocates, who had long complained about RAC's narrow composition. For example, MIT Professor Jonathan King, a vocal critic of the research, had charged back in 1975 that the committee was designed to "protect geneticists, not the public," and that having the committee chaired by recombinant DNA scientist David Hogness was akin to "having the chairman of General Motors write the specifications for safety belts" (Wade, 1975:769). Faced with such criticism, RAC added a few nonscientists in 1976, but with little enthusiasm. (The committee's chairperson wrote candidly to NIH: "Like many other present members of the committee, I'm not sure [a nonscientist] could contribute to the deliberations, but I am sure that we need one for the purpose of being able to say we have one when there are complaints" (Wade, 1977b:89). And, indeed, nonscientists remained in the minority on RAC, even after 1978, and had little if any impact on key policy decisions: containment levels were steadily lowered and public accountability remained largely symbolic. Although community involvement in local biosafety committees has likewise had no dramatic effect on policy trends, it does suggest that such participation is both feasible and generally constructive. The presence of nonscientists seems to have encouraged broader discussion and more critical scrutiny of research proposals (Dutton and Hochheimer, 1982). According to one committee chairman, "the public members proceeded to sensitize the entire committee to issues that they would otherwise not have considered" (Porter, 1981).

Sometimes demands couched in terms of public rights converged with arguments based on better results. One example was the involvement of laboratory workers in safety decisions. Critics argued that workers had a special right to participate in safety decisions because they would suffer greatest harm if health hazards developed; and, furthermore, that their familiarity with day-to-day safety practices would improve the final decisions.[19] Broader public involvement was also defended on similar grounds. To strike the proper balance between costs and benefits, public interest advocates contended, decision making should involve both those potentially at greatest risk (the larger public and laboratory workers) as well as those likely to receive the most direct benefits (researchers and corporate officials).[20]

That these various demands, which clearly implied a shift in existing patterns of authority, provoked a struggle for power was not in itself surprising. Yet, the intensity of this struggle led some observers to fear a fundamental clash between expertise and democracy. As a widely cited article appearing in the *Atlantic Monthly* concluded, "The ultimate question is not whether bacteria can be contained in special laboratories, but whether scientists can be contained in an ordinary society" (Bennet and Gurin, 1977:67). Tension between expertise and democracy was also evident in the other cases in attempts to suppress dissent. For instance, after Ford administration officials refused to debate Sydney Wolfe about the swine flu immunization program, Wolfe protested to the Secretary of HEW: "You want to stifle public debate on these serious problems? . . . If HEW can't live with such debate, perhaps its leaders and Mr. Ford should consider whether they are comfortable living in a democratic society" (Wolfe letter, 1976). It is perhaps peculiarly American to place such trust in "due process" and democratic decision making. But with profound disagreement about the "right" decisions for complex issues of science and technology, a fair and open process may be the only way to arrive at results viewed as sound and socially acceptable.

The Impact of Public Efforts

Although public involvement has often led to more discussion and a broader view of issues and options, it has had less effect on policy outcomes than proponents would have liked. Yet the impact should not be underestimated. The swine flu program went forward, but adverse publicity generated by public interest critics and dissident experts undoubtedly lowered immunization rates. Research on the artificial heart continues, surgical heroics are still glamorized in the popular press, and there is no mechanism for public involvement in the program's direction. Yet, federal funding for research on the nuclear-powered heart was discontinued after strong opposition from the largely nonmedical Artificial Heart Assessment Panel of 1973.

In the case of recombinant DNA research, although no federal regulatory legislation was ever passed and commercial applications of the research have mushroomed, a number of cities and towns have passed local ordinances to regulate the growing commercial market. And, while broader representation in federal policymaking has not appreciably altered previous policy trends, community participation in local biosafety committees has been shown to be feasible and generally effective.

For DES, the picture is likewise mixed. The FDA has done little to curb the use of DES or other estrogens as a morning-after pill, and most DES victims receive no compensation for their injuries or expenses. On the other hand, activities at the state and local levels have done a great deal to inform and help DES victims. Most of the credit for these activities belongs to an organization called DES Action. The accomplishments of this organization, almost entirely the product of local consumer-based efforts, are worth recounting briefly.

The roots of DES Action go back to 1974, when several women in Berkeley, California—dismayed at the continuing lack of information and resources for DES victims—decided something had to be done (Bryant, 1979). They formed a group and set about developing an informational pamphlet. This pamphlet circulated widely through informal networks, and as the information spread, so did concern. By 1978, at least five other DES groups had formed around the country, and they decided to set up a national network. They agreed on a common name, DES Action, and common objectives. Their motto: "Don't Mourn, Organize!!" (*DES Action Voice*, 1979).[21]

This motto could hardly have been more apt. As of summer 1983, there were thirty-seven DES Action groups around the country and three abroad. Their activities have been manifold, ranging from public and professional education to the development of technical resources such as audiovisual materials and physician referral lists. Two national DES newsletters now provide information on the latest medical, legal, and legislative developments (*DES Action Voice*; *DES National Quarterly*). And, due to lobbying by DES groups, more than fourteen states have considered or passed bills or resolutions dealing with DES, and three (New York, California, Illinois) have also appropriated funds (*DES Action Voice*, 1981). The New York legislation has been particularly successful, setting up special DES-screening centers around the state and a voluntary DES registry for research and follow-up. An intensive statewide media campaign succeeded in almost doubling public awareness of DES (Glebatis and Janerich, 1981).

DES advocates have been active nationally as well, testifying at various congressional hearings. In 1978, lobbying by Fran Fishbane, then president of DES Action National, was instrumental in creating the HEW Task Force on DES. DES Action may also deserve at least indirect credit for the climate of opinion that led to precedent-setting judicial decisions responding to the special needs of DES victims. A 1979 Massachusetts decision allowed class-action suits by DES daughters (*Payton v. Abbott Labs*, 1979), and in 1980 the California Supreme Court removed a major roadblock to lawsuits by allowing DES daughters to sue the major manufacturers of DES without having to identify the particular brand alleged to have caused the injury (*Sindell* v. *Abbott Labs*, 1980). Not surprisingly, the pharmaceutical and insurance industries strongly opposed this decision and, with backing from the business and medical communities, introduced state legislation to overturn it. The bill was defeated, but only by a narrow margin. Another industry-backed bill was introduced in 1981 and again defeated. Press coverage gave credit for this defeat to "DES victims," citing DES Action's opposition in particular (*San Francisco Chronicle*, 1980, 1982).

A crucial factor in the success of DES Action has been the intense commitment of women personally affected by DES. The risks of DES exposure are frightening and potentially tragic. Ties to the women's health movement, in turn, have helped transform these personal fears into political action. Women's health activists—all too familiar with being marginal to mainstream medicine, financially threatening to the drug industry, and low priority for the federal government—have schooled DES advocates in the tactics of self-help through collective action, sharing resources, and contacts. DES Action has also benefited greatly from the involvement of concerned physicians.[22] But it is ties to the local community which are the greatest source of DES Action's effectiveness. This community base has kept the organization accountable while allowing it to flourish entirely outside any formal structure of government, academia, or industry. With this base, DES Action has shown growing numbers of women how to take social as well as personal control of their medical destinies.

Keys to Public Involvement and Influence

Public interventions have had varying degrees of impact on policy, even in the DES and recombinant DNA cases. From these experiences, we can identify certain factors which tended to promote broader and more effective involvement.

Both DES and recombinant DNA research posed real or potential health risks which first sparked public concern and activity. As these issues came to reflect public rather than scientific priorities, the focus on risks typically expanded to encompass a wider spectrum of concerns: the long-run social, ethical, and political implications of recombinant DNA research, the actual problems of the morning-after pill, and various medical, emotional, and financial needs of those exposed to DES.

Along with this natural broadening of focus, interested groups also made a deliberate attempt to relate specific concerns to larger issues in order to create working coalitions. Recombinant DNA was linked with environmental and occupational health problems, and DES was related to women's health issues. Although some new ties were temporarily forged, most organizations retained a predominantly single-issue focus.

Adequate access to technical resources and expertise was critical in allowing nonexperts to take part in disputes that were often highly technical. After scientists and medical experts had first called attention to risks, only a few "dissident" experts were willing (sometimes at considerable personal sacrifice) to work with lay groups as the controversies evolved.[23] Women's groups working on DES allied with sympathetic physicians; and public-interest advocates in the recombinant DNA debate depended heavily on a small number of scientist-critics. This expertise was crucial in interpreting technical developments and it lent credibility to the arguments of lay groups.

Also important were the organized constituencies and political contacts of the public groups active in the DES and recombinant DNA issues. Concerned scientists (some associated with Science for the People), activists in the women's health movement, and environmental, labor, and consumer groups had all dealt with political controversies before, and they made use of the skills and networks they had developed. Their constituencies helped supply added political pressure.

Barriers and Boundaries

A number of significant barriers to public participation are also apparent from these case studies. Most notably, in government decision making, formal opportunities for outside involvement were limited and often severely constrained. Public representatives were usually a small minority, often could not vote, and typically had the fewest financial and technical resources.[24] Local involvement was more feasible, but less likely to influence national policy.

Much formal participation thus turned out to be largely symbolic, allowing token contributions without any real control over decisions. The nonscientists and critics added to the Recombinant DNA Advisory Committee in 1978 comprised a small fraction of the total membership, and could neither slow the steady dismantling of the guidelines nor convince the committee to consider ethical issues or questions about the technology's commercial exploitation. Yet, while these members privately questioned their own effectiveness on the committee, their presence created the public image of balanced, broadly based policymaking. By silencing complaints about exclusion of dissent in this way, symbolic participation may, in fact, serve to legitimize the status quo.[25]

There were also formidable obstacles to informal public intervention. It was difficult for outsiders, especially those with controversial views, to penetrate the massive and complex policymaking bureaucracy. Even the boldest and most persistent efforts by DES and recombinant DNA activists had relatively little impact on national decisions. In turn, bureaucratic and ideological obstacles were compounded by apathy and cynicism in a citizenry accustomed to powerlessness, especially vis-à-vis science and technology. If "let the experts decide" was no longer the comfortable solution it once seemed, ready alternatives were for the most part not apparent.

Another barrier was the incomplete and uncertain data available, particularly on the "soft" issues that were often of greatest public concern—the human, social, and ethical aspects of policy decisions. Because such issues were also difficult to integrate with the standard, more quantitative criteria, a common (if hardly optimal) solution was simply to exclude them altogether from official policy deliberations.[26] Furthermore, the diffuse and uncertain character of issues meant that, like many health matters, they were not high priority for most people—until problems arose. DES did not lack for a mobilized public once the cancer link was discovered, but by then much of the damage was done. On the other hand, public concerns about the risks of recombinant DNA (as with nuclear power and weaponry) suggest an increasing effort to *prevent* future tragedies rather than merely patch up their consequences. But preventive efforts still do not match the catalyzing effects of a known disaster.

Public interventions that were effective, on the other hand, invariably produced a powerful backlash from established interests. In California, medical and industry groups twice tried to pass legislation to overturn the court decision facilitating DES suits. Similarly, once awakened to the prospect of stricter federal regulation of recombinant DNA research, scientists mounted a lobbying effort which succeeded in derailing proposed national legislation. There has also been a backlash against individual "dissident" scientists working with public groups. Many were ostracized by the scientific establishment, and the more faint-hearted lapsed into "monklike silence" fearing for their careers (*Time*, 1977).

Finally, developments in the private sector, a major source of biomedical innovation, were essentially off limits to public groups. The Artificial Heart Assessment Panel could recommend the discontinuation of federal support of research on the nuclear-powered artificial heart, but was powerless to stop corporate research from continuing. Private industry is well represented on government advisory committees, and has considerable direct influence on government decisions. Corporations also have a great deal of indirect influence, spending 50 to 100 times as much as consumer groups lobbying federal agencies in 1977 (U.S. Senate, 1977).[27] Promised commercial benefits of biotechnology clearly accelerated the push for rapid and unfettered development of recombinant DNA research; pharmaceutical and bioengineering firms joined with scientists in defeating federal regulation in 1978, and have lobbied heavily against state regulation. These events serve to demarcate definite boundaries as to what citizen groups can accomplish within the present social context.

Arguments For and Against Public Participation

In the case studies, the most common justification for public participation was the right of citizens in a democracy to have a voice in major social issues. Biomedical policy has become just such an issue, in that many developments now reap significant benefits *and* risks for the general public and the research often entails large expenditures of public funds.

There are major arguments against public participation. Some have questioned whether it is possible to represent public interests effectively in what has been called an "imbalanced political market" (Marmor and Marone, 1980). With constituencies typically diffuse, unorganized, resource poor, and relatively inexperienced, and with no easy way to assure that participating individuals are accountable to these constituencies, citizen organizations are at a substantial disadvantage compared to well-endowed corporate and professional groups with a direct stake in the issue. Special programs and resources to correct this imbalance are necessary to prevent dominance by special interests. A related problem is participation's inherent bias against the disadvantaged. Global issues such as biomedical policy simply do not have the same priority for people worried about the next paycheck as they do for the more affluent. Again, without specific measures to counteract this bias, opportunities for direct involvement are likely to be of least benefit to those with the greatest health needs.

Opponents of citizen participation have also argued that yet another layer of bureaucracy will paralyze an already tortuous policymaking process. Wider involvement is not only more cumbersome administratively but, more significantly, it introduces new views and priorities that are bound to conflict as previously excluded groups fight for their share of the shrinking biomedical pie. Yet, in a democracy, conflict over divergent priorities is presumably preferable to a consensus based on repression of interests and exclusion of dissent—even if it does slow things down.

However, the most common argument against public participation is more basic: it is that science and medicine are so highly specialized that only experts are qualified to make competent judgments. Many scientists believe this very deeply, and view public intervention as a harmful intrusion of inexpert and alarmist ideas. For instance, Philip Handler (1980), former president of the National Academy of Sciences, has argued that "most members of the public usually don't know enough about any given complicated technical matter to make meaningful informal judgments. And that includes scientists and engineers who work in unrelated areas." In his view, such judgments should be left to "knowledgeable wise men" serving as trusted representatives of the public; citizens should assess the options determined by established government institutions and communicate their opinions to elected decision makers.

As this argument implies, the debate over how science should be governed is closely related to the larger question of how society should be governed. At the heart of this question is the role of citizens in a democracy. According to the so-called classical theory of "participatory democracy," often identified with such philosophers as Mill and Rousseau, direct citizen involvement in political decisions is critical in assuring wise and legitimate decisions and, equally important, in allowing for the continuous education of citizens about important issues and for the sustenance of their sense of political "efficacy." Indeed, this theory holds that the human development which results from the participatory process is essential for the survival of democracy. By contrast, many contemporary political theorists contend that democracy is quite compatible with a much more limited role for citizens, who should be confined essentially to selecting and rejecting leaders through the vote. In their view, leaders are the critical element of the system and the competition for leadership by elites is the defining characteristic of democracy.[28]

This contemporary view of democracy was widely embraced after World War II by political theorists seeking to explain and justify declining trends in voter participation. Schumpeter (1943), Huntington (1975), and others argued that direct participation in government was neither feasible nor desirable in the modern age—that inactivity on the part of a majority increases political stability. "The effective operation of a democratic political system," Huntington wrote, "usually requires some measure of apathy and noninvolvement on the part of some individuals and groups." Others noted that the noninvolvement of lower socioeconomic groups, believed to have "authoritarian" personality traits, was especially functional in maintaining stability (Dahl, 1970).

Recent examples of public involvement in science policy have extended this larger debate into a new arena. But many of the issues and problems are the same, despite the esoteric nature of modern research; the parallels help put current arguments in perspective. For example, since the late 1700s, each successive extension of voting rights—first to all white males and eventually to women, blacks, and youths—was opposed on virtually the same grounds as many now oppose public involvement in science: that the disenfranchised group was too ignorant, disinterested, and unreliable to be allowed to participate; and that the group's participation would be too costly or disruptive to the system's efficiency and stability (Rosenbaum, 1978). Yet today, universal suffrage is essentially unquestioned as a political right, even though never fully realized in political practice.

Evidence from the four cases likewise casts doubt on dire predictions about the consequences of broader public participation in science policy. Many citizens and public groups clearly wanted more of a voice in biomedical issues and were capable of making useful and responsible contributions. And, as participatory theory would suggest, when there was greater involvement, it usually resulted in more comprehensive consideration of issues, greater attention to potential risks and possible alternatives, and a more realistic assessment of likely benefits. Although outsiders were often critical of existing policy, in general they were not trying to block progress but rather to force decision makers to incorporate a wider range of social values and priorities in policy choices. Nor do other experiences with lay involvement in policymaking support the view that the public is antiscience and wants to stop scientific and technological progress. Polls show that although most people recognize the harmful effects of science and technology, they nevertheless view science as instrumental in achieving important social goals (Nelkin, 1980). Moreover, freedom of inquiry has never been absolute, but has been balanced against a variety of other considerations.

But, the skeptic asks, what about the dangerous and irresponsible passions of particular groups? Even if the majority of the public is trustworthy, should decisions about medical science be vulnerable to those with views that many consider extreme or wrong-headed? (Favorite examples cited here include fluoridation, saccharin, creationism, and the Moral Majority.) To the advocate of public participation, there is no better response than Thomas Jefferson's reply to similar concerns:

> I know of no safe depository of the ultimate powers of this society but the people themselves; and if we think them not enlightened enough to exercise their control with a wholesome discretion, the remedy is not to take it from them, but to inform their discretion. [Thomas Jefferson, Letter to William Charles Jarvis, 28 September 1820]

With the "ultimate power" that science now has in society, this response is as valid today as it was in Jefferson's time.

Any significant effort to encourage citizen involvement in biomedical policy will certainly lead to new questions and problems; and it will clearly involve added time and expense. But with confidence faltering in science along with other major institutions, these costs may be a small price to pay if they help to build a more secure and responsive relationship between science and society.[29]

Notes

1 The panel's final report states, "We were not asked to consider specifically the question of whether a totally implantable artificial heart should be developed or whether there is a reasonable likelihood that it will be" (Artificial Heart Assessment Panel Report, 1973:15, hereafter "Assessment Panel Report").

2 In 1962, the *Consumer Bulletin* demanded that "DES should not be permitted in treatment of animals, in their feed or by implantation" (p. 10). In 1971, the National Resources Defense Council sued both the USDA and the FDA to try to force a ban on DES as a feed additive. DES was banned in 1972, but the ban was phased in over a six-month period and was overturned two years later. A group called DOOM (Drugs Out of Meat) opposed the six-month delay and collected 25,000 signatures in support of an immediate total ban. The group demanded that "FDA immediately ban all forms of diethylstilbestrol, liquid, powder, implant, etc. from being used in livestock meant for our dinner tables" and concluded "we are fed up with this complacency in the face of increased cancer deaths" (reprinted in *Regulation of Diethylstilbestrol*, see U.S. House, Committee on Government Operations, 1972:438–39).

3 Some critics have argued for a total ban on the use of DES as a morning-after pill, while others have argued for proper experimental safeguards, with use restricted to physicians who have filed an Investigational New Drug Application with the FDA and who will test it in well-designed studies with complete disclosure of risks and proper informed consent (FDA Ob-Gyn Advisory Committee meeting, 1973). Although the use of DES as a morning-after pill has been most controversial, similar concerns have been raised for other estrogens used for the same purpose. As early as 1975, Dr. Peter Greenwald of the

New York State Cancer Control Bureau warned, "some people have shifted to other estrogens, a drug called Premarin, mainly because it is not as controversial, but we do not have any idea it does not have the same risk. It just is not studied" (U.S. Senate, 1975:15). After summarizing evidence on the relation between estrogens and cancer, Sydney Wolfe told the FDA Ob-Gyn Advisory Committee: "The animal evidence doesn't let one pick and choose among estrogens . . . we do not know of any estrogen, natural or synthetic, that is safe and that protects someone from the risk of cancer. They all need to be assumed to be both animal and human carcinogens" (FDA Ob-Gyn Advisory Committee, 1978:19, 28–29).

4 At Senate hearings in 1975, Nancy Belden, of the San Francisco Coalition for the Medical Rights of Women, testified: "We know that it is widely used in doctors' offices, on college campuses and elsewhere in situations where the term 'emergency' may be very liberally interpreted" (U.S. Senate, 1975:56). High rates of use continued at least through 1975. At the same hearing, Dr. Peter Greenwald of the New York State Cancer Control Bureau reported: "In 1973 and again in 1974 we surveyed 45 large hospitals, college health services and planned parenthood organizations in New York State. . . . Two-thirds of the responding institutions used DES as a morning-after contraceptive" (U.S. Senate, 1975:14).

5 Study cited is by Lucile Kuchera (1971:562). Cowan testified: "It may surprise the Subcommittee to learn that there has not been one scientifically controlled efficacy study of the morning-after pill. Dr. Kuchera's study of more than 1,000 college students at the University of Michigan was retrospective. There was no control group. I have interviewed many of these students. They were not told they were part of an experimental study. Further, many were not even followed up to see if they were pregnant. Dr. Kuchera's claims of 100 percent effectiveness is wishful thinking, and the FDA know this" (U.S. House, 1975:50–51).

6 The report was later published by Marluce Bibbo et al. (1978:763–67).

7 Technically, the disagreement was over whether a one- or two-tailed t-test was the appropriate measure of statistical significance. The general rule is that a one-tailed test is appropriate when differences are expected in only one direction, whereas the two-tailed test is appropriate when differences in both directions are equally likely. Wolfe argued that given animal studies and other evidence, higher rates of breast cancer were expected among the DES-exposed women (and indeed lower rates were biologically implausible).

8 For further discussion of scientists' responses to risks, see Sheldon Krimsky (1979:227–53).

9 Mead testified: "There are no strong reasons for hurry beyond that of competitiveness among commercial laboratories, or between scientific laboratories who wish to get Nobel Prizes" (1977:166).

10 Ethan Signer elaborated on the potential impact of human genetic engineering at a congressional hearing in 1977: "Those who are powerful in society will do the shuffling; their own genes will get shuffled in one direction, while the genes of the rest of us will get shuffled in another" (U.S. House, p. 80). In a more sober vein, Clifford Grobstein asked: "Is it safe, in the present state of our society, to provide means to intervene in the very essence of human individuality. . . . Can genetic destiny, whether of human or other species, wisely be governed by human decision?" (1976:1134).

11 The bishops urged reflection on, among other things, "the correlation between the scien-

tific advance possible through recombinant DNA research and human progress adjudged by a variety of criteria" (National Conference of Catholic Bishops, 1977).

12 Speaking at the 1977 National Academy of Sciences public forum, Harvard biologist Ruth Hubbard stated: "There are lots of questions that we have to answer in order to lick diabetes. . . . But what we don't need right now is a new, potentially hazardous technology for producing insulin that will profit only the people who are producing it. And given the history of drug therapy in relation to other diseases, we know that if we produce more insulin, more insulin will be used, whether diabetics need it or not" (p. 169).

13 For example, David Baltimore, a Nobel Laureate, stated: "If there is a revolutionary idea anywhere in here, it's the idea that there is a responsive science someplace that is different from the biomedical science we're doing now. That responsive science is not going to be discovered by a group of basically science-oriented people getting together and discussing their own disciplines" (1977:125). Baltimore went on to suggest that scientists meet with lawyers and representatives of unions and the poor people's movement to discuss the "appropriate end products of science and medicine."

14 Concerns about the possible negative consequences of scientific breakthroughs was quite widespread for a time within the scientific community. As David Baltimore observed: "We all grew up with the question of the correctness of using the atomic bomb as one of the great moral dilemmas of the second part of the twentieth century. And I don't think that any of us are untouched by that" (1974:2).

15 One member of the panel, Dr. Kaplan, criticized the notion of societal informed consent, arguing that: (1) society has a broader range of choices than consent to or refusal of biomedical innovation; (2) the panel was not asked to answer the central question, "Should the development of the artificial heart continue?"; and (3) the panel had no authority to make a decision for society at large (Adess, 1973:223–27).

16 Besides Cambridge, local ordinances regulating recombinant DNA research were also enacted in Amherst (Massachusetts), Princeton (New Jersey), and Berkeley (California). New York and Maryland passed state legislation regulating the research. However, after the NIH guidelines were relaxed in 1978, many of these states and localities abandoned the additional safeguards they had enacted. Other states and localities that have considered enacting regulations or have debated the issue in public forums and hearings include Shrewsbury (Massachusetts), San Diego (California), Madison (Wisconsin), Ann Arbor (Michigan), New York City, and the states of California, Wisconsin, Illinois, Massachusetts, and New Jersey (Krimsky and Ozonoff, 1979:1252–59).

17 For a full description of the lobbying effort, see John Lear (1978); also Harold M. Schmeck, Jr. (1977). Although some prominent scientists remained opposed to any form of federal legislation, Halvorson and his allies chose to support limited federal legislation consistent with the agreed-on principles, rather than pursue what then seemed to be the hopeless goal of defeating all legislation. The nine principles are summarized in Halvorson's testimony (1977a:142). Professional lobbyists counseled Halvorson not to appear arrogant in Congress, advice that he passed along to colleagues in a lead editorial in *Science* warning them not to " 'come on too strong' with self-serving pronouncements and overzealous protective positions" (1977b). Despite this advice, however, some members of Congress were dismayed by what Representative Richard Ottinger, a member of the House Committee on Science and Technology, called "the arrogance and anti-

democratic spirit of which the 'established' scientific community . . . has shown itself capable." Ottinger continued: "Those who lobbied so hard to prevent the Congress from taking steps many of us are convinced need to be taken to protect public health and safety have shown that they think themselves omniscient and infallible. 'We are the experts' the saying goes, 'and you can't possibly understand whereof you speak.' I resent that, and I resent it extremely, and the American public will destroy you if you take that attitude" (Walgate, 1978:698).

18 Sidney Udenfriend, director of the Roche Institute for Molecular Biology (an affiliate of Hoffman-LaRoche), explained: "I'm afraid there's going to be some brush fires if we get communities involved in deciding biohazards. If we permit non-scientists to question our work in one area (DNA), we'll open ourselves to all kinds of things" (Park and Thatcher, 1977:29). Also, see statements of Joseph Stetler, president, Pharmaceutical Manufacturers Association, and Ronald E. Cape, president, Cetus Corporation (1977).

19 Jonathan King testified: "Those most at risk are the laboratory workers who daily will be handling new types of organisms, most of which have never before occurred on earth. If we cannot prevent them from being infected, we cannot protect ourselves" (1977:295). And OCAW's Tony Mazzochi argued that "those who know [about safety procedures] are the people out there who work in the factories" (1977b:141–45).

20 For example, Ruth Hubbard, a vocal critic, testified before Congress: "Obviously one has to balance risks against benefits, but one has to also balance to whom the risks accrue and to whom the benefits accrue, and as long as these decisions are made by the people who are most likely to reap the immediate benefits and the people who are equally likely to reap the risks are not involved in the decision-making process, then the process itself is flawed" (1977b:93).

21 Pat Cody recalls the informality of this first national meeting: "We met in someone's apartment, still with no funds, getting acquainted, trading ideas, discussing ways to spread the word, giving ourselves a name" (Bryant, 1979:22).

22 For example, Dr. Geraldine Oliva has worked closely with DES Action in San Francisco. Nancy Adess, president of DES Action National, has noted that Oliva's communication of information was a teaching process for lay members, who now have a good command of the relevant technical issues themselves. Adess also feels that Oliva's participation added to the group's legitimacy, especially in the early stages.

23 For further discussion of the role of activist-scientists in modern technical controversies, see Dorothy Nelkin (1979); also Joel Primack and Frank von Hippel (1974).

24 Despite the existence of over 1200 public advisory committees with more than 22,000 members in 1975, a Senate committee report found that in more than half of all formal federal regulatory agency meetings, there was no public participation at all, nor was there virtually any public involvement in informal agency proceedings (U.S. Senate, 1977:vii).

25 A congressional investigation of FDA advisory committees concluded that their predominantly medical composition was "conducive to resolving issues in a manner more favorable to the practicing physician than to the public at large," and that the "FDA has increasingly used advisory committees to gain support in the medical community for regulatory decisions thought desirable by the agency's leadership" (U.S. House Committee, 1976:6). Another form of tokenism is the appointment of well-known public figures

or "leaders" in their fields, who may not represent all of the interests affected, particularly those of less elite groups with whom they have had little contact. Moreover, agencies do not always appoint individuals favored by consumer constituencies, especially those known to be forceful critics of government policies. Most advisory committees skirt the issue of representing opposing viewpoints, concentrating instead on the less controversial representation of specified demographic and geographic categories. (See, for example, Gage and Epstein [1977]; also, U.S. Senate [1977]).

26 One study of public participation in science and technology observed that expert "decision-making bodies traditionally accustomed to receiving technically competent, legally reasoned briefs often find it difficult to cope with qualitatively different types of testimony. Intervenors expressing strong social, political, or emotional points of view are therefore often termed 'technically incompetent' or, simply, 'uninformed' " (Nichols, 1979).

27 Although the Federal Advisory Committee Act requires that committees not be "inappropriately influenced by the appointing authority or by any special interest," no enforcement provisions are specified. Thus, for example, a 1976 survey of sixteen federal energy agency advisory boards found that almost half of the board members represented industry, while consumer and environmental representatives each comprised less than 5 percent of the members (unpublished report by J. Sullivan, cited in Nelkin [1980:488]). And a 1977 Senate committee report concluded: "In the Food and Drug Administration, for example, which has 54 advisory committees composed almost exclusively of academic scientists, there is an endemic problem that stems from the dependence of academic institutions on the Government and the drug industry for research funds. The choice of experts by an agency will most likely be influenced by the informal network of contact and association which grows up around an agency and *will tend to exclude experts with differing perspectives.*"

28 These arguments are elaborated in Carole Pateman (1970).

29 This essay is based on material to appear in *Do No Harm: Health Risks and Public Choice* (working title), by Diana B. Dutton and contributors, University of California Press, forthcoming. An earlier draft was prepared by Malcolm Goggin and Ralph Silber, as part of a collaborative research project. The research was funded by the National Science Foundation's Program in Ethics and Values in Science and Technology, and by the National Endowment for the Humanities, with additional support from the Rockefeller Foundation. Natalie Fisher and Kathy McFadden provided secretarial and administrative services.

An earlier version was presented at the Sixth Annual meeting of the Society for the Social Studies of Science, Atlanta, Georgia, 5 November 1981.

References

Adess, Nancy. 1973. *The Totally Implantable Artificial Heart: Legal, Social, Ethical, Medical, Economic, Psychological Implications.* National Heart and Lung Institute, Department of Health, Education and Welfare Pub. No. (NIH)74–191, June.

———. 1978. *Notes of Task Force Meeting.* September 21. Artificial Heart Assessment Panel Report.

Baltimore, David. 1974. "Some of These Artificial Recombinant DNA Molecules Could Prove Biologically Hazardous." *National Academy of Sciences News Report* (August–September):2.

———. 1977. *Biomedical Research and the Public.* Subcommittee on Health and Scientific Research, U.S. Senate (May):125.

Bazelon, David. 1979. "Risk and Responsibility." *Science* 205:277–80.

Bennet, William, and Gurin, Joel. 1977. "Science That Frightens Scientists: The Great Debate Over DNA." *Atlantic* (February):67.

Bibbo, Marluce; Haenszel, William; Wied, George; Hubby, Marian; and Herbst, Arthur. 1978. "A Twenty-Five-Year Follow-up Study of Women Exposed to Diethylstilbestrol during Pregnancy." *New England Journal of Medicine* 298:763–67.

Bishops Committee for Human Values. 1977. "Statement on Recombinant DNA Research." National Conference of Catholic Bishops (May 2).

Bryant, Dorothy. 1979. "The DES Odyssey of Pat Cody." *San Francisco Sunday Examiner Chronicle, California Living* (March 18):21.

Business Week. 1981. "Can Gene-Splicers Make Good Neighbors?" (August 10).

Carnoy, Martin, and Shearer, Derek. 1980. *Economic Democracy: The Challenge of the 1980s.* New York: Sharpe.

Chargaff, Erwin. 1976. "On the Dangers of Genetic Meddling." Letter to the Editor, *Science* 192:938.

Clem, David. 1977. *Recombinant DNA Research Act of 1977.* U.S. Senate Hearings (April 6):173.

Coalition for Responsible Genetic Research. n.d. *Position Statement on Recombinant DNA Technology.*

Cohen, Victor. 1977. "DNA Research Control Dims." *Washington Post* (September 28).

Consumer Bulletin. 1962. "Harmful Drug in Meats?" (May):10.

Crawford, John D. 1981. "Meat, Potatoes, and Growth Hormone." Editorial, *New England Journal of Medicine* 305:163–64.

Culliton, Barbara. 1978. "Recombinant DNA Bill Derailed: Congress Still Trying to Pass a Law." *Science* 199:274–77.

Dahl, Robert. 1956. *A Preface to Democratic Theory.* Chicago: University of Chicago Press.

DES Action Voice. 1979. "Report on National DES Conference, New York, April 30, 1977." Vol. 1 (January).

———. 1981. "DES Legislation: Effective and Far-Reaching." Vol. 3 (Fall):1.

Dutton, Diana B., and Hochheimer, John L. 1982. "Institutional Biosafety Committees and Public Participation: Assessing an Experiment." *Nature* 297:11–15.

Federal Drug Administration Ob-Gyn Advisory Committee. 1973. *Statement of Health Research Group.* Meeting held January 26.

———. 1978. Meeting held January 30–31.

Fishbane, Fran. 1979. "The Role of DES Action in Federal Legislation." Paper presented at a session on *Medical Innovation and Public Policy: The Case of DES.* Annual Meeting of the American Association for the Advancement of Science, January 4, Houston, Texas.

Gage, Kit, and Epstein, Samuel. 1977. "The Federal Advisory Committee System: An Assessment." *Environmental Law Reporter* 7(2):5001.

General Secretaries, National Council of Churches, Synagogue Council of America, U.S. Catholic Conference. 1981. International Conference in Holland of the World Council of Churches (June).

Glebatis, Donna M., and Janerich, Dwight T. 1981. "A Statewide Approach to Diethylstilbestrol: The New York Program." *New England Journal of Medicine* 304:47–50.

Goodell, Rae. 1979. "Public Involvement in the DNA Controversy: The Case of Cambridge, Massachusetts." *Harvard Newsletter on Science, Technology and Human Values* (Spring).

Grobstein, Clifford. 1976. "Recombinant DNA Research: Beyond the NIH Guidelines." *Science* 194:1134.

Halvorson, Harlyn. 1977a. "Recombinant DNA Regulation Act, 1977." Testimony before the U.S. Senate, April 6, pp. 140–42.

———. 1977b. "Recombinant DNA Legislation: What Next?" *Science* 198:28.

Handler, Philip. 1980. "In Science, 'No Advances without Risks.' " *U.S. News and World Report* (September 15):60.

Herbst, Arthur L.; Ulfelder, Howard; and Poskamzer, David. 1971. "Adenocarcinoma of the Vagina: Association of Maternal Stilbestrol Therapy with Tumor Appearance in Young Women." *New England Journal of Medicine* 284:878–81.

———. 1978. *Clinical Week* (January 18).

Hubbard, Ruth. 1977a. "Potential Risks." *Research with Recombinant DNA: An Academy Forum,* Washington, D.C. (March 7–9):169.

———. 1977b. *Recombinant DNA Research Act of 1977.* House Hearings, 95th Congress, 1st Session (March 15,16,17):93.

Huntington, Samuel. 1975. *The Crisis of Democracy: Report on the Governability of Democracies.* New York: University Press.

Jefferson, Thomas. 1820. Letter to William Charles Jarvis (September 28).

Johnson, Anita, and Wolfe, Sidney. 1973. "Quality of Health Care: Human Experimentation." U.S. Senate.

Jones, Vicki. 1978. FDA Ob-Gyn Advisory Committee (January 30–31):72–78.

Jonsen, Albert. 1980. Interview (January 23).

Katz, Jay. 1980. Interview (January 15).

Kennedy, Edward. 1977. *Recombinant DNA Regulation Act.* U.S. Senate (April 6):2–3.

King, Jonathan. 1975. *Recombinant DNA Research Act of 1977.* House Hearings (March 15,16,17):295.

Knox, Richard. 1977a. "Layman Is Center of Scientific Controversy." *Boston Globe* (January 9).

————. 1977b. "Cambridge Panel OK's Genetic Experiments at Harvard, M.I.T." *Boston Globe* (January 6).

Krimsky, Sheldon. 1979. "Regulating Recombinant DNA Research." In *Controversy: Politics of Technical Decisions*, ed. Dorothy Nelkin. Beverly Hills: Sage Publications, pp. 227–53.

Krimsky, Sheldon, and Ozonoff, David. 1979. "Recombinant DNA Research: The Scope and Limits of Regulation." *American Journal of Public Health* 69:1251–59.

Kuchera, Lucile. 1971. "Postcoital Contraception with Diethylstilbestrol." *Journal of the American Medical Association* 218:562.

————. 1973. "The Morning-After-Pill." Letter to the Editor, *Journal of the American Medical Association* 224:1038.

————. 1974. "Postcoital Contraception with Diethylstilbestrol: Updated." *Contraception* 10:49–54.

La Porte, Todd, and Metlay, Daniel. 1975. "Technology Observed: Attitudes of a Wary Public." *Science* 188:121–27.

Lear, John. 1978. *Recombinant DNA: The Untold Story*. New York: Crown, pp. 172–203.

Marmor, Theodore R., and Morone, James A. 1980. "Representing Consumer Interests: Imbalanced Markets, Health Planning, and the HSAs." Milbank Memorial Fund Quarterly/ *Health and Society* 58:125–65.

Mazzochi, Anthony. 1977a. *Recombinant DNA Act of 1977*. Testimony to the House of Representatives (March 15–17):467.

————. 1977b. "Health Hazards to Labor." *Research with Recombinant DNA: An Academy Forum*, Washington, D.C. (March 7–9).

Mead, Margaret. 1977. "Regulation of Recombinant DNA Research." Testimony to Senate (November 2,8,10):166.

Nelkin, Dorothy. 1979. "Science, Technology and Political Conflict: Analyzing the Issues." In *Controversy: Politics of Technical Decisions*, ed. D. Nelkin. Beverly Hills: Sage Publications.

————. 1980. "Science and Technology Policy and the Democratic Process," in *The Five-Year Outlook: Problems, Opportunities and Constraints in Science and Technology*, vol. 2, p. 488. Washington, D.C.: National Science Foundation.

New York Times. 1977. Editorial (October 9).

Nichols, K. Guild. 1979. *Technology on Trial: Public Participation in Decision-Making Related to Science and Technology*. Paris: Organisation for Economic Co-operation and Development.

Park, Robert, and Thatcher, Richard. 1977. "Dealing with Experts: The Recombinant DNA Debate." *Science for the People* 9:29.

Pateman, Carole. 1970. *Participation and Democratic Theory*. Cambridge: Cambridge University Press.

Payton v. Abbott Labs. 1979. 83, F.R.D. 382, Massachusetts.

Porter, David L. 1981. Personal correspondence (July 28).

Primack, Joel, and von Hippel, Frank. 1974. *Advice and Dissent: Scientists in the Political Arena.* New York: Basic Books.

Rosenbaum, Nelson M. 1978. "The Origins of Citizen Involvement in Federal Programs." In *Anticipatory Democracy: People in the Politics of the Future,* ed. Clement Bezold. New York: Random House, pp. 139–55.

Rudman, Daniel; Kutner, Michael; Blackston, Dwain; Cushman, Robert; Bains, Raymond; and Patterson, Joseph. 1981. "Children with Normal-Variant Short Stature: Treatment with Human Growth Hormone for Six Months." *New England Journal of Medicine* 305: 123–31.

San Francisco Chronicle. 1980. "Victims of DES Win Victory in Assembly." (August 27):10.

———. 1982. "A Legislative Victory for DES Victims." (January 21):24.

Schmeck, Harold M., Jr. 1977. "Scientists Seek to Influence Legislation on Gene Research." *New York Times* (July 6).

Schumpeter, Joseph. 1943. *Capitalism, Socialism and Democracy.* London: Allen and Unwin.

Signer, Ethan. 1977a. *Recombinant DNA Act of 1977.* House of Representatives (March):80.

———. 1977b. "Recombinant DNA: It's Not What We Need." *Research with Recombinant DNA: An Academy Forum,* March 7–9. Washington, D.C.: National Academy of Sciences, p. 232.

Sindell v. *Abbott Labs.* 1980. 26 California 3d 588.

Slovic, Paul; Fischhoff, Baruch; and Lichtenstein. 1980. "Risky Assumptions." *Psychology Today* 14:44–48.

Smithies, Oliver. 1977. "Regulation of Recombinant DNA Research." U.S. Senate (November 2,8,10):248.

Stetler, Joseph, and Cape, Ronald E. 1977. "Regulation of Recombinant DNA Research." Senate hearing (November 2,8,10):252, 329–31, 337–46.

Swazey, Judith; Sorenson, J.; and Wong, C. 1978. "Risks and Benefits, Rights and Responsibilities: A History of the Recombinant DNA Research Controversy." *Southern California Law Review* 5(6):1019–78.

Time Magazine. 1977. "Doomsday: Tinkering with Life." (April 18):33.

Tribe, Laurence H. 1972. "Policy Science: Analysis or Ideology?" *Journal of Philosophy and Public Affairs* 2(1):66–110.

Tversky, Amos, and Kahneman, Daniel. 1981. "The Framing of Decisions and the Psychology of Choice." *Science* 211:453–58.

Udenfriend, Sidney. 1976. Drug Research Reports (December 3).

———. 1977. "Dealing with Experts: The Recombinant DNA Debate." *Science for the People* 9:29.

U.S. House. 1972. "Regulation of Diethylstilbestrol." Hearings before the Committee on Government Operations, 93rd Congress, 2d Session (August 15):438–39.

———. 1976. "Use of Advisory Committees by the FDA." Hearings of the Committee on Government Operations, p. 6.

———. 1977. *Recombinant DNA Research Act of 1977*. Hearings on March 15,16,17, p. 80.

U.S. House and Senate Subcommittees on Appropriations. 1964–79. Testimony and discussion.

———. 1967–72. Testimony and discussion.

U.S. Senate. 1975. "Regulation of Diethylstilbestrol, 1975." Washington, D.C.: Government Printing Office.

———. 1977. *Study on Federal Regulation. Volume 3: Public Participation in Regulatory Agency Proceedings*. Committee on Governmental Affairs, July. Washington, D.C.: Government Printing Office, p. vii.

Wade, Nicholas. 1975. "Recombinant DNA: NIH Group Stirs Storm by Drafting Laxer Rules." *Science* 190:769.

———. 1977a. "Gene-Splicing: Critics of Research Get More Brickbats than Bouquets." *Science* 195:466–68.

———. 1977b. *The Ultimate Experiment*. New York: Walker and Company, p. 89.

———. 1978. "Gene-Splicing Rules: Another Round of Debate." *Science* 199:33.

Walgate, Robert. 1978. "The Expert Has No Clothes." *Nature* 271:698.

Watson, James. 1977. *Chemical and Engineering News* (May 30):26.

Weiss, Kathleen. 1973. "Quality of Health Care: Human Experimentation." U.S. Senate Hearing, pp. 300–313.

Wolfe, Sidney. 1976. Letter to F. David Matthews, Secretary of DHEW, dated October 14.

———. 1978. "Evidence of Breast Cancer from DES and Current Prescribing of DES and Other Estrogens." Statement made before the FDA Ob-Gyn Advisory Committee, January 30.

10

Solving Political Problems of Nuclear Technology: The Role of Public Participation

Randy J. Rydell

Introduction

Recent national developments in science and technology are straining our political institutions and raising questions about the adequacy of methods we use to comprehend technological change. This is particularly true of large-scale projects focused on the development of high technologies in the areas of energy, space, national defense, transportation, and communication. Massive public investments in these areas have increased demands being made on courts, legislatures, and executive agencies, which have proven far more adept as vehicles for the communication of organized interests than as forums for the resolution of conflict. These investments at times seriously affect the economy. They have environmental impacts. They shape people's attitudes toward both technology and government. And they often carry international implications, affecting "literally billions of people who have had no say in those scientific and technological developments nor in their application" (Brooks and Skolnikoff, 1978).

Nowhere are these propositions more evident than in the controversies surrounding nuclear power, an area which epitomizes much of the complexity found in other areas of public controversy involving high technology. The difficulties governments have had in resolving such nuclear power issues as the proliferation of nuclear weapons, the safe disposal of nuclear waste, and building public confidence in safety measures are due not only to technical difficulties but also to the growing number of political actors with stakes in the resolution of these problems.

As pressures grow both nationally and internationally for changes in the regimes and institutions governing nuclear power, it becomes increasingly important to comprehend the critical roles that are and will be played by new participants in this political process of responding to technological challenges. This essay will outline a framework of analysis that should be useful to interest group strategists, policy makers, and the lay citizen concerned with this complex but intelligible process.[1] The more governments intervene in the national process of technological development, and the more this intervention yields effects which spill across national borders and down into private homes, the greater is the need for such a framework.

The Process of Research and Development

Technological development is not an end-state but an ongoing process. Governmental intervention in this process similarly produces not one, but a variety of effects, some more visible and enduring than others. Often these are intended effects, as for example when an aerospace industry is created to respond to political calls represented in such slogans as a "man on the moon," or "closing the missile gap." Yet unintended effects, what economists call negative externalities, often take center stage in the guise of unemployment, environmental degradation, international mistrust, or economic injustice. Although both centrally planned and capitalist governments try to anticipate these effects, they inevitably must cope with unforeseen problems as they arise. What thus begins as a grand design, a comprehensively planned introduction of a specific technology, often becomes an exercise in day-to-day bargaining where organized groups struggle to maximize their own vested interests often at the expense of broader social objectives.

When the focus is shifted downward from national technological development to the advancement of specific projects, the conventional literature on technology policy refers to the "R&D" (research and development) process (Villers, 1964). This process is usually represented as a linear and stepwise progression of a certain project from basic and applied research to development, demonstration, and commercialization.

Using this framework, a specific high technology "advances" from an idea, to a subject of empirical research, to the development of prototypes, to a larger-scale project that purportedly demonstrates its growing commercial appeal, and finally to wider introduction to the economy and society. Many questionable assumptions underlie this view of R&D:

1   *A unitary goal exists: commercialization.* The possible existence of other goals (e.g., individual and group self-interest, or national prestige) is not recognized in this view.

2   *The various "stages" of R&D are separable.* In fact, however, it is often difficult to distinguish basic from applied research, or development from demonstration.

3   *Scientific information serves to increase understanding of technological problems.* The instrumental use of scientific information by organizational actors is neglected.

4   *Transitions between stages are based on technical judgments.* Political or ideological motivations are not acknowledged.

5   *R&D reduces uncertainty.* Uncertainties often grow as unanticipated consequences materialize from past decisions.

The conventional R&D process thus is perhaps best perceived as an ideal type, a tool to be employed by project managers to gauge progress toward some fixed goal, to simplify the complex real world in order to attain narrow objectives, and to facilitate gross international and/or intercorporate comparisons. It is virtually useless as a means of comprehending public participation in technological controversies or the diverse political "missions" given to specific technological projects.

Because R&D often does lead to intense conflicts between values and to vast numerical expansion of relevant participants, an alternative conception of the R&D process is in order. The alternative emphasizes the roles of increased participation, value diversification, decision making in face of uncertainty or high risk, and shifting goals.

The R&D Process: Three Levels of Interaction

The alternative framework begins by positing that public technological enterprises essentially involve coordinated activity in four problem areas: understanding, exploitation, control, and integration. *Understanding* refers to the search for scientific explanation of regularities in nature and is attained by iterative research and experimentation. *Exploitation* concerns the utility that various segments of society derive from past and future investments. For civilian technologies, it usually involves active roles by industry, special interest groups, and local governments. *Control* involves insuring that exploitation occurs within an agreed-upon set of social values. And *integration* refers to the role government plays in assuring that policies are consistent and complementary. Regardless of time, culture, or governmental structure, these four problem areas are addressed (with varying degrees of emphasis) by political actors in the R&D process.

Several activities take place within each problem area in an R&D process:

1   *Problem definition.* A "problem" is an organization's interpretation of a social need. Created through a process that combines scientific analysis with political bargaining, "problem definitions" tell organizations what is most important about that need, which actors really count, what values are at stake, and how effects follow from specific causes.

2   *Solution.* "Solutions" consist of what an organization actually does to respond to a problem. The process of solution differs from the customary notion of implementation only in its closer association with organizational interests. Systems analysts will recognize solutions as organizational "outputs."

3   *Diffusion of a problem.* When solutions fail to accomplish their objectives or when they aggravate a problem, a problem is diffused, i.e., it grows in intensity or expands to involve new issues, values, or actors.

4   *Evaluation.* Evaluation is a bureaucratic process whereby solutions are reviewed and adjusted on the basis of incoming information about the evolution of the social need.

Problems and solutions therefore differ by problem area: a scientist in pursuit of understanding will not ask the same questions or perform the same activities as a project manager concerned with meeting deadlines, a company president bent on profit maximization, or an environmentalist worried about genetic disorders. Presidents, legislators, judges, civil servants, indeed all political actors develop their own conceptualizations of the problems requiring their attention. These problem definitions can often be molded by organizational settings, but often they cannot.

Problem-solving *activities* are thus deeply interdependent: an actor who sees the threat of nuclear war as the dominant problem underlying a particular technology will search for information, methods, and resources to enable him to devise solutions consistent with this problem definition. Similarly, an actor who fears the prospect of his own unemployment might search for "solutions" which have no relation whatsoever to the formal goals of his or her organization. Problem *areas* are also interactive: knowledge gained through the organized pursuit of "understanding" influences subsequent efforts at control and exploitation. In the nuclear field, for example, narrow national preoccupations with engineering applications and basic science were accompanied by a neglect of alternative technologies and long-term risks (e.g., from waste disposal and nuclear theft or terrorism). Subsequent belated efforts to cope with these problems were greatly constrained by these early problem definitions.

Another level of interaction is evident in the international effects produced by national technological investments, and in the growing importance for national projects of information or events from abroad. A nuclear explosion by India in May 1974, for example, triggered a major reevaluation of U.S. nuclear export policy and led to an international search for more "proliferation-resistant" technology. Similarly, the accident at Three Mile Island led to massive demonstrations in Europe, including one in Germany involving thousands of protestors shouting, "We all live in Harrisburg."[2] Despite this linkage between national technological developments and international society, most studies of R&D continue to neglect international influences on R&D policy.

This framework, the "interactive R&D process" can be summarized graphically:

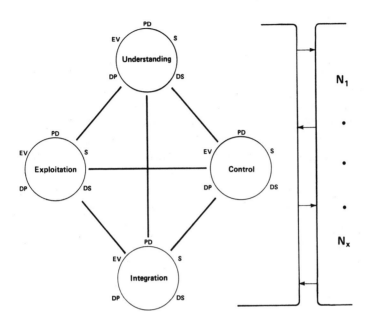

. . . where U, E, C, and I refer to problem areas; PD, S, DP, and EV* refer to the various problem-solving activities; $N_1 \ldots N_x$ refers to events and information emanating from abroad, and solid lines signify interaction. This process is multidimensional, nonlinear, dynamic (rather than steady state), and reflective of the interplay between diverse actors and values.

Public Participation in the R&D Process

Viewed in the above framework, the key questions for analysis become: How do problems get defined? And, how are priorities set between problem areas? Participation emerges as a critical variable influencing patterns of interaction in both of these areas. This is quite clear in the ongoing debate over the future of nuclear power. The entire political history of nuclear power can be effectively summarized in terms of shifts between dominant problem areas. At times these shifts came as a result of governmental

---

*Literally, problem definition, solution, diffusion of problem, and evaluation.

initiatives, at times a product of sustained pressure from below.

Prewar research and experimentation (U) was governmentally applied to military purposes (E_{mil}), then civil uses (E_{civ}); these were followed by a growing concern at various levels of society and government about adverse environmental, social, and political consequences (C) and an ever-apparent need to harmonize nuclear policies (I) with other public objectives. During the Carter administration, the United States advocated a strong emphasis on C as a basis for the new nuclear regime; that is, American diplomacy was heavily oriented toward grappling with the problems of nuclear proliferation and reactor safety. In contrast, the Reagan administration has stressed E_{mil} and E_{civ} as major themes of nuclear R&D policy. European policy makers largely share the Reagan problem definitions, whereas environmental and public interest groups in these countries give least emphasis to the problem of exploitation, or attempt to redefine the problem to include the pursuit of smaller-scale energy technologies.

These shifts between problem areas were in large measure due to the increased involvement of nongovernmental groups in the nuclear R&D process. In the late 1960s and early 1970s, the American legislative process was overwhelmed with appeals for action on growing environmental problems apparently linked with nuclear power. Institutional and legal reforms brought new values, information, and ideas into what was hitherto a rather closed decision-making process. The National Environmental Policy Act mandated environmental impact statements on all major public projects; citizen groups were permitted to contest (in administrative and legal arenas) exports of nuclear fuel and technology; and individual R&D projects were subject to growing public scrutiny.[3] New actors emerged, an antinuclear movement was rejuvenated, and considerable regulatory legislation followed apace. Following the Indian nuclear explosion, dissensus within the scientific community about the problems of C led to the mobilization of think tanks and universities; expert was pitted against expert in public hearings and the press. Under the aegis of problem areas C and I, groups of experts sponsored by the Ford Foundation issued lengthy studies which had a profound impact on government policy (Ford Foundation, 1974 and 1977). Media events such as the fire at the Browns Ferry reactor and the accident at TMI further expanded participation in the process by heightening public awareness of issues, stakes, and values.

The rapid expansion of participation domestically was matched by increasing calls from nuclear "have-not" countries for greater equity in the norms regulating international nuclear commerce and a greater participatory role in the formulation of these norms. In such forums as the five-year reviews of the Nuclear Nonproliferation Treaty, the United Nations, and ad hoc conferences, developing nations sought increased transfers of nuclear technology and less emphasis on "barriers" to proliferation that also restrain trade. To these countries, as is also the case in Europe although in a somewhat different light, the paramount issue on the international agenda is problem area E.

Public Participation in Three
Nuclear Power Controversies[4]

Three Mile Island　On 28 March 1979, a technical problem or "trip" (automatic shutdown) occurred in the secondary pump feeding coolant water into the TMI-2 reactor near Harrisburg, Pennsylvania. At the time the accident occurred, the $1 billion reactor complex was under the control of four high school graduates who were all veterans of the nuclear navy. Through a series of technical and operator-related problems, a portion of the core of the reactor was uncovered and partially melted. Radioactive water flooded the reactor confinement buiding and within hours the accident was being reported around the country as the "nation's worst nuclear accident" and, in Walter Cronkite's words, as a "nuclear nightmare." Antinuclear groups in Europe organized rallies, citing the accident as symptomatic of the environmental problems posed by nuclear power and the elitist nature of the public decisions concerning its development. Although the immediate technical problems were eventually brought under control, the accident and the partial evacuation of the vicinity of the reactor led to a major reappraisal of the safety of the nation's nuclear power installations, a review which included a presidential commission under Dartmouth's President John Kemeny.[5]

According to the Kemeny Commission, the accident pointed to the need for major changes in the procedures and institutions responsible for ensuring the public safety; in particular, the commission suggested that "human factor engineering" be given greater emphasis in future licensing in light of the inadequate training and human error evident in the accident. In Congress and the media, however, the accident was widely depicted as the result of a dangerous and unthinking attachment to a technology whose risks, while remote, can be potentially catastrophic.

What caused the issue to spread so quickly over several issue areas? Why was this technical incident to become an international event? The answers emerge largely through the examination of the roles of nongovernmental groups.

Although human error in handling the technical problems unquestionably exacerbated the controversy, other organizational factors contributed to the same result. Contradictory advice was given to the public by responsible but poorly informed officials; the public did not know whose facts to listen to during the crisis. The news media, based only a short distance from the reactor in New York, gave the accident immediate national visibility. Moreover, the popular film, *China Syndrome*, had just been released which warned of an accident that would jeopardize an area "half the size of the state of Pennsylvania." The order to evacuate pregnant women and preschool children raised the stakes considerably. Expert statements on the radiological dangers posed also helped widen the debate.

The administration and the industry clearly preferred to treat the accident as a problem requiring administrative, legal, and technical solutions. This is evident in postaccident administrative efforts to frame the issue as one of training and procedures. Thus, the head of the NRC resigned; the nuclear industry set up a study group on training problems; and the Kemeny Commission called for a reorganization of the NRC under a single head appointed by the president. Yet many members of Congress, local groups, environmental and antinuclear groups, and the media sought to stimulate the debate. In light of the de facto moratorium on reactor licensing following the accident, the latter groups had succeeded in at least buying time for further study of safety questions. In short, the problem of c had been vigorously asserted onto the public agenda, along with the problems of u and i.

Clinch River Breeder Reactor (CRBR) CRBR is an advanced nuclear reactor currently under debate for possible construction near Oak Ridge, Tennessee. Its purpose is to "demonstrate" (i.e., prove to public utilities and nuclear industry) the commercial viability of a breeder, a reactor designed to produce large quantities of plutonium while generating electricity. Plutonium is a valuable and efficient fuel for breeders and can thus help alleviate the fears of those who doubt the long-term availability of uranium fuel. However, plutonium is also extremely toxic and a major component of nuclear explosives. On 20 April 1977, President Carter announced that because of the risks that breeders pose for nuclear proliferation, the U.S. will terminate CRBR and restructure its breeder program to emphasize less risky (and more efficient) prototypes.[6]

This case involves a wide array of issues and actors. It is a controversy that not only expanded to new issue areas, but that also caused major international repercussions. Although the Reagan administration has indicated some support for this project, it is not yet clear that CRBR will be built or, if it is, which criteria will govern its construction and operation. In recent years, congressional debate has shifted considerably from a concern for maintaining international leadership in technology, to a greater concern for letting the market determine the timing for introducing the breeder.

The news media has played a modest role in informing the public about this reactor. Because of its technical complexity, however, most Americans have never heard of CRBR or the issues it represents. A far greater role has been played by public interest groups, which have raised the issues repeatedly in legislative hearings, regulatory forums, and in the courts. The Natural Resources Defense Council and the Scientists' Institute for Public Information have been most successful in obtaining legal sanction for the view that an environmental impact statement must be prepared both for CRBR and the entire U.S. breeder program.[7] Expert testimony in congressional hearings and conflicting analyses of the technical and economic issues also helped expand the conflict to new levels (national to international) and to new issue areas (technical to political). International events (e.g., the May 1974 Indian explosion, and an enormous German-Brazilian nuclear deal in 1975) helped link CRBR to the wider international debate over the plutonium economy.

Considerable evidence suggests that a new administrative and technical consensus is developing in government along the following lines: the U.S. will permit, even encourage, international use of plutonium, but only for R&D uses and only in countries that can demonstrate a compelling need to conduct this R&D (Smith et al., 1980). Presidential support of this new consensus may well succeed in confining the controversy to limited problem areas capable of resolution. But the success or failure of this compromise will largely depend upon its political reception by the numerous influential groups pressing for greater attention to the problems of C, U, and I.

The control of nuclear proliferation Nuclear nonproliferation—preventing the spread of nuclear weapons—has been a central goal of U.S.

foreign policy for thirty-six years. In 1945, the American "Baruch Plan" proposed that all sensitive steps of the nuclear fuel cycle be placed under international control and ownership. Numerous attempts have since been made to reaffirm the international norm against the development of nuclear weapons in nonweapons states: the 1953 "Atoms for Peace" policy of President Eisenhower assured the world of the availability of civilian nuclear power technology in exchange for promises to eschew atomic weapons; the 1968 Nonproliferation Treaty extended this global bargain to include a promise by the superpowers to reduce their strategic arsenals; in 1978 a group of nuclear-exporting countries announced new restrictive standards to regulate international trade in nuclear technology and materials; and in 1980 a two-year international study called INFCE was completed, which reinforced national perceptions of the need for nuclear power while also finding no technical fix to the problem of nuclear proliferation.

In the 1970s Europe and Japan viewed technological prestige, concerns for energy security, and economic needs as paramount in encouraging expanded efforts to sell sensitive nuclear technology (like enrichment and reprocessing plants). In the United States and Europe, antinuclear groups used proliferation as another tool to attack nuclear power (and in some instances high technology, in general). The nuclear industry attempted to define proliferation as a political and motivational problem that had no direct relevance to exports. The Carter administration approached the problem from a standpoint of national motivations for acquiring nuclear weapons and national capabilities to achieve that goal. The Reagan administration, meanwhile, will perhaps be best noted for candidate Reagan's remark during the 1980 presidential election campaign: "It's not our problem." Continued proliferation in such areas as South Africa, Pakistan, Iraq, and Libya can only guarantee that national R&D programs will continue to be deeply influenced by international considerations.

Strengths and Limitations of a
Pluralist R&D Process

High technology R&D in the public sector is inevitably somewhat elitist, for the technical complexity drives away more potential political actors than it attracts. Nevertheless, national R&D systems differ in their degree of openness to new information, actors, and values. The American nuclear R&D process is presently more decentralized, pluralistic, and open than ever before, certainly more so than in most foreign R&D processes. The Madisonian "checks and balances" character of American R&D, although by no means a guarantee that problems U, C, E, and I will be addressed in a socially responsible way (i.e., open and accountable), nevertheless structures participation in patterns that potentially encourage greater adaptiveness.

Public participation was critical in bringing about a reexamination of the problem definitions undergirding American policies for nuclear development and control. For example, new ideas about the relationships between nuclear exports and proliferation evolved largely because of the mobilization of groups of experts, citizen lobbies, local governments, and professions (e.g., public interest lawyers and physicians). The successful call for revised or new problem definitions was due in large part to the mobilization of scientific knowledge by politically astute individuals and groups. Although to date most policy changes have occurred as problem reformulations (i.e., shifts in tactics or means) rather than as radical problem redefinitions, the continued testing of the legitimacy and accuracy of existing problem definitions can only occur in a governmental system that permits widespread participation stemming from access to technical and scientific resources.

The great danger, of course, is that the major countervailing blocs within the R&D establishments—i.e., industry, government, academia, national laboratories, and umbrella public interest groups—will themselves negotiate problem definitions which, although amenable to their own separate organizational interests, are not effectively scrutinized or debated by nonparticipants in this process. There is no guarantee that the sum of particular interests in a community will approximate the general will of that community, as Rousseau so often pointed out.

Participation can also be a convenient means by which government can build support for or legitimate a prior decision, rather than a means of informing public choices. In England, for example, local "public inquiries" have been (or will be) organized to deliberate prior decisions on the expansion of the Windscale nuclear reprocessing plant, the selection of a pressurized water reactor, and (soon) the development of a commercial fast breeder reactor. The major focus of these inquiries has been limited to discussing the scientific merit of alternative means of implementing prior decisions, rather than to reconsidering the fundamental premises (re: "problem definitions") of the decision.[8]

The great difficulty with large-scale, capital-intensive projects involving high technology is that once the initial decisions have been made—once problem definitions are set in place and institutions are mobilized accordingly—it becomes increasingly difficult to reverse these prior commitments. The reversibility of these commitments is jeopardized as organizational interests multiply in existing patterns of resource allocation. For most industrialized countries, nuclear power is no longer even an energy option. Unions, whole industries, local governments, major cities, national public agencies, and individual politicians have too much at stake to permit any radical reversal of past commitments to nuclear power.

Open participation is also no guarantee that present commitments to a particular technology (or decisions not to commit) will be in the interests of future generations. Peter Bachrach (1975) has defined "democratic participation . . . [as] a process in which persons formulate, discuss, and decide public issues that are important to them and directly affect their lives." Yet the problem with nuclear wastes is that the major "effects" are likely to be long term and will fall primarily on future (i.e., nonparticipating) generations. There should thus be no delusions about public participation in the R&D process: at times it will delay needed projects, exacerbate conflicts by rendering issues more difficult to disentangle, legitimize prior decisions, and advance special interests. The most important role that citizens and public groups can play in an open R&D process is to assure that the right questions are being asked about the fundamental problem definitions underlying R&D decisions.

Notes

1 The framework was initially developed for the author's doctoral dissertation on the politics of developing the breeder reactor in Britain and the United States. See Randy J. Rydell, "Decision Making on the Breeder Reactor in Britain and the United States: Problems and Solutions in the Plutonium Economy," Department of Politics, Princeton University, October 1979, soon to be published by the University of California Press.

2 For two excellent reviews of the roles of public participation in nuclear power debates, see Dorothy Nelkin and Susan Fallows, "The Evolution of the Nuclear Debate: The Role of Public Participation," *Annual Review of Energy*, ed. Jack M. Hollander et al. Palo Alto, California: Annual Reviews, Inc., 1978, pp. 275–312; and Dorothy Zinberg, "Public Response to Nuclear Energy," in *Nuclear Nonproliferation: The Spent Fuel Problem*, ed. Frederick C. Williams and David A. Deese (New York: Pergamon, 1980), pp. 179–94.

3 For further details on this legislation, see Nelkin and Fallows, "The Evolution of the Nuclear Debate."

4 These particular controversies were discussed further in Robert F. Rich and Randy J. Rydell, "The Problem of Closure in Three Nuclear Power Controversies," paper pre-

sented to Hastings Center Conference on "The Closure of Scientific Disputes," Hastings-on-Hudson, 31 May 1980, pp. 10–16.

5 See *A Report to the Commissioners (of the NRC) and to the Public on Three Mile Island,* Mitchell Rogovin, Director (Washington, D.C.: NRC, January 1980); and *Report of the President's Commission on the Three Mile Island Accident,* John Kemeny, Director (Washington, D.C.: Kemeny Commission, November 1979).

6 For a useful overview of the current issues about CRBR, see "The Clinch River Breeder Reactor: An End to the Impasse," White Paper prepared for the U.S. Congress, 11 May 1979 (Washington, D.C.: White House, 1979).

7 *Calvert Cliff's Coordinating Committee* v. *United States Atomic Energy Commission,* 449 F. 2d 1109 (1971); and *Scientists' Institute for Public Information* v. *Atomic Energy Commission,* 481 F. 2d 1079 (1973).

8 For a useful survey of the Windscale proceedings, see David Pearce, Lynne Edwards, and Geoff Beuret, *Decision Making for Energy Futures* (London: Macmillan, 1979).

References

Bachrach, Peter. 1975. "Interest, Participation and Democratic Theory." In *Participation in Politics,* ed. J. Roland Pennock and John W. Chapman. New York: Lieber-Atherton.

Brooks, H., and Skolnikoff, E. 1978. "Science, Technology and International Relations." Paper presented at NATO Science Committee Conference, April 12.

Ford Foundation. 1974. *No Time to Choose.* New York: Ballinger.

————. 1977. *Nuclear Power: Issues and Choice.* New York: Ballinger.

Smith, Marcia; Behrens, Carl; Donnelly, Warren; Raleigh, Lani; and Civiak, Robert. 1980. "Nuclear Energy Policy." Issue Brief #IB78005. October 17. Washington, D.C.: Congressional Research Service.

Villers, Raymond. 1964. *Research and Development: Planning and Control.* New York: Financial Executives Research Foundation.

11

Public Interest Group Participation in Congressional Hearings on Nuclear Power Development

Jane C. Kronick

The literature on the nuclear energy debate has focused either on the need for adequate energy sources or on the hazards of nuclear energy. At a more general level, the limitations of the American structure of government for problem solving have been identified (Lindblom, 1977; Sharpe, 1973; Thurow, 1980) and the operation of power politics clearly documented (Dahl, 1956). Recent work has questioned the role of the voter (Nisbet, 1976) and noted the predictable cycle of voter support for social legislation (Frey, 1978). Relatively little attention, however, has been given to the importance of legislative hearings and the representations that are made in this forum. The analysis of nuclear energy includes studies of the safety of nuclear energy for domestic use

(Rasmussen, 1975), of the effects of radiation on human health (U.S. House, 1979a), of the hazards of nuclear energy production (Environmental Action Foundation, 1979), and of the origins and actions of nuclear protest groups (Nelkin and Pollak, 1980). This essay will examine the history of participation by different interest groups in the hearings on critical legislation to promote the development of nuclear power and will document the limited nature of the participation by "public interest" groups.

The 1970s was a time of a rapidly expanding awareness of the need to contain toxic substances in the environment. Virtually continuous debate was in process throughout that decade within the subcommittee structure of Congress. Major acts were passed by Congress that established national policy on issues of responsibility for hazardous activities. Chief among these is the Toxic Substances Control Act, passed in 1976, which defines the joint responsibility of industry and government to contain the introduction of toxic substances into the environment. In the development of these acts, public interest groups played an important role in identifying the threat to the collective welfare and arguing for government response.

At the same time that policies were developing to prevent undesirable industrial activities, legislation hastening the development of nuclear power was progressing. Domestic production of nuclear power generates several different kinds of risks to the population: the unknown risks associated with continual release of low-level radiation, the risk of exposure to radioactive materials in the workplace, the potential for catastrophic disaster following an accident at a nuclear plant, and the dilemmas posed by radioactive wastes. The hearings on the Toxic Substances Control Act were held in 1975 and occurred midway between the hearings on the two critical acts promoting nuclear power development, the 1973 hearings on the Energy Reorganization Act and the 1978 hearings on the Nuclear Siting and Licensing Act. The hearings on the Toxic Substances Control Act provide a base from which to compare and identify the role of public interest groups in hearings on activities involving public risk and to establish their relative role in the hearings on the domestic development of nuclear power.

In such a process, specific questions are addressed: Who has participated in hearings on domestic production of nuclear power? What role do submissions in legislative hearings play in the legislative process? Does it make a difference what interests are represented? What constraints exist

on participation in hearings in general, and are the unwritten rules governing the hearings on nuclear energy different from other rules of participation? Are there costs to participation in nuclear energy hearings for certain
groups? To what degree and why have the nuclear energy hearings been
relatively closed hearings? Are there identifiable consequences to the constraints placed on participation in these hearings, particularly in light of
accidents like Three Mile Island?

American politics are interest group politics: the arena where legislation
is made is one of bargaining and influence. Some of the process of interest
group politics is hidden, occurring in congressional offices, party headquarters, and the halls of Congress. At other points in the legislative process, the operation of interest group representation is open to scrutiny.
One such point is the hearings held by congressional committees. I have
examined representations made in hearings by different interest groups to
a wide range of legislation involving national response to environmental
hazards, including legislative hearings, oversight hearings, and budgetary
hearings. These hearings have involved problems of defective consumer
products, energy development, occupational hazards, and toxic substances (Kronick, 1980). This paper will draw upon the data generated by
a formal content analysis of the hearings on the Toxic Substances Control
Act, the Energy Reorganization Act (which established the Nuclear Regulatory Commission), and the Nuclear Siting and Licensing Act.

All material in these submissions has been analyzed.[1] Each submission
was divided into discrete units, every one of which represented an argument with respect to a different issue. Data were recorded under five variables for each unit of analysis: the identity of the person making the submission, the issue addressed, the position taken regarding that issue, the
facts offered in support of that position, and the values invoked. On two of
these variables—the issue addressed and the position taken—the categories for the variables were idiosyncratic to the hearings examined. The
other variables, identity of the interest group, facts offered, and values invoked, were categorized to allow both analysis across hearings and cross-
cultural comparison.[2] All coding was done by one research assistant. The
entire coding was replicated by the author. Less than 1 percent discrepancy
occurred between the coders in terms of category assignment. Comparison
of the coding, however, extended the data base by approximately 10 percent, a reflection of a "fatigue factor" and a tendency to skip sentences
after several hours of work. These data were then cross-tabulated to obtain variation by interest group. Since total population data have been

analyzed, no tests of significance were applied. These data have been used in the context of a Glaser-Strauss constant comparative method of induction (Glaser and Strauss, 1967) to generate statements regarding the relative importance of public interest group participation.

Does It Matter Who Participates in Hearings?

Legislative hearings are not agenda setting forums. At the point hearings are held, specific legislation is under review. Hearings provide an opportunity for interested parties to respond to action that is in progress. Participants, therefore, are severely limited in the extent to which they can initiate action. They can, however, play an important role in shaping the final bill presented to Congress. They can cause alteration in the wording of the bill, be instrumental in having sections added to or deleted from it, and even provide momentum for major change in the provisions of the legislation. In addition, submissions to hearings can provide material for the rhetoric of defense of the legislation on the floor of Congress.

Hearings on specific legislation occur in the context of the legislation that already exists. Options are equally constrained by legislation that does not exist. For example, the absence of a national health program is a pervasive handicap for legislation involving public health programs as well as for all legislation involving the compensation of injured or disabled persons. Similarly, curtailment of the fault doctrine cannot be considered as a means of controlling health costs attributable to the threat of malpractice suits because, without recourse to the courts, many individuals would have no possibility of insuring adequate health care for their misfortunes (Gaskins, 1980). Both the legislation under review in hearings and the responses to the proposed legislation are shaped in the understanding of current laws and the programs already in existence.

Submissions to hearings follow a relatively uniform format. Issues are identified and a position is taken that is defended with reference to both facts and values. In the United States interest groups differ not only with respect to the issues identified and position taken, but also with respect to the values used in support of their positions.[3] While a common position is shared by different representatives within an interest group, different interest groups contribute uniquely to the development of the discourse. Because each interest group is likely to differ on all dimensions in its statement on a given piece of legislation, the parameters of the debate are determined by the range of interest groups participating. It would be naive to assume that all statements in hearings have equal weight. The legislation passed by Congress reflects the interests of some groups in society more than others. This does not mean, however, that some contributions are either fruitless or unimportant.

Submissions play an important role in determining what values surround a specific piece of legislation. This is the forum where alternate frames of reference can be introduced, where the boundaries of the debate can be extended, and where it is possible to force recognition of alternative positions. Clearly articulated arguments, especially when they rest on differing values or on differing interpretations or applications of similar values, remain in the domain of the debate. That which is not stated can be overlooked. What has been stated, however, is less easily ignored. Because interest groups represent sharply diverging points of view, loss of a relevant interest group in a hearing will result in a debate that contains a less than complete representation of the value frame in circulation in the nation. Limited representation around critical pieces of legislation may mean that concerns vital to the health of the nation are not considered and important values are ignored.

The past fifteen years have witnessed a rapid growth in organizations representing areas of the public interest. These include organizations representing special categories of the public interest such as the environmental protection groups, organizations representing previously unorganized sectors of the citizenry such as the consumer or the aged, and special groups created to represent categories of injured citizens such as the Vietnam victims of Agent Orange. Some organizations have restricted activity primarily to local organization and self-help efforts (the Eastern Service Workers Association), others have sought through confrontation strategies to influence public opinion (the nuclear protest groups); some have used legal challenge to require enforcement of existing legislation (the public interest law firms), and some have presented their case in the legislative arena. During this period of rapid expansion of groups representing citizen interests, national protective legislation has also rapidly expanded, partially in response to specific problems (black lung disease, lead poisoning, the PBB [polybrominated Biphynyls] disaster in Michigan) and partially in response to the combined needs of government and industry (Kronick, 1980). Few would argue with the perception that the growth of the petrochemical industry following World War II, combined with the rapid acceleration of energy production and consumption, has created a world of new, expanding, and partially unknown hazards for mankind (Council on Environmental Quality, 1977).

Despite the growth of public interest groups and of regulatory legislation, the present situation is far from comfortable. Toxic waste dumps permeate the nation; funds to correct the problems they pose are limited. Manmade environmental hazards, most of which are created by the industrial process, are having an impact on Americans that is both insidious and precipitous. The risk of cancer has been steadily rising at a time when other major causes of death such as heart disease have been declining (National Center for Health Statistics, 1980). Toxic hazards in the environment involve risks to the health of a majority of the citizens, death to a substantial number, the loss of an adequate level of living to the victims and to their dependents, cross-generational genetic damage, widespread erosion of the quality of life, and the threat of catastrophic disasters, a sufficient threat in the case of the operation of nuclear power plants to make it necessary to plan for mass evacuation. Major dimensions of the public interest are at stake in the debate over government regulation and control of hazardous processes. The record of the government to date, as made evident by such public calamities as those created by PBB contamination of cattle feed in Michigan, the toxic dump at Love Canal, or Tris in children's pajamas, is not such as to suggest that public surveillance is unnecessary, that public concern is not needed.

The Honorable William M. Brodhead, representative from Michigan, speaking in the hearings on the adverse effects of PBB offered this succinct summary of the adequacy of current responses to public catastrophes:

> In the face of this public health disaster in Michigan, the Federal Government's response has been highly inadequate—a tragic example of governmental insensitivity. Michigan consumers found that they could not count on the Federal government to insure the quality of their food. Farmers learned that they could expect little help in identifying what caused their families to get sick and their animals to die. Mothers received no guidance on the safety of breast feeding their children or the advisability of serving Michigan meat or dairy products on their tables. . . . Unfortunately . . . [of] the actions that HEW proposes to implement, the most important of these recommendations are not adequate to meet the need. [U.S. House, 1975a:3]

In the hearings on the major regulatory legislation passed in the 1970s,

public interest groups have made a significant contribution by representing the risks to the general population and the threat to collective welfare
that these risks represent. In the case of nuclear power generation, however, they have not been equally visible.

Public Interest Group Participation in Hearings
on Toxic Substances

Of the regulatory legislation passed in the 1970s, one critical act is the
Toxic Substances Control Act, which mandates testing of new materials
before they are placed into production and provides for testing of existing
compounds. Hearings on this act were held just two years after the hearings on the Energy Reorganization Act, an act that created the nuclear regulatory commission to promote the development of nuclear power. These
hearings were three years prior to the hearings on the Nuclear Siting and
Licensing Act, an act passed only months before the accident at Three Mile
Island and designed to hasten the licensing process for nuclear power
plants. The hearings on the Toxic Substances Control Act provide a perspective on the participation of interest groups with which the hearings on
the acts promoting nuclear power development can be contrasted.

Like other acts to control environmental hazards, the Toxic Substances
Control Act represents governmental intervention in the operation of the
market to specify conditions under which the private market will function,
in this case to require manufacturers to test new compounds for carcinogenic, teratogenic, and mutagenic properties and to report these findings
to the government. Although the act provides also for government testing
of materials, initiative remains primarily in the private sector with the government playing the role of modifier of the "rules of the game" by which
the private market will function. The act was prompted by the inadequacy
of existing regulatory legislation (e.g., the Clean Air Act of 1963 and the
Occupational Safety and Health Act of 1970) to prevent the occurrence
and spread of toxic chemicals, many of which (like asbestos) were discovered to be carcinogenic years or decades after they were widely dissemi-
nated in the environment, when effective prevention of widespread harm
was impossible and removal of the product was costly to the range of
industries now dependent on the product.

In the hearings on this act, each interest group had substantial representation. These included industrial representatives, government departments, Congressmen, labor unions, professional associations, civic associ-

ations, and public interest groups. Submissions from public interest groups include those from the Health Research Group, the Sierra Club, the Center for Science in the Public Interest, the Audubon Society, the National Wildlife Federation, the Environmental Defense Fund, Resources for the Future, and Friends of the Earth. In addition, seven different union representatives made submissions to these hearings. Of the forty-seven different statements, one-third came from either labor unions or public interest groups.

In these hearings, the argument centers around the proper role of government; all interest groups are in agreement on the need for some governmental regulation. Industry, using efficiency arguments, argues for limited government intervention with its primary concern being for costs and protection of trade secrets, technological development, and the private market. Pressure for expansion of government involvement comes from other interest groups. Two interest groups, labor unions and the public interest groups, consistently introduce in the hearings concern for collective welfare and argue for government responsibility to that collective welfare. They contribute a countervailing pressure to industry's concern for cost criteria and industrial protection and to government's pragmatic orientation. In addition, only the public interest groups raise the question of the public's right of access to information. The perspective added by these two interest groups prevents these hearings from focusing only on narrowly defined efficiency considerations, that is, the immediate costs to industry,

Table 1
Dominant Value Introduced by Different Interest Groups in the Hearings
on the Toxic Substances Control Act

Interest group	Value
Industry	Efficiency
Government departments	Pragmatism
Congressmen	Collective welfare
Labor Unions	Collective welfare
Public interest groups	Collective welfare/Responsibility
Civic associations	Responsibility
Professional associations	Efficiency

and forces expansion of cost considerations to include total costs to the nation. Without their contributions, the argument would appear quite different.

These hearings occurred in the context of agreement by all parties that new rules were necessary. The argument concerned not the intent of the legislation but the details of the rules. As in the later Solid Waste Disposal Act, it was in the interest of all parties, including industry and government, to contain the negative effects of toxic substances. The forum is open, no apparent "costs" accrue to those who participate, and no restrictions are placed on the content of submissions. In contrast to parliamentary hearings of other countries, however, individual citizens representing only themselves do not participate in congressional hearings. (Occasionally individuals are brought to the hearings by an interest group and are asked by them to "tell their story.") The absence of individual participation in hearings parallels the definition of collective welfare as involving the well-being of the nation as a whole, not the well-being of specific individuals. In the hearings on environmental hazards it seems justified to say that no representation of individual welfare has been made and no serious consideration has been given to what happens to those who become victims of technological progress (Kronick, 1980, pp. IV–141–48).

The Context of Nuclear Power Legislation

The context in which legislation promoting nuclear power has developed differs from that of the regulatory legislation around control of toxic substances. The role of government has been defined not as one of adjusting the rules governing the private market but as one of primary actor. The national defense implications of nuclear power have placed government in the central position of controlling the development and spread of nuclear technology. The availability of nuclear materials, the licensing of private plants, the availability of sources of funding, and the control of liability for negative consequences of such operations have all been determined by government action. Decisions reached around nuclear materials have been cloaked in secrecy with access to information, access to technological knowledge, and access to the decision-making arena carefully guarded (Farley, 1980). The decision to promote the domestic use of nuclear power was made in response to projected inadequacies in the traditional energy sources and government's interest in protecting a vital national goal, economic growth. Thus, Secretary of Energy James Schlesinger summarized

the need for nuclear power in the hearings on the Nuclear Siting and Licensing Act: "We are faced with a national energy problem. The solution
to that problem bears upon the future social and political health of this
country, on the standing of the dollar, on the capacity of the United States
to have reasonable latitude in the formation of its foreign policy" (U.S.
House, 1978:54). In addition, as the hearings indicate, government representatives were more than uneasy at the possibility that the available supply of electricity would be inadequate on a specific day so that the light
switch would not turn on a light, a fear that was augmented by black-outs
and brown-outs in major cities. A steady, unbroken availability of electric
power is viewed as essential to securing minimal levels of trust in the efficacy of government. From the government's point of view, vital government interests were at stake in the development of domestic use of nuclear
power.

In the decision to promote nuclear power development, basic national
goals are in conflict. On the one hand, government is committed to the protection of economic growth; on the other, the known and unknown hazards of nuclear power generation—from uranium mining, from the operation of the plants, from the location of radioactive wastes—pose a threat
to the health and safety of the population. That is, in Lester Thurow's
terms, a situation in which no choice can be made if the forum is open to
full debate, since two goals are in conflict and any choice will require the
allocation of significant loss to some sector of society. As a consequence,
nuclear power development has been subject to definite constraints on the
conditions under which the public can participate.

The Energy Reorganization Act represents a move on the part of government to actively promote the domestic use of nuclear power. The act is
a revision of the older Atomic Energy Act. The military and domestic applications of nuclear energy are separated in the Energy Reorganization
Act, and the Nuclear Regulatory Commission is created to oversee the
domestic development of nuclear power. The Nuclear Siting and Licensing
Act addresses the problem of increasing delays in the licensing process and
attempts by constraining opportunities for objection to expedite the process. Both acts intend to achieve more rapid development of domestic
nuclear power.

Public Interest Group Participation
in the Hearings

The participation of public interest groups in the hearings on the development of nuclear power provides a sharp contrast to their participation on
legislation to curb environmental hazards. Despite the fact that nuclear
power has been feared even before the first bomb was dropped on Hiroshima (Weart, 1980) and that the hazards of radiation to human health
and the environment have been documented since Marie Curie first handled radium and subsequently died of cancer, public interest groups have
paid only limited attention to the legislation promoting nuclear development. In the submissions to the Energy Reorganization Act, only one was
made by a public interest group, Friends of the Earth, supported by the
Sierra Club. This is a relatively brief submission in which Friends of the
Earth argues for equal consideration of the development of all energy
sources and protests the proposed structure that fails to include oversight
by a specific congressional committee. The submission does not address
directly the question of the promotion of nuclear power or the potential
conflict between national goals of energy development for economic
growth and the health and safety of the population. Rather it focuses on
the need for an opportunity for such conflicts to be explored around specific proposals as would be provided, presumably, with congressional
oversight. In the 1973 hearings, no one speaks clearly to the threat to collective welfare posed by nuclear power development. In the 1978 hearings,
public interest group participation had expanded to include representation of five public interest groups, a number still below public interest
group participation in the 1975 hearings on the Toxic Substances Control
Act. In addition, labor unions are effectively absent in these hearings.
There was no submission by a labor union in the 1973 hearings on the
Energy Reorganization Act and only one in the hearings on the Nuclear
Siting and Licensing Act. The major participants in the Energy Reorganization Hearings and in the Nuclear Siting and Licensing hearings were
representatives of government departments involved with nuclear power
(the Atomic Energy Commission, the Nuclear Regulatory Commission),
national laboratories, and public utilities. The limited participation by
public interest groups and labor unions allowed a dialogue between government and industry, a dialogue in which the need to achieve adequate
energy sources was the dominant concern.

Jane C. Kronick

Why Limited Participation?

The reasons for the limited participation of labor unions are self-evident;
the limited participation by public interest groups is less easily understood.
The intent of nuclear power development is the securing of an adequate
supply of energy for industry. Associated with industrial development are
jobs. Few labor leaders would be eager to take a public position against expansion of the labor market or in favor of the possible curtailment of that
market. On the issue of the generation of adequate supplies of power, as
with all cases where control of environmental hazards threatens jobs,
labor unions are stuck. Workers are always more at risk than any other
single group from the hazards of the industrial process, yet unemployment
and poverty extract an immediate toll in both health and general welfare.
Labor unions can promote safety only when economic conditions are such
that unemployment is no serious threat. The 1970s was not a decade that
permitted such concerns.

Limited participation by public interest groups is more complex and involves at least four different considerations. In the case of nuclear power,
the probability of having a significant impact on the course of legislation
was more limited, the rules for participation were more demanding, the
financial cost of participating effectively was higher, and the potential loss
in other areas was considerable. By the time of the hearings on the Energy
Reorganization Act, the nation was perceived to be entering a period of
crisis in the availability of energy. Commissioned studies as well as the
independent commentary by such groups as the Club of Rome and the
public utilities confirmed both the need for new energy resources and, in
the case of government-sponsored studies, the relative safety of nuclear
power stations. Nuclear power plants were under construction and the decision had been made to continue this development. Public interest groups
were unlikely to have much opportunity to alter the course of development
of nuclear power in these hearings. In addition, according to information
from interviews with public interest law firms, public interest groups were
discovering that the judiciary was most reluctant to entertain cases involving nuclear power—cases that, if entertained, would place the judiciary in potential opposition to the executive on matters of national goals.
(This is confirmed in the Nuclear Siting and Licensing hearings when
Representative Bauman of Maryland states, "In effect, the Court has told
the Federal Court to stay out of the Nuclear Regulatory Commission's

business" [U.S. House, 1978:57].) For public interest groups, nuclear power was even more of a "no-win" game than most issues.

Participation in legislative hearings on nuclear power is more constrained, more demanding of the participant, than participation in other hearings. Nuclear power involves a complex technology—available only to those with training in nuclear physics and engineering. Effective argument requires that technical issues be engaged, and to do that requires expert testimony. The public cannot, according to the implicit rules of the game governing these hearings, simply appear and register personal disapproval of the legislation. (Nor can the public do so at any point in the licensing hearings; all objections must have a technical base.) In the Nuclear Siting and Licensing Act hearings there is a rare committee response to the completed testimony of Ralph Nader that demonstrates the narrow boundaries of acceptable participation that have been drawn around hearings on nuclear power. Nader had responded to the intent of the bill to hasten the licensing of nuclear power plants by arguing that the intent was in error—that the demand for power generation had altered dramatically by the end of the 1970s, that more generating plants were costly and unnecessary, and that the problems lay with the distribution network for existing power plants. He therefore argued for a moratorium on the licensing of nuclear power plants. Following his submission, committee members note that he failed to address the question before the hearings, namely how to hasten the licensing process. In effect, they rule his submission out of order (U.S. House, 1978:217–28).

The provisions of the Nuclear Siting and Licensing Act are designed to limit the potential participation of the public in licensing hearings by setting further requirements on relevancy of the content, by setting forth procedural rules that establish points at which certain objections, based on technical data, can be made, and by ruling out any subsequent introduction of these objections irrespective of their validity. They are indicative of the thrust of nuclear power hearings to limit public participation, to establish narrow rules of what are relevant and acceptable submissions, and to further contain participation by parliamentary and procedural rules. Participation by interest groups virtually required acceptance of the position voiced by Alice Rivlin as director of the Congressional Budget Office, "that new technology has, to some extent, come of age; that the risks are now better known; and that it is more of a stable technology about which there is some history; and that it is time to see whether some of the delays could not be reduced with little risk to the public" (U.S. House, 1978:146).

Public interest groups have limited funds and a wide agenda. To effectively participate in the nuclear energy hearings would require paying for expert consultation and the development of expert testimony. The pay-off for this investment would be limited, compared to what might be achieved in the more open arenas of other environmental hazards.

In addition, there were further risks to public interest group participation. Nuclear protest had become synonymous with the civil disobedience that some nuclear protest groups fostered at the site of nuclear plants. Popular support for civil disobedience was limited, and the increasing conservatism of the electorate was reflected in increasing disapproval of such protest strategies. If other public interest groups engaged the nuclear power question, they ran the risk of confusion of their intent with the activities of civil disobedience of other nuclear protest groups. Their credibility was at stake. Not only might they have little impact on the course of nuclear development, but participation would be both financially and socially expensive. Their effectiveness in other areas of public concern might be significantly reduced by their participation in issues of nuclear power.

The Consequences of Limited Public Interest Group Participation

It is predictable from the result of the analysis of other hearings that the absence of participation by labor unions and the limited participation of public interest groups would result in a limited development of issues of collective welfare involved in the risks of nuclear power. In other words, the benefits rather than the costs of nuclear power are dominant and little attention is paid to questions of the need for reimbursement to those who encounter the risks. The limited participation of these groups allowed the acceptance of the image of nuclear power as "known . . . stable . . . and with little risk" (U.S. House, 1978:146). A limit on the liability of nuclear power plants for damages that might occur from a nuclear accident had been in place since 1954. The potential cost of nuclear power in damages to the public is raised in the Nuclear Siting and Licensing Act hearings not by a public interest group but by Donald Allen of the New England Electric System: "I can only suggest that the amount that Congress has seen fit to put into protecting the health of miners and taking care of miners who have black lung injury is an enormous bill, which in the broad frame of reference you give, I think puts the cost of nuclear fuel cycling from an insurance [point of view] . . . vastly more expensive than anything we know likely to come into the nuclear fuel cycle" (U.S. House, 1978:210). This is an isolated view in these hearings.

The limited participation allowed legislation to be passed that promoted a solution to the energy crisis. Only one national goal was addressed. Wider engagement with questions of health, safety, damage to the environment—the trade-offs necessary in the promotion of nuclear energy—were avoided or limited by the restricted participation in the hearings. This has meant that little legislative attention has been directed to the extent of responsibility for potential serious accidents, to questions of what are compensable losses, of how losses should be determined, and of who should bear the burden of meeting these responsibilities. Rather than a considered judgment with a well-informed public who have had access to the decision-making arena, with recognition of the costs involved, and with preparation to meet these costs in the case of an accident, nuclear power development has been allowed to develop with an understanding that accidents can be prevented. When Three Mile Island compromised that understanding, another, equally improbable, panacea was invoked—mass-evacuation plans.

The Challenge of Three Mile Island

On 28 March 1979, primarily as a result of human error in conjunction with difficulties inherent in the design of the control panel and the information it made available, a major nuclear accident occurred that caused the release of radioactive materials, the formation of a hydrogen bubble in a reactor, and the probable partial melt-down of its core at the Three Mile Island nuclear plant in eastern Pennsylvania. This accident threatened the safety of the metropolitan population of the eastern seaboard from New York City to Washington, D.C. For one week, the condition of the reactor and the difficulties of achieving "cold shut-down" placed the area in a crisis situation. The official advisory to pregnant women and small children to leave the immediate five-mile radius of the reactor remained in effect until April 9 (U.S. House, 1979b). This accident demonstrated the inadequacy of emergency preparations to handle nuclear emergencies. For the people of the area who have experienced a variety of difficulties since the accident, the events of the ensuing months read like an unfortunate parallel to the experiences of the victims of the PBB disaster in Michigan (Del Tredici, 1980), with the government intervening, not to help but rather to suppress information.

The official response to the accident has had several components:

1 The repetitive set of inquiries or investigations of the accident. These include the special commission appointed by the president, the special commission appointed by the governor of Pennsylvania, oversight hearings of the House subcommittee on Energy Research and Development, special reports commissioned by the Nuclear Regulatory Commission, as well as independent studies funded by the different divisions of government. The thrust of most of these investigations is on what went wrong at Three Mile Island—why the accident occurred.

2 Anger over the involvement of the public through the information carried in the press. This annoyance with the press has prompted repeated analyses of the newspaper coverage beginning with the president's commission to determine "wrong-doing" or distortion by the press. No such claim has been supported by the investigations (President's Commission, 1979:57–58, esp. no. 9, p. 58).

3 Attempts to "cool out" the public by public meetings of NRC and Metropolitan Edison officials in local communities surrounding the power plant. These were discontinued after a 19 March 1980 meeting in Middletown that erupted in public anger (Del Tredici, 1980:47–53).

4 Late, reluctant, and limited attempts to measure the extent of damages in the communities surrounding the plant. Despite the partial evacuation, the loss of earnings this represented, and the demonstrable loss of property values, the first official report on the accident, the president's commission report, claimed that the effects of the accident were "immediate, short-lived mental stress" (President's Commission, 1979:35). The negative effects of the accident are now known to be considerably more extensive and long lasting than this initial report would indicate. But it seems fair to say that no systematic and reliable measure currently exists of the full costs of the accident to the people of that region.

None of these reactions suggests that the government is prepared to deal rationally and fully with the negative consequences of costs to health, safety, and property rights of nuclear power generation.

Conclusions

The history of the development of nuclear power represents the application of a strategy to solve an insoluble dilemma where national goals are in conflict with each other and a choice cannot be made without allocating costs to large segments of the nation. In the case of nuclear power, the choice has been made through a simple strategy of ignoring the existence of costs in one sector, of allocating costs by not counting them or recognizing their existence.

Successful application of this strategy has been possible because of the limited participation of public interest groups (and labor unions) in the hearings on legislation to promote the development of nuclear power which has allowed the dialogue to progress between industry and government with an attendant limited range of issues addressed and values considered. Such limited participation has resulted because of the difficulties of participation and the tangible potential costs to the groups participating.

The success of this strategy is questionable. A choice made between conflicting national goals allocates costs whether or not these costs are recognized. Proceeding not by rationally considering options and provision for the likely loss but by ignoring potential outcomes has resulted in lack of preparation for a disaster (as can be seen at Three Mile Island), in unwillingness to recognize and respond to loss, in public anger, and in loss of confidence in government representatives.[4]

Notes

1 Sampling material from hearings would be a risky process. Although the pages of a hearing may appear voluminous, each submission is a relatively parsimonious statement of a position. In addition, each interest group is represented by relatively few submissions. Reduction of the material analyzed would pose the risk both of omission altogether of an interest group and of omission of a critical component of an interest group's argument. Because one of the functions of a hearing is to establish the parameters of the debate, loss of part or all of a position will seriously compromise the conclusions drawn from the analysis.

2 The work presented here is part of an ongoing analysis of hearings in the United States and in New Zealand. The categories for the analysis together with detailed methodological discussion of the problems of measuring values and the theoretical framework informing the analysis of values are contained in the two final reports to the National Science Foundation (Kronick, 1978 and 1980).

3 In earlier work, I have applied content analysis to hearings on personal injury held in

New Zealand. Unlike the hearings in the United States, interest groups shared similar objectives and similar values in New Zealand. In this case, the lack of participation by an interest group would have less effect on the content of the hearings because other interest groups will make the argument (see Kronick, 1978).

4   The research on which this paper is based has been supported by Grants No. oss78–18023 and No. oss79–25663 from the National Science Foundation and the National Endowment for the Humanities. Any opinions, findings, and conclusions or recommendations expressed in this paper are those of the author and do not necessarily reflect the view of the National Science Foundation, the National Endowment for the Humanities, or other members of the research group.

References

Council on Environmental Quality. 1977. *Environmental Quality–1977*. Washington, D.C.: Government Printing Office.

Dahl, Robert A. 1956. *A Preface to Democratic Theory*. Chicago: University of Chicago Press.

Del Tredici, Robert. 1980. *The People of Three Mile Island*. San Francisco: Sierra Club Books.

Environmental Action Foundation. 1979. *Accidents Will Happen*. New York: Harper and Row.

Farley, Noel. 1980. "Regulation and the Special Case of Nuclear Energy." In Kronick (1980).

Frey, Bruno. 1978. *Modern Political Economy*. New York: John Wiley.

Gaskins, Richard. 1980. "Compensation and Responsibility in Public Health Programs." In Kronick (1980).

Glaser, Barney, and Strauss, Anselm. 1967. *The Discovery of Grounded Theory: Strategies for Qualitative Research*. Chicago: Aldine.

Kronick, Jane C. 1978. *Community Responsibility: The New Zealand Accident Compensation Act as a Value Response to Technological Development*. Final report to NSF.

———. 1980. *Value Issues in the Control of Technology-Related Damages*. Final report to NSF.

Lindblom, Charles E. 1977. *Politics and Markets*. New York: Basic Books.

National Center for Health Statistics. 1980. *Annual Vital Statistics of the United States*, vol. 2, *Mortality*. Washington, D.C.: Government Printing Office.

Nelkin, Dorothy, and Pollak, Michael. 1980. "Ideology as Strategy: The Discourse of the Anti-Nuclear Movement in France and Germany," *Science, Technology and Human Values* 15:3–13.

Nisbet, R. 1976. "Public Opinion vs. Popular Opinion," *Public Interest* 41:166–92.

President's Commission. 1979. *Report on the Accident at Three Mile Island*. Washington, D.C.: Government Printing Office.

Rasmussen, N. 1975. *Reactor Safety Study*. U.S. Nuclear Regulatory Commission WASH–1400 (NURG 75/014).

Sharpe, L. J. 1973. "American Democracy Reconsidered: Part II and Conclusions," *British Journal of Political Science* 3:129–67.

Thurow, Lester C. 1980. *The Zero-Sum Society*. New York: Basic Books.

U.S. House. 1973. Subcommittee of the Committee on Government Operations. *Energy Reorganization Act of 1973, Hearings*, 93rd Congress, 1st Session. Washington, D.C.: Government Printing Office.

———. 1975a. *Adverse Effects of Polybrominated Biphenyls (PBB), Hearings*, Serial #95–65. Washington, D.C.: Government Printing Office.

———. 1975b. *Toxic Substance Control Act, Hearings*, Serial 94–24. Washington, D.C.: Government Printing Office.

———. 1978. Subcommittee on Energy and the Environment. *Nuclear Siting and Licensing Act, Hearings*, 95th Congress, 2nd Session. Washington, D.C.: Government Printing Office.

———. 1979a. *Health Effects of Low-Level Radiation, Hearings*, Serial No. 96–41. Washington, D.C.: Government Printing Office.

———. 1979b. Committee on Interior and Insular Affairs, Subcommittee on Energy and the Environment. *Accident at the Three Mile Island Nuclear Power Plant, Hearings*, Serial No. 96–8. Washington, D.C.: Government Printing Office.

Weart, Spencer R. 1980. "Nuclear Fear: A History and an Experiment." Presented at the Hastings Center Conference on the Closure of Scientific Disputes, May 1980.

12

Nonviolent Protest and Third-Party Public Opinion: A Study of the June 1978, Seabrook, New Hampshire, Antinuclear Power Protest

John P. Hunt and
Neil H. Katz

Introduction

Political protest and nonviolent struggle have had a long history in the United States, dating back to colonial times. During the nineteenth century, nonviolence was associated with such causes as abolition, temperance, antimilitarism, and women's suffrage. More recently, the nonviolent tactics and strategies used in the civil-rights and antiwar movements of the 1950s and 1960s spawned similar activity on a diverse array of issues, including urban poverty, Native American rights, welfare reform, homosexuality, women's rights, and environmental pollution. Although many of these movements have been chronicled and protest has been recognized as an effective method for influencing political and social policy, less is known about the ways by which protest operates to exert such effects.

One aspect of this process, the ability of protesters to influence third-party observers, forms the focus of the present study. Surveying the data collected shortly after the 1978 demonstration against the construction of the Seabrook, New Hampshire, nuclear power plant provides an opportunity to examine the views of local townspeople toward the antinuclear protesters. Specifically, this research addresses the following four groups of questions:

1   How did third-party observers view construction of the Seabrook nuclear power plant and how did they view demonstrations against construction in terms of legitimacy and appeal?
2   Did third parties perceive the protesters as immature troublemakers or as responsible citizens, and did third parties view the protest as mostly violent or mostly peaceful?
3   To what extent did the protest group's ability to contact the public and legitimize its issue increase its appeal? Furthermore, how were the protest group's abilities to contact the public, to legitimize its issue, and to generate public appeal interrelated?
4   How did the social and ideological backgrounds of third-party observers relate to the ways in which they perceived protest?

Citizen Participation, Nonviolent Action, and the Exercise of Political Influence

A substantial amount of research has taken place concerning the ways through which individual citizens participate in American politics (see, for example, Milbrath, 1965; Verba and Nie, 1972; Milbrath and Goel, 1977). In general, these analyses start from the premise that citizens act in politics in order to exert influence. Although some findings (Verba and Nie, 1972:299–333) have indicated that such participation does have an impact on policy decisions, power should not necessarily be assumed to follow from such activity. In their review of participation research, Robert Alford and Roger Friedland argue that conventional types of participation (i.e., voting, petitioning, contacting, campaigning, etc.) tend to be ineffective means for low-status social groups to influence political decisions. They write: "Participation by the poor is encouraged at points in the political system where policy making does *not* take place, thus limiting the potential effects of participation to spasmodic challenges of the ways public policies are conventionally implemented" (Alford and Friedland, 1975: 464). Their inability to influence decisions through conventional means has caused some people to seek other, nonconventional ways for obtaining a voice in policy deliberation. One nonconventional method whereby low-status people have achieved influence on policy is through political protest and nonviolent direct action.

Several analyses have looked at political protest and nonviolent action techniques in terms of their ability to help groups obtain tangible political ends. James Wilson examined protest as a means through which groups can establish bargaining positions. He defined protest as "the exclusive use of negative inducements (threats) that rely, for their effect, on sanctions which require mass action or response" (Wilson, 1961:292). Through these means, otherwise powerless groups can obtain the necessary power with which to bargain with more powerful adversaries. Gene Sharp sets forth a theory of nonviolent action based on the view that "power is pluralistic, and that political power is fragile because it depends on many groups for reinforcement of its power sources" (Sharp, 1973:18). From this theoretical basis, Sharp argues that nonviolent action offers a concrete response to the problem of how to act effectively in politics, especially how to wield power effectively.

One of the ways through which nonviolent action confers power onto its users is through its activation of third-party sympathy, support, and, at times, active participation on behalf of the grievance group. Sharp refers to this process, in which nonviolent action operates to turn the power of a stronger opponent against itself, as political jujitsu. Due to political jujitsu effects, according to Sharp, "wider public opinion may turn against the opponent, members of his own group may dissent, and more or less passive members of the general grievance group may shift to firm opposition" (Sharp, 1973:658).

Other researchers have reached similar conclusions concerning the importance of third-party opinion in determining the outcome of nonviolent struggle. Louis Kriesberg writes that "insofar as one side can garner support from previously uncommitted groups, it has a better chance of getting the outcome it seeks" (Kriesberg, 1973:226). Irving Janis and Daniel Katz (1959) point to favorable attitude changes among spectators as an important aspect in the operation of nonviolent struggle. According to Michael Lipsky (1968), the activation of third-party leverage is the primary means through which protest groups can exert influence. Sidney Perloe et al. (1968) discuss a number of psycho-sociological mechanisms through which nonviolent action can produce favorable attitude changes among both participants and observers. Finally, Neil Katz and John Hunt (1979) found third-party opinion change to have exerted significant influence in the resolution of a nonviolent conflict in Albany, Georgia.

Thus the use of political protest and nonviolent direct action is one of the ways challenging groups in American society can obtain political influence. In addition, the literature suggests that one of the more important mechanisms by which nonviolent action operates to confer power upon its users is through its impact on third-party observers and public opinion.

The Public Perception of Political Protest

Ralph Turner (1969) has suggested five factors that are useful in explaining the ways in which people perceive public events. These include perceived credibility, appeal and threat messages, conciliation, coalition, and bargaining. Concerning credibility, Turner states that for observers to perceive protesters as credible, those taking action must be seen as part of a group whose grievances are already well documented, who are believed to be individually or collectively powerless, and who show some signs of moral virtue that render them deserving. Perception of appeal and threat messages, according to Turner, involves combinations of personal involvement, proximity, and the ability to perceive the events realistically. Conciliation, coalition, and bargaining all concern third-party assumptions about the existence of a conflict situation and the grievance group's ability to project itself as an influential actor.

Marvin Olsen's (1968) analysis of data from a 1965 Ann Arbor, Michigan, survey found that educational attainment and two measures of political alienation (political incapability and political discontentment) were related to the acceptance of social protest actions. A curvilinear relationship existed between education and approval of protest with the level of approval increasing with greater amounts of education until a point was reached where it leveled off. On both alienation measures, the less alienated showed more acceptance of protest. In their 1971 publication, Vincent Jeffries and his colleagues developed and tested measures of protest definition, credibility, appeal, threat, and conciliation. Their findings are most consistent and strongest in the case of credibility theory involving a sensitizing experience or predisposing ideology (Jeffries et al. 1971:450).

In a different study of the credibility of protest, David Altheid and Robert Gilmore (1972) examined survey data concerning reactions to a student demonstration in Colorado. They found support for Turner's contentions that perceived credibility increases the willingness to evaluate a group's actions as protest. Employing a similar analytical framework, Franklin Wilson and Robert Day (1974) found perceived threat to be the most important variable mediating protest interpretation. In their examination of survey data collected in the United States and Sweden, Marvin Olsen and Mary Anna Baden (1974) concluded that education, age, media exposure, association participation, and political efficacy are all positively related to the willingness to grant legitimacy to protest activities. Finally, Stan Kaplowitz (1977) presented national survey data findings concerning the influence of moral considerations on the perception of civil-rights actions. His results show that as the perceived morality of an action increases, so too does the perception that it will help the actors achieve their goals.

In sum, the above literature suggests that the public perception of political protest depends on a number of factors. The ability of the protest group to project appeal and legitimacy to its actions are the most immediate precursors of a favorable view toward the protest. However, predisposing ideologies and favorable social positions vis à vis the protest group may also help sway third parties to the grievance group's side during the course of a protest action.

The Seabrook Study

During the weekend of June 24, 1978, an antinuclear power demonstration involving approximately four to six thousand protesters, and at times up to fourteen thousand other participants, occurred at the site of a nuclear power plant in Seabrook, New Hampshire. Organized by the Clamshell Alliance, an umbrella organization of New England area antinuclear power groups, the June 1978 demonstration was the largest antinuclear power protest in North America up to that time.

After reaching agreement with the State of New Hampshire and the Public Service Company of New Hampshire to hold a weekend rally and alternative energy fair (open to the public on Sunday, June 25), Clamshell Alliance protesters occupied an eighteen-acre parcel of land adjacent to the

Seabrook nuclear plant. Following the weekend actions, the demonstrators peacefully left the Seabrook site, thereby upholding the controversial negotiated settlement and contradicting claims of opponents that the Clamshell Alliance could not keep its "lawless mobs" from initiating violence.[1]

In order to assess the impact of this nonviolent action on local public opinion and to explore the public perception of protest, a telephone survey was conducted between June 28 and July 11, 1978, using a random sample of residential listings drawn from the Seabrook area telephone directory. Interviewers spoke to one person eighteen years old or over at each phone number, attempting to maintain an equal sex ratio among respondents. The original sample of 242 residential listings yielded 144 complete interviews (completion rate = 60 percent).[2]

Table 1

Percentage Distributions for Items Measuring the Perception
of the Protest Issue and Events

Questions	Responses	Percent*
Would you say that the recent actions taken by the Clamshell Alliance in Seabrook have been violent, have most of them been peaceful, or have some been violent and others peaceful?	(1) Most violent	0.0
	(2) Some violent, some peaceful	16.9
	(3) Most peaceful	83.1
Would you describe the recent actions of the Clamshell Alliance at the nuclear power plant site in Seabrook as	(1) an attempted revolution	0.9
	(2) a rebellion against authority	1.5
	(3) a few troublemakers causing trouble	0.0
	(4) a bunch of people out to have a good time	4.4
	(5) a demonstration or protest	93.2
Do you strongly favor, favor, oppose, strongly oppose the construction of a nuclear power plant in Seabrook, or do you feel neutral?	(1) strongly favor	5.9
	(2) favor	22.6
	(3) neutral	32.8
	(4) oppose	19.0
	(5) strongly oppose	19.0

Do you think that the recent actions taken in Seabrook by the Clamshell Alliance have on the whole helped their cause or hurt their cause?	(1) helped	58.3
	(2) helped some, hurt some	11.8
	(3) hurt	17.4
The recent actions taken by the Clamshell Alliance have made local people more opposed to the construction of the Seabrook nuclear power plant. Do you	(1) strongly agree	5.3
	(2) agree	37.0
	(3) feel neutral	28.0
	(4) disagree	21.2
	(5) strongly disagree	4.5
The Clamshell Alliance has stimulated local people to take action against the Seabrook nuclear power plant. Do you	(1) strongly agree	9.6
	(2) agree	40.0
	(3) feel neutral	20.7
	(4) disagree	24.4
	(5) strongly disagree	1.5
The Clamshell Alliance does not have respect for the law. Do you	(1) strongly agree	0.7
	(2) agree	5.9
	(3) feel neutral	12.6
	(4) disagree	59.3
	(5) strongly disagree	17.8
In their opposition to the Seabrook nuclear power plant, the Clamshell Alliance has a legitimate grievance. Do you	(1) strongly agree	23.1
	(2) agree	51.5
	(3) feel neutral	11.2
	(4) disagree	8.2
	(5) strongly disagree	1.5
The Clamshell Alliance has sincerely attempted to use legal means in its efforts to stop construction of a nuclear power plant in Seabrook. Do you	(1) strongly agree	18.7
	(2) agree	49.3
	(3) feel neutral	15.7
	(4) disagree	6.0
	(5) strongly disagree	0.7

*Not sure, no opinion, and "refuse" responses are not presented; thus, percentages may not total 100.

These results show that the Seabrook area residents in our sample tended to oppose more than favor the construction of the nuclear power plant. With regard to their perception of the protest events, 83.1 percent of the respondents saw them as mostly peaceful. Similarly, an overwhelming majority of the people in our sample called the actions a demonstration or protest as opposed to an attempted revolution, a rebellion against authority, or a bunch of people out to have a good time. These findings are in stark contrast to Clamshell's opponents' characterization of the demonstrations and the findings of David Altheide and Robert Gilmore (1972) who reported much less acceptance of a student protest.

Regarding appeal, a majority of our sample thinks that "the recent actions taken in Seabrook by the Clamshell Alliance have on the whole helped their cause." Almost twice as many agree or strongly agree, rather than disagree or strongly disagree, that "the recent actions taken by the Clamshell Alliance have made local people more opposed to the construction of the Seabrook nuclear power plant." To the statement "The Clamshell Alliance has stimulated local people to take action against the Seabrook nuclear power plant," third parties answer "strongly agree" or "agree" about twice as often as they disagree or strongly disagree.

Third parties tend to rate the Clamshell Alliance high on questions concerning legitimacy. Over 77 percent disagree or strongly disagree with the statement, "The Clamshell Alliance does not have respect for the law." Almost three-quarters of the respondents agreed or strongly agreed that "in their opposition to the Seabrook nuclear power plant, the Clamshell Alliance has a legitimate grievance." Finally, by a more than ten to one margin, respondents agree or strongly agree with the assertion that "the Clamshell Alliance has sincerely attempted to use legal means in its efforts to stop construction of a nuclear power plant in Seabrook."

Bivariate correlations among the two dependent variables (attitude toward the protest actions and attitude toward the Seabrook plant), the intervening social, psychological, and political orientations, and the independent demographic variables are presented in table 2. Among the four demographic variables, only age and sex show significant relationships with any of the measures of the perception of protest issues and events. For these variables, the bivariate results suggest that opponents of constructing the plant tend to be female ($r = .20$), and that younger respondents experience greater appeal ($r = -.20$), had more contact with the protest organization ($r = -.19$), identify more strongly with the Democratic than with the Republican party ($r = -.24$), and hold more liberal ideology positions ($r = -.23$).

Legitimacy possesses the strongest bivariate relationship with view toward the plant ($r = .42$). Appeal ($r = .32$), ideology ($r = .32$), contact ($r = .21$), and party ($r = .19$) also hold significant correlations with this variable. These results indicate that opponents of the plant tend to be female, politically liberal, to have had contact with the Clamshell organization, have considered the protest legitimate, and have received some appeal from the actions.

For appeal, these bivariate results suggest connections to high legitimacy ($r = .33$), contact ($r = .19$), and a Democratic party orientation ($r = .16$). Results for legitimacy show correlations with contact ($r = .21$) and liberal ideologies ($r = .25$). In addition, contact also correlates with liberal ideologies ($r = .20$), as does Democratic partisanship ($r = .26$).

Table 3 sets out multiple regression coefficients for attitude toward the Seabrook plant, legitimacy, and appeal. These measures provide a view of the impact of each independent variable on the dependent variables while controlling for other variables. In addition, the R^2 provides a measure of how much of the variation in each dependent variable is explained by a set of independent variables. These multiple regression findings indicate that women and political liberals tend to oppose the plant more than men and conservatives. In addition, both appeal and legitimacy have significant impact on view toward the plant. Contact, however, has only an indirect

Table 2
Zero-Order Correlation Coefficients for Social and
Political Position, and Perception Variables*

Attitude toward Plant (X_1)	X_1	X_2	X_3	X_4	X_5	X_6	X_7	X_8	X_9
Appeal (X_2)	$.32^3$								
Legitimacy (X_3)	$.42^3$	$.33^3$							
Contact (X_4)	$.21^1$	$.19^1$	$.21^1$						
Party (X_5)	$.19^1$	$.16^1$	$.10$	$.03$					
Ideology (X_6)	$.32^3$	$.12$	$.25^2$	$.20^1$	$.26^2$				
Social Class (X_7)	$-.04$	$-.11$	$.00$	$.06$	$-.06$	$.03$			
Age (X_8)	$-.09$	$-.20^1$	$-.15$	$-.19^1$	$-.24^2$	$-.33^3$	$.03$		
Education (X_9)	$-.02$	$-.02$	$.12$	$.14$	$-.01$	$.08$	$.27^2$	$-.21^1$	
Sex (X_{10})	$.20^1$	$.12$	$.02$	$-.05$	$-.14$	$.20^1$	$.03$	$-.03$	$-.07$

[1]Significant at 0.05 level.
[2]Significant at 0.01 level.
[3]Significant at 0.001 level.
*N=122.

impact on attitude toward the Seabrook plant, through its effect on legitimacy.

In addition, the data show direct linkages between age and ideology and age and appeal. Younger respondents tend both to be more liberal and to perceive more appeal from the protest events. Respondents' ideological orientations influence their degree of contact with Clamshell activities and their willingness to grant legitimacy to the protest actions. Further, the regression results indicate that contact with the Clamshell organization influences the degree of perceived legitimacy, and that increased legitimacy engenders increased appeal.

Table 3

Standardized Multiple Regression Coefficients for Predicting Perceived Legitimacy, Appeal, and Attitude toward Plant*

Dependent variable:		Legitimacy	Appeal
Independent variables:	Sex	−.017	.122
	Age	−.051	−.168[1]
	Ideology	.199[2]	.004
	Contact	.161[1]	.166[1]
	R^2	.090	.082

Dependent variable:		Attitude toward Plant	Attitude toward Plant
Independent variables:	Sex	.153[1]	.137[1]
	Age	.036	.082
	Ideology	.263[3]	.201[3]
	Contact	.172[2]	.094
	Legitimacy		.306[3]
	Appeal		.175[2]
	R^2	.146	.288

[1] Significant at 0.05 level.
[2] Significant at 0.01 level.
[3] Significant at 0.001 level.
*N= 122; class identification, education, and party had no significant betas and were dropped from the analysis.

John P. Hunt and Neil H. Katz

Discussion and Conclusions

For the most part, the data presented in the above section support and further refine the general conclusions for the public perception of protest discussed earlier. Consistent with Olsen and Baden (1974), age plays an important role in the way people perceive protest. The present data do not, however, point to education as having a significant role. Possibly this is due to the fact that nonviolent struggle had been going on in Seabrook for over two years and the protest group had affected people at many different educational levels. The finding that women tend to oppose the plant more than men follows findings by Allan Mazur (1975) that women were more likely than men to oppose technological innovations.

Among the intervening psycho-sociological variables, legitimacy emerged as the central factor. It had the strongest impact on appeal and on attitude toward the Seabrook plant and is in turn significantly influenced by both ideology and contact. Indeed, we have a contact-legitimacy-appeal hierarchy. Thus, along the lines of both Turner (1969) and Wilson and Day (1974), the ability of protesters to move third-party observers revolves largely around their ability to convey credibility and legitimacy to their actions. This finding also supports Stan Kaplowitz's (1977) conclusion that the perceived morality of an action influences the perception that it will help the actors achieve their goals. That political liberals are more likely than conservatives to view the protest as legitimate follows from a similar finding by Jeffries et al. (1971). A new finding in the present study is that contact with the grievance group through literature and personal discussion does influence the tendency to view protest action as legitimate.

In general, the data presented in this paper suggest that the Seabrook protest did have an impact on local public opinion. Although respondents were fairly evenly divided on support or opposition to the plant, they viewed the demonstration as mostly peaceful and rated the protesters and their actions high on measures of appeal and legitimacy. The protest group's ability to convey both a sense of legitimacy and appeal is the most important factor mediating a favorable issue evaluation. Thus, the data demonstrate the ability of nonviolent action to influence third-party behavior and attitudes and suggest that political protest may operate most effectively when it can be interpreted on a broad scale as credible and supporting a legitimate grievance.

The importance of ideological orientation suggests that grievance groups would do well to take into account the types of appeal their actions will have to people from different political viewpoints. In the data presented here, people with liberal ideologies were more favorably influenced by the protest actions. The data, however, do not supply sufficient information from which to judge whether holding a liberal ideology connects more to approval of protest in general or to the approval of the specific protest issue. Were the latter the case, we might expect conservatives to incline more favorably toward protest used to pursue goals more in line with a conservative orientation.

In addition, the findings point to a highly significant role for contact. Particularly, the interrelationships among ideology, contact, and legitimacy suggest that contact with the activist group may act to reinforce and strengthen ideological predispositions toward perceiving protest actions as legitimate. The results indicate that persons with predisposing ideological orientations in support of the protest issue tend to experience greater contact with the activist group. People so contacted, in turn, more often view protest activities as legitimate. The importance of contact in this linkage between ideology and perceived legitimacy suggests that grievance group actions of a grassroots nature can have a significant impact.

In conclusion, four points deserve mention. First, in general, third parties viewed the Seabrook protest favorably in terms of legitimacy and appeal. Second, in the explanation of the public perception of protest, these data indicate that perceived legitimacy plays the most crucial role. Third, important linkages among ideology, contact, legitimacy, and appeal suggest that protest groups would do well to place emphasis on direct contact with third-party observers. Fourth, protest issues may attract support from particular population segments (in this case, women and youth). Thus, when examining or planning protest, researchers and activists should consider the multiplicity of factors that influence a favorable impression of protest by third parties.

Notes

1 For a discussion of the controversial negotiated settlement (commonly referred to as "the Rath Agreement,") and for a discussion of Clamshell's opponents' predictions of violence, see Katz and List, 1981.

2 The full breakdown on completion rate is as follows: complete or partially complete—60 percent (N=144); no answer—6 percent (N=14); refusal—34 percent (N=84). Towns in New Hampshire and Massachusetts from which listings were drawn included Amesbury, Byfield, Newbury, Newburyport, Plum Island, Seabrook, and West Newbury. The

John P. Hunt and Neil H. Katz

authors would like to thank Christopher Kruegler, David Goldsman, and David List for their help in the data collection phase of this project.

For the most part, our sample appears relatively representative of the Seabrook area population as it was measured in the 1970 census. Women, older people, and more educated people appear slightly overrepresented.

3   This is a revision of a paper presented at the annual meetings of the Society for the Study of Social Problems (1980). The authors gratefully acknowledge the assistance of the Research and Equipment Fund of Syracuse University which provided financial assistance for this research (Grant No. RE–78–B6). We also wish to thank Louis Kriesberg, Allan Mazur, and David Goldsman for their advice on earlier drafts of this article.

References

Alford, Robert R., and Friedland, Roger. 1975. "Political Participation and Public Policy." *Annual Review of Sociology* 1:429–79.

Altheide, David L., and Gilmore, Robert P. 1972. "The Credibility of Protest." *American Sociological Review* 37:99–108.

Duncan, Otis D. 1966. "Path Analysis: Sociological Examples." *American Journal of Sociology* 72:1–16.

———. 1975. *Introduction to Structural Equation Models*. New York: Academic Press.

Heise, David R. 1975. *Causal Analysis*. New York: John Wiley and Sons.

Janis, Irving L., and Katz, Daniel. 1959. "The Reduction of Intergroup Hostility: Research Problems and Hypotheses." *Journal of Conflict Resolution* 3:85–100.

Jeffries, Vincent; Turner, Ralph H.; and Morris, Richard T. 1971. "The Public Perception of the Watts Riot as Social Protest." *American Sociological Review* 36:443–51.

Kaplowitz, Stan A. 1977. "The Influence of Moral Considerations on the Perceived Consequences of an Action." *Journal of Conflict Resolution* 21:475–500.

Katz, Neil H., and Hunt, John P. 1979. "Nonviolent Struggle in Albany, Georgia." In *Nonviolent Action and Social Change*, ed. Severyn T. Bruyn and Paula M. Rayman. New York: Irvington, pp. 128–46.

Katz, Neil H., and List, David. 1981. "Seabrook: A Profile of Anti-Nuclear Activists, June 1978." *Peace and Change: A Journal of Peace Research* 7:59–70.

Kriesberg, Louis. 1973. *The Sociology of Social Conflicts*. Englewood Cliffs, New Jersey: Prentice-Hall.

Land, Kenneth C. 1969. "Principles of Path Analysis." In *Sociological Methodology 1969*, ed. Edgar C. Borgatta. Washington, D.C.: Jossey-Bass, pp. 3–37.

Lipsky, Michael. 1968. "Protest as a Political Resource." *American Political Science Review* 62:1144–58.

Mazur, Allan. 1975. "Opposition to Technological Innovation." *Minerva* 13:58–81.

Milbrath, Lester. 1965. *Political Participation*. Chicago: Rand McNally.

Milbrath, Lester, and Goel, M. L. 1977. *Political Participation*. Chicago: Rand McNally.

Olsen, Marvin E. 1968. "Perceived Legitimacy of Social Protest Actions." *Social Problems* 15:297–310.

Olsen, Marvin E., and Baden, Mary Anna. 1974. "Legitimacy of Social Protest Actions in the United States and Sweden." *Journal of Political and Military Sociology* 2:172–89.

Perloe, Sidney L.; Olton, David S.; and Yaffee, David L. 1956. "Attitudes and Nonviolent Action." In *Nonviolent Direct Actions*, ed. A. Paul Hare and Herbert H. Blumberg. Washington, D.C.: Corpus, pp. 407–46.

Sharp, Gene. 1973. *The Politics of Nonviolent Action*. Boston: Porter Sargent.

Turner, Ralph H. 1969. "The Public Perception of Protest." *American Sociological Review* 34:815–31.

Verba, Sidney, and Nie, Norman H. 1972. *Participation in America: Political Democracy and Social Equality*. New York: Harper and Row.

Wilson, Franklin D., and Day, Robert C. 1974. "White Students' Evaluation of a Black Student Protest Organization: A Test of a Model." *Social Science Quarterly* 55:690–703.

Wilson, James Q. 1961. "The Strategy of Protest: Problems of Negro Civic Action." *Journal of Conflict Resolution* 5:291–303.

Afterword

James C. Petersen

The dozen chapters in this work provide both theoretical assessments and empirical accounts of the diverse means by which citizens may attempt to influence issues with strong scientific or technical components. Some of these means are highly formalized, including the legislative hearings discussed by Jane Kronick, the governing boards of Health Systems Agencies reviewed by Barry Checkoway, and the devices—such as litigation, referenda, public hearings, and advisory boards—examined by both Dorothy Nelkin and Sheldon Krimsky. Others are more emergent, as in the grassroots Chipko protests described by Jayanta Bandyopadhyay and Vandana Shiva or in the Seabrook antinuclear demonstration studied by John Hunt and Neil Katz. A few of the mechanisms remain proposals that have yet to receive a full trial. Among these are Frederick Rossini and Alan Porter's notion of adversary technology assessment and such approaches as the science court and citizen court.

It seems clear that many of the authors expect the demand for significant citizen input in policy making on scientific and technical matters to intensify. Despite the traditional hostility of those who have dominated the science policy process toward public involvement, the authors perceive a broad and growing base of support within society for citizen participation in this sector. Among the sources of this support are the public's changing image of science and expertise, the increased recognition of the risks posed by technology and by some scientific inquiry, and the expectations developed by citizen participation programs and participatory movements in other sectors of society. Some political leaders and scientists have also contributed through the public interest science movement, through recognition of the contributions that citizens can make to problem identification, and through pragmatic acceptance of the need for greater public involvement to attain increased legitimacy for policy decisions.

Twenty years ago sociologists were describing faith in science and rationality as a dominant American value. Today, many Americans are agnostics, if not nonbelievers, on the question of whether science will save us. With increased recognition that science and technology produce significant risks along with their obvious benefits, the view that those who bear the risks should have a say in the decisions that create them has attracted many supporters. The rise of "big science" with huge expenditures of public funds creates a further justification for a more democratic decision-making process.

This intensified demand for citizen input has the potential of yielding real benefits for science, technology, and the larger society. At the same time, we should acknowledge, as I and several other authors have done in our chapters, that public involvement can carry with it costs in the form of delay and unwise decisions. Still, the benefits clearly outweigh these risks. Krimsky and Diana Dutton have provided extensive analyses of the justifications for public involvement and the common arguments used to limit public access. That in a democratic society one is still compelled to develop justifications for citizen participation in decisions that are of great importance to much of the public is itself an indication of the extent to which technical experts continue to dominate the resolution of science-related issues.

The central argument against citizen participation in issues of a scientific or technical nature, although often cloaked in more muted tones, is that such decisions must be left to technical experts because the issues are too complex and the public too ignorant. Such statements are a convenient justification by those who currently dominate decision making and wish to retain power. As several of the chapters point out, the boundaries between the technical and the political are, at best, indistinct in many technical controversies and science-related issues. Furthermore, citizens have shown remarkable capacity to deal successfully with highly complex issues. The Cambridge (Massachusetts) Experimentation Review Board that examined the public health hazards of recombinant DNA research is but one example. This citizen review board, described by both Krimsky (a member of the board) and Dutton, contained no practicing scientists; at the beginning of their deliberations most members knew nothing about recombinant DNA work. The report issued by the board after much self-education, presentation of expert opinion, and debate, has been widely praised for its intelligence and fairness.

The argument that nonscientists are unable to understand the issues in questions of science policy seems weak in light of the Cambridge experience. In any case, this argument is reminiscent of the attacks on the ability of the public that have always been made by those uncomfortable with democracy. As both Krimsky and Dutton point out, the participatory process provides numerous opportunities for citizens to gain knowledge and expertise. Democracies may never attain a fully informed electorate. Still, the pursuit of such a goal yields benefits for society, and the actual gains in knowledge made by individual citizens represent significant accomplishments.

It is unrealistic to demand that meaningful citizen input on science-related issues be postponed until all the public is fully equipped to handle such matters. Furthermore, such delay is unnecessary. Segments of the public are currently well informed, and the number of knowledgeable citizens can be increased through improved science education and science journalism, through greater availability of technical assistance for citizens, and through many of the participatory mechanisms described in this book.

Even in the absence of such actions, citizen participation has often helped to reshape policy questions. This book is replete with accounts of such successes. For example, Randy Rydell observes that public participation has been critical in producing a reexamination of the assumptions underlying American policies on nuclear development and control, and Dutton describes how public input on a series of biomedical issues has broadened and humanized health policy. No one could read this book, however, and see all the cases described as success stories for citizen participation. Several of the accounts depict processes that largely excluded the public or mechanisms for input that were clearly inadequate.

If there is great unanimity on the desirability of greater public participation, there is much less certainty that a democratic science and technology policy can actually be achieved. Kronick's account of the role of public interest groups in legislative hearings on nuclear power development makes clear that the hearings have been manipulated in order to contain debate and restrict the policy impact of these groups. In his examination of Health System Agencies, Checkoway notes that even though consumers have a legal right to a majority of positions on each HSA board, effective control of these boards has often been seized by health-care providers. Rachelle Hollander's description of the short-lived Science for Citizens experiment points to the tenuous support for many participatory mechanisms. While a number of the authors remain optimistic that effective mechanisms for citizen input can be developed, none would expect those who have monopolized decision making on science and technology policy to welcome limitation of their power.

Increased recognition of the social costs attached to exclusion of the public may, however, help to bring about change. In his chapter on the United States's "War on Cancer," Daryl Chubin suggests that manipulation of the public has provoked anger and cynicism resulting in intense public criticism of current health policy. Kronick's analysis of hearings on nuclear power development demonstrates that the restriction of public interest group participation resulted in a nuclear policy that paid scant attention to the risks of nuclear power or to related issues of responsibility for accidents and reimbursement for damages. These examples, along with others provided in the book, make it clear that societies often pay high prices for practices that limit policy decisions to technical experts.

To be effective and meaningful, citizen participation must have certain characteristics. The public must be able to enter the decision-making process at an early stage. Too often citizen input follows the public hearing model, where citizens are provided with a setting in which to react to a decision that has already been made. Such procedures severely circumscribe the options of the public and may make it impossible to introduce issues of central concern. Participation of this type is often only symbolic and may contribute to increased public cynicism.

Furthermore, meaningful citizen participation requires that all segments of the public have the opportunity to participate in the policy formulation process. Outreach efforts will be necessary to ensure participation by the poor and minorities. Care must be taken that the location or scheduling of meetings does not exclude whole segments of a community.

In some instances, technical assistance will be necessary to provide citizens access to existing scientific knowledge and to collect and analyze new data. The NSF-funded public service science centers described by Hollander provide a useful model of how such technical assistance could be provided. With the elimination of federal funding for these centers, however, new sources of support or new approaches to technical assistance will have to be found.

Finally, participatory mechanisms that provide citizens with real opportunities to influence the resolution of science-related conflicts must be institutionalized. A certain amount of citizen input will always have a spontaneous and emergent character. Scientific and technical change occurs too fast, however, to permit citizens to create a new participatory structure for each issue that must be faced. If the public is to have early and regular access to the decision-making process, the mechanisms for this input must be in place. No challenge facing citizen activists is of greater significance than the establishment of such structures.

Contributors

Jayanta Bandyopadhyay obtained his Ph.D. in physical metallurgy from the Indian Institute of Technology, Kanpur, in 1975. He is now a member of the faculty at the Indian Institute of Management, Bangalore. His research interest is in political economy and technological change, innovation and transfer of technology in third world countries, and systems analysis of natural resource utilization.

Barry Checkoway is Associate Professor of Social Work at the University of Michigan, where he teaches courses in community organization, social planning, and citizen participation. His publications include the edited book, *Citizens and Health Care: Participation and Planning for Social Change* (Pergamon Press, 1981).

Daryl Chubin is Associate Professor in the School of Social Sciences and director of the Technology and Science Policy Program at Georgia Institute of Technology. Trained as a sociologist, he specializes in the social and political dimensions of science and technology. He is co-author of *The Cancer Mission: Social Contexts of Biomedical Research* (Sage, 1980) and the author of *Sociology of Sciences: An Annotated Bibliography on Invisible Colleges, 1972–1980* (Garland, 1983).

Diana Dutton received a Ph.D. in urban social policy from the Massachusetts Institute of Technology. She is currently Assistant Professor in the Department of Family, Community and Preventive Medicine, Stanford University School of Medicine, where she is completing a book on medical innovation and public decision making.

Rachelle Hollander received her Ph.D. in philosophy from the University of Maryland in 1979, with a specialization in applied ethics. She manages the program on Ethics and Values in Science and Technology at the National Science Foundation, which supports research on ethical implications and value assumptions in the roles of scientific and technological research and development in United States society.

John P. Hunt received a doctorate in interdisciplinary social science from Syracuse University in 1980. He has engaged in research evaluating federally funded youth employment programs, taught sociology and computer science, and currently plans to pursue further research on political behavior and nonviolent struggle, youth and generations, and social science computer applications.

Neil H. Katz is director of the Program in Nonviolent Conflict and Change and Associate Professor of Public Affairs in the Maxwell School of Citizenship of Syracuse University. He is the author of more than a dozen books, book chapters, and articles on nonviolent struggle, conflict resolution, and radical pacifism.

Sheldon Krimsky is Associate Professor of Urban and Environmental Policy at Tufts University. He served on the NIH Recombinant DNA Advisory Committee for two and a half years, and on the Cambridge Experimentation Review Board, which drafted the first legislation regulating recombinant DNA research in the United States. His recent book, *Genetic Alchemy: The Social History of the Recombinant DNA Controversy*, was published by MIT Press.

Jane C. Kronick is a professor in the Graduate School of Social Work and Social Research, Bryn Mawr College, where she teaches courses in quantitative and qualitative data analysis and the process of national policy formation. She has been the project director of three cross-cultural, interdisciplinary studies of the role of values in shaping national policy for environmental hazards funded by the EVIST program in the National Science Foundation and the National Endowment for the Humanities.

Dorothy Nelkin is a professor in the Program on Science, Technology and Society at Cornell University. Her many publications on controversies over science and technology include *The Creation Controversy* (W. W. Norton, 1982), *Technological Decisions and Democracy* (Sage, 1977), and *Controversy: Politics of Technical Decisions*, 2d edition (Sage, 1984).

James C. Petersen is Associate Professor of Sociology and Associate Director of the Center for Social Research at Western Michigan University. He is president of the Association of Voluntary Action Scholars and co-editor (with Gerald Markle) of *Politics, Science, and Cancer: The Laetrile Phenomenon* (Westview, 1980).

Alan L. Porter is Associate Professor of Industrial and Systems Engineering at Georgia Institute of Technology. His primary professional interests are impact assessment and technology and public policy issues. He serves as secretary of the International Association for Impact Assessment and has just completed a term as co-editor of the *Impact Assessment Bulletin*.

Frederick A. Rossini is Professor of Social Sciences, associate director of the Office of Interdisciplinary Programs, and director of the Technology Policy and Assessment Center at Georgia Tech. His main areas of interest are impact assessment, technology and social forecasting, and technology and science policy issues. A founder of the International Association for Impact Assessment, his books include *A Guidebook for Technology Assessment and Impact Analysis* and *Integrated Impact Assessment*.

Randy J. Rydell is an international political analyst at the Lawrence Livermore National Laboratory. His current research focuses on the political economy of nuclear proliferation, with special reference to Western Europe. He is working on a book about the politics of the breeder reactor in Britain and the United States.

Vandana Shiva obtained her Ph.D. in philosophy of physics from the University of Western Ontario, Canada, in 1978. She currently heads the Research Foundation for Science, Technology and Natural Resource Policy in Dehradun. Her research interest is in rationality in non-Western sciences, scientific community structure in India, and ecological limits of modern technology.

Index

Library of Congress Cataloging in Publication Data
Main entry under title:
Citizen participation in science policy.
Bibliography: p.
Includes index.
1. Science and state—United States—Citizen participa-
tion. 2. Technology and state—United States—Citizen
participation. I. Petersen, James C.
Q127.U6C5   1984   361.2'5   84–246
ISBN 0–87023–433–1
ISBN 0–87023–434–X (pbk.)